# Pekingese

# PEKINGESE

## AN OWNER'S COMPANION

Vandella Williams
and Adele Summers

The Crowood Press

First published in 1990 by
The Crowood Press
Ramsbury, Marlborough,
Wiltshire SN8 2HE



British Library Cataloguing in Publication Data

Williams, Vandella
Pekingese.
1. Pekingese dogs
I. Title II. Summers, Adele
636.7'6

ISBN 1 85223 262 5

We should like to dedicate this book to the late
ALEXANDREA CONSTANCE WILLIAMS
Without her, and the success of the foundation of the original
Toydom strain, this book would never have been written.

Line-drawings by Aileen Hanson

Typeset by Chippendale Type Ltd, Otley, West Yorkshire
Printed in Great Britain by Redwood Press Ltd, Melksham, Wilts

# Contents

# Acknowledgements

We should like to take this opportunity to thank the following people for their help in relation to this book. Each and every one has played an important part in various ways.

First of all we should like to thank the following photographers:- Thos. Fall for Figs 21, 41, 65, 66, 81, 83, 91, 93–6, 102; Francis Pilgrim for Figs 15, 20, 73, 80, 97, 101; Roger Chambers for Fig 23; Michael Trafford (Australia) for Fig 70; Bingham for Fig 89; Russell Fine Arts for Fig 77; Risbey for Fig 85; Steinar Moen for Figs 74 and 103; Dave Freeman for Fig 69; Anne Roslin Williams for Fig 79; Hartley for Fig 63; McChesney for Fig 30; Stephen Ball for Figs 13, 16, 28, 29, 32–8, 40, 42–5, 49–62, 68, 71, 72, 75, 77, 78, 82, 90, and also for the front cover photograph. We should like to offer a special thank you to Stephen Ball who, over the last few months, has offered his help and advice and possessed a wealth of patience in helping to produce the desired photographs.

We should like to thank Russell Y. Christie MRCVS, BVMS, for his professional advice in the compiling of Chapters 11, 12 and 13. Also, to everyone who was kind enough to entrust into our keeping their very precious photographs for reproduction in this book, we are very grateful. Thank you Terry Nethercott for allowing us to photograph his grooming demonstration, aided by Ch. Jay Trump of Sunsalve and Ch. Toydom Modesty Permits. Many thanks to the other half of the Sunsalve partnership Eddie Hurdle whose word processor has been of invaluable help in this exercise. Thanks must go also to Erica Crouse for her assistance in the drawings seen in this book (E. Renalt).

We should also like to thank Yvonne Border for her assistance with proof-reading together with her secretarial expertise and Shirley Border for assisting with the presentation of the pedigrees in such an artistic way. Last but not least, we thank June Grant, whose help in keeping the Toydom Pekingese looking in tiptop condition whilst this book was underway has been invaluable.

# Introduction

Over the years several books both in the United Kingdom and abroad have been written on this very popular breed, the Pekingese, in which various aspects of present-day kennels have been covered by experts and top breeders. In this book, *Pekingese: An Owner's Companion*, we introduce you to the kennels of yesterday as well as those of today, taking you through the first beginnings of the breed in the United Kingdom right up to the dogs that you will recognize winning or in the pedigrees of the modern-day Pekingese.

If you are just venturing into this breed we hope that this book will be of assistance, from buying a new puppy right through to the time that you may possibly enter the show ring.

The United Kingdom has been regarded as having some of the top Pekingese in the world. People flock from far and wide to shows such as Cruft's, ensuring usually that there is 'standing room only' around the ring as the overseas fanciers watch the dogs that they have read so much about.

Competition in many countries is becoming much stronger. In the United States, for instance, there are top winning dogs that could hold their own in competition quite ably against some of the dogs in the United Kingdom. The same can be said of some other top winning dogs from Canada, Australia, New Zealand, Scandinavia and countries within the European community and it is sad that borders and distance sometimes discriminate against international competition.

The Pekingese that you see winning in the show ring today have changed from the dogs that were first brought into the country all those years ago. The oriental dogs that left their homeland in the mystic East to travel across continents and oceans to reach these shores were different in appearance to those of today. Inwardly, however, their lion hearts, dedication and devotion remain, for these dogs win the hearts of those from the lowest in the land to the highest.

Nowadays, Pekingese have flatter faces than their ancestors had, their coats are probably more profuse today and they are shorter in leg. Many of the original Pekingese dogs were smaller in type to those of today, probably resembling more the Sleeve Dog, as they are known in the breed.

Throughout the book, for convenience, the Pekingese has, except where inappropriate, been referred to as masculine. This does not mean to be sexist but is merely an expression of common usage.

For those of you who are already 'possessed' by a Pekingese we hope that in some small way we can pass on to you some of the knowledge that we have learnt along the way. For those of you who are about to enter into sharing your life with one of these enchanting, affectionate, if stubborn, dogs whether as a show dog or, equally important, purely as a companion, we hope that the following pages will be of some benefit to you also.

The most enjoyable and challenging side of owning a Pekingese, or even showing and breeding, is that there is always something new to be learnt. We would not be so presumptuous to say that we know the answer to everything, for one thing we have discovered is that there is always room for learning. This is one of the most fascinating features of being involved with dogs. All we hope is, that if there is anything we have gleaned over the years that may in the future be of assistance to you, then that in itself has made the publication of this book worthwhile.

# 1
# The History of the Breed

In order to introduce you to this delightful breed that we all share, the Pekingese, it is necessary to go back in time so that you will have a little insight into their origin. We will also reveal how it was that they came to our shores from that far-off mystical land, China.

Several earlier books on our breed have covered the breed's history in great depth; in fact, a couple of really early editions, written near enough at the beginning of this century, were almost 'straight from the horse's mouth', so to speak. So, without disappearing beneath a catalogue of multiple dates and a myriad of descriptions, let us return to the mid-seventeenth century and Peking.

In 1644, from the north-east of China came the Manchurians who established the Ch'Ing dynasty on the Imperial Throne. Before they had invaded the Throne a mention was made in the annals of Chinese history of a small dog in the Imperial Palace, referred to as *fu-lin* dogs. It is also known that the Manchurians themselves brought with them from their homelands their own *harbo-go* dogs. However, as with a lot of our breed's history, the facts around this period are unfortunately more than a little hazy.

During the reign of the Emperor Tao-Kuang (1821–50), there is a reference to a Pekingese type. There was the long-haired type and the *lo-sze*, a short-haired pug, and it is thought that there is more than a strong possibility that the two types were crossed. It is also considered that the Shih Tzu or rough-coated Tibetan Lion Dog was most probably crossed with these two dogs.

On the death of the Emperor, his son Hsian Feng succeeded him and, upon his death, his wife Tzu-An, together with Yehonala, the mother of his son, were accorded the title of Dowager Empress. Yehonala became known as Tzu Hsi, a name that has become synonymous with the Pekingese as much of today's ancient breed history revolves around her.

However, we return now to 1857, a time when there was serious discontent without the country of China due to the stringent trading restrictions imposed by the Chinese on the outside world. The final straw eventually came when the British Trading Quarter was literally burnt to the ground by some of the local inhabitants, and because of this Britain and France launched an expeditionary force that captured the city of Canton in the same year. After an unsuccessful request for more lenient trading terms, the army continued its march until it eventually reached the Imperial City itself.

On reaching the Summer Palace it was discovered that the Emperor, together with his entourage, had already fled, although it is rumoured that one of his relatives was found dead, guarded by her little dogs.

In the conclave, three members of the British Force, Lord John Hay, Lieutenant Dunne, and Sir George Fitzroy, eventually came upon five little dogs.

Lord John Hay took possession of two of the little dogs who became known as Schlorff, a male, and Hytien, a black and white bitch. Hytien he presented to his sister, the Duchess of Wellington, while Schlorff remained with him, living to a ripe old age of eighteen.

Sir George Fitzroy's two little acquisitions were also given as gifts; he presented them to his relations the Duke and Duchess of Richmond and Gordon. It is not known quite what happened to these two dogs, except that their son Lord Algernon Gordon-Lennox and his wife became one of the pioneers of the breed, establishing the now famous strain of Goodwood. In fact, one day this good gentleman and his wife were amazed to see, while walking down a London street, two more specimens of the breed. They consequently introduced themselves to their owners, Mr and Mrs Douglas Murray.

It transpired that Mr and Mrs Murray had imported their two dogs from the Imperial Palace; they were the famous Ah-Cum and Mimosa. Eventually these two partnerships got together and produced the very first English Champion, Goodwood Lo.

The last little dog to be taken from the Palace was brought home to England and was presented to Queen Victoria by Lieutenant Dunne; and this was the aptly named Looty.

As the years passed by, several more dogs found their way to Britain from China. In 1893, Captain Loftus Allen, the master of a trading ship, managed to buy a dog for his wife who was already an avid fan of Japanese Spaniels, and this dog became known as Pekin

Peter. It is thought that he was more than likely smuggled out of the Imperial Palace before being sold to the Captain. It has to be remembered that these little palace dogs were so highly revered by the Royal Family and the hierarchy that anyone trying to purloin one of them would have suffered the direst consequences.

However, Pekin Peter safely reached the shores of England and not long after his arrival here he was exhibited at the Chester Show. Three years later the Loftus Allens acquired two more specimens, a dog and bitch, Pekin Prince and Pekin Princess, who were both black.

Another very important bitch who played a part in the development of the breed here was Fantails. She had been brought into the country in 1889 and was a very pretty parti-colour. She was a present to Mrs Browning from Commander Gamble and it was from this little girl that the Brackleys emerged.

Fantails had actually been born in China and bred by a Mr George Brown who had been assigned to the British Consul out there. On his return home he put a bitch named Pinkee, whom he had produced from a bitch called Siaorr'h by an unknown sire, to Ah-Cum. The result of this alliance was a bitch called Tai Tai who was eventually owned by a Mrs A. Gray. Tai Tai was then put to a dog named Pekin Paul, who was a son of Pekin Prince and Pekin Princess, and the result of this was the production of the breed's first Bitch Champion, Champion Gia Gia.

Champion Gia Gia was owned by a Mrs Lilburn MacEwen who, together with two puppies from matings of Mimosa to Ah-Cum and later to Champion Goodwood Lo, also established a niche in the breed with her Manchu prefix.

From the Manchu dogs came one of the early greats, Sutherland Avenue Ouen Teu T'ang, a prominent stud dog in those early days. Champion Gia Gia also proved to be strong in the foundation of the breed for, not only was she the first bitch Champion, her grandson was the famous Champion Chu-Erh of Alderbourne owned by Mrs Ashton Cross, who established a Pekingese dynasty.

Another name in the breed that must not be passed over is Greystones. A dog and a bitch, Chang and Lady Li, were presented to Major Heuston in recognition of his service in China by a highly respected minister of that time, Li Hung Chang. They made their home with their new master in Ireland eventually.

It was in 1898 that the Kennel Club first officially recognised the breed and a Standard of points was drawn up. Also, in that same year, classes were scheduled for the first time at the Ladies Kennel Association show where Ah-Cum won his class, as did Pekin Pretty. Two years later, in 1900, that famous show, Cruft's, decided to put on classes, but in those infant years just one dog was entered, Pekin Yen – how different from the classes of today!

While the breed was beginning to take root here, things were far from quiet in their country of origin. Once again there was unrest, this time from a group commonly known as the Boxers. These latter-day terrorists were hell-bent on driving the 'foreign devils' from their land. They eventually besieged Peking, the Diplomatic Legation being the prime target, and the occupants of this quarter were placed in a desperate situation for quite some time until the arrival of a relief column eased their plight. On the force's arrival at the City, it was once again discovered that the Royal Family had quickly taken their leave.

On the previous occasion the allied troops had entered Peking, they had raided the Summer Palace alone. This time they entered the Forbidden City itself. It is not thought that many dogs were found on this occasion; however, two Pekingese did leave the Palace. Shortly before the force gained entry to the city a Major Gwynne was amongst the army surrounding the palace. Prince Ch'ing, a highly influential member of the palace hierarchy from inside the palace made a bargain with the Major. This was not a pact entered into lightly on the Prince's part for he requested safe passage from the palace through the lines, and, in return, the Major requested a pair of the palace dogs. After much consideration, the Prince finally agreed for, as we mentioned before, these little dogs were practically gods to the inhabitants. The dog and the bitch became known as Boxer and Quaema. It is thought that these are virtually the last two dogs to have come directly out of the old Imperial Palace.

With the breed firmly establishing itself in the British Isles, it must not go without saying that it was becoming equally popular in the United States. In fact, the Dowager Empress, Tzu Hsi, gave several of her little companions away to selected people. One of these was the American artist Miss Carl who had been commissioned to paint the Dowager Empress. The Empress rewarded her with parti-colour Melah. Another of these generous gifts was presented to Dr Mary Cotton and called Chaou Ching Ur, destined to become the first female Champion in the USA.

Several other Pekingese were imported into America but it is not thought that many of these were bred from to a great degree, many of the original winning blood lines coming from Pekingese imported from the United Kingdom. In 1905, in the USA, classes were put on for the breed at the Westminster Show and shortly afterwards America's first Champion was made up: Champion Tsang of Downshire.

Back in Britain, in 1902, the Japanese Spaniel and Asiatic Spaniel Association divided. Originally known as the Japanese Spaniel Club, it had been formed in 1898 and was one of the major influences on the breed involved in the drawing up of the Standard of points. After the division, the Pekingese Club was founded by twenty-nine members and two years later the Pekin Palace Dog Association was formed. Both societies are still in operation. However, they lived a little more grandly perhaps in those days – the committee meetings of the Pekin Palace were held in the Ritz!

When the Pekingese Club was originally formed they had placed within their Standard a weight limit of 10 pounds (4.5 kilograms). Over the years this was altered by a majority vote for the weight limit not to exceed 18 pounds (8 kilograms). A short time after, the weight limit was scrapped altogether. This would appear to be one of the reasons for the formation of the Pekin Palace Dog Association. Two of the club's founder members were Mrs Ashton Cross and Lord Gordon-Lennox, and the club set a Standard which included the reintroduction of the 10-pound weight limit.

Mention must be made at this point of a Colonel Barratt who was serving with the Indian Army in Peking. On returning home to India he took with him two Pekingese, a dog and a bitch – Jabberwock and Howdie, the result of their eventual liaison being Chinky-Chog who was brought to England where he gained his title and went on to become extremely influential as a stud dog.

Chinky-Chog was a bigger type (as was Boxer) than many of the dogs brought over originally. For instance, Schlorff and Hytien weighed a mere 5 pounds (2.3 kilograms) apiece. Pekin Princess weighed 6 pounds (2.7 kilograms) although Pekin Peter was 2 pounds (1 kilogram) heavier. Ah-Cum and Mimosa, it is thought, weighed 5 pounds and 3 pounds (2.3 and 1.4 kilograms) respectively.

This particular chapter would be incomplete without the reputed words of the late Dowager Empress Tzu Hsi about her beloved 'Lion Dogs' that had become a very integral part of life in the Imperial Palace. They were favourites of the Dowager Empress and many of the high court officials and eunuchs, although it is believed that the latter were less than scrupulous on many occasions in some of their methods of husbandry. These little dogs were guarded and cared for in the confines of the palace with a passion, and as we mentioned previously, anyone attempting to spirit one away suffered the dire consequences of his or her action. Small wonder that Prince Ch'Ing dallied over his decision with Major Gwynne.

Therefore, let us close these first few pages with the 'pearls' that are reputed to have 'dropped from the Lips of Her Imperial Majesty Tzu Hsi, Empress of the Flowery Land' concerning the Imperial Pekingese:

> Let the Lion Dog be small; let it wear the swelling cape of dignity around its neck; let it display the billowing standard of pomp above its back.
>
> Let its face be black; let its forefront be shaggy; let its forehead be straight and low.
>
> Let its eyes be large and luminous; let its ears be set like the sails of a war junk; let its nose be like that of the monkey god of the Hindus.
>
> Let its forelegs be bent, so that it shall not desire to wander far, or leave the Imperial precincts.
>
> Let its body be shaped like that of a hunting lion spying for its prey.
>
> Let its feet be tufted with plentiful hair that its footfall may be soundless and for its standard of pomp let it rival the whick of the Tibetans' yak, which is flourished to protect the Imperial litter from flying insects.
>
> Let it be lively that it may afford entertainment by its gambols; let it be timid that it may not involve itself in danger; let it be domestic in its habits that it may live in amity with the other beasts, fishes or birds that find protection in the Imperial Palace.
>
> And for its colour, let it be that of the lion – a golden sable, to be carried in the sleeve of a yellow robe; or the colour of a red bear, or a black and white bear, or striped like a dragon, so that there may be dogs appropriate to every costume in the Imperial wardrobe.
>
> Let it venerate its ancestors and deposit offerings in the canine cemetery of the Forbidden City on each new moon.
>
> Let it comport itself with dignity; let it learn to bite the foreign devils instantly.
>
> Let it be dainty in its food so that it shall be known as an Imperial dog by its fastidiousness; sharks fins and curlew livers and the breasts of quails, on these may it be fed; and for drink give it the tea that is brewed from the spring buds of the shrub that groweth in the province of Hankow, or the milk of the antelopes that pasture in the Imperial parks.

Thus shall it preserve its integrity and self-respect; and for the day of sickness let it be anointed with the clarified fat of the legs of a sacred leopard, and give it to drink a throstle's eggshell full of the juice of the custard apple in which has been dissolved three pinches of shredded rhinoceros horn, and apply it to piebald leeches.

So shall it remain – but if it die, remember thou too art mortal.

# 2

# Pedigree

For those of you taking your first tentative steps into the world of pedigrees and Pekingese let us firstly take a look at the official Pekingese Breed Standard as laid down by the Kennel Club.

Every breed is guided by a Breed Standard that is drawn up by the aforementioned body. The Kennel Club, in their quest for a unified Standard, also consult several of the Breed Clubs for their points of view. It must be said at this point that in some cases it has been an extremely controversial subject!

The Breed Standard is basically a guide for breeders, exhibitors and judges to consult in their pursuit of the ideal Pekingese. The old adage goes that the perfect Pekingese has yet to be born. One always feels that this will never happen, for in the search for perfection one should be more than a little hypercritical. Beware that person who thinks that they have that perfect specimen, for their neighbour may not agree with them. It is always best to be more critical of your own stock and, at the same time, try not to be overcritical of your fellow exhibitor's dogs.

## The Pekingese Breed Standard

### *General Appearance*

Small, well-balanced, thickset dog of dignity and quality.

### *Characteristics*

Leonine in appearance with alert and intelligent expression.

### *Temperament*

Fearless, loyal, aloof but not timid or aggressive.

## *Head and Skull*

Head large, proportionately wider than deep. Skull broad, wide and flat between the ears; not domed; wide between the eyes. Nose short and broad, nostrils large, open and black; muzzle wide, well wrinkled with firm underjaw. Profile flat with nose well up between the eyes. Pronounced stop. Black pigment essential on nose, lips and eye rims.

## *Eyes*

Large, clear, round, dark and lustrous.

## *Ears*

Heart-shaped, set level with the skull and carried close to the head, with long, profuse feathering. Leather not to come below line of muzzle.

## *Mouth*

Level lips, must not show teeth or tongue. Firm underjaw essential.

## *Neck*

Very short and thick.

## *Forequarters*

Short, thick, heavily boned forelegs; bones of forelegs slightly bowed, firm at shoulder. Soundness essential.

## *Body*

Short, broad chest and good spring of ribs, well slung between forelegs with distinct waist, level back.

## *Hindquarters*

Hind legs lighter but firm and well shaped. Close behind but not cow-hocked. Soundness essential.

## *Feet*

Large and flat, not round. Standing well up on feet, not on pasterns. Front feet slightly turned out.

## *Gait/Movement*

Slow dignified rolling gait in front. Typical movement not to be confused with a roll caused by slackness of shoulders. Close action behind. Absolute soundness essential.

## *Tail*

Set high, carried tightly, slightly curved over back to either side. Long feathering.

## *Coat*

Long, straight with profuse mane extending beyond shoulders forming a cape round the neck; top coat coarse with thick under-coat. Profuse feathering on ears, back of legs, tail and toes.

## *Colours*

All colours and markings are permissable and of equal merit, except albino or liver. Parti-colours evenly broken.

## *Weight and Size*

Ideal weight not exceeding 5kg (11 lbs) for dogs and 5.5 kg (12 lbs) for bitches. Dogs should look small but be surprisingly heavy when picked up; heavy bone and a sturdy well-built body are essentials of the breed.

## *Faults*

Any departure from the foregoing points should be considered a fault and the seriousness with which the fault should be regarded should be in exact proportion to its degree.

## *Note*

Male animals should have two apparently normal testicles fully descended into the scrotum.

(Copyright: The Kennel Club)

To help you visualise this Standard we will now go through each section and help you to picture the dog mentally as it is described. However, it should be pointed out at this stage that each individual will paint a slightly different picture as each person can interpret the standard in a fractionally different way.

Provided, of course, that the dog is within the guide-lines of this official Standard there is no need to worry. That is why we have judges. Judge A, for instance, may not entirely agree with Judge B if they happened to have the same few dogs in front of them. One might reverse the decision of the other as regards first or second position. This is what showing is all about, and we cover this in more detail in Chapters 9 and 10.

## General Appearance

The Standard states that the dog should be small and well balanced, thickset and of great dignity and quality. It is a well-known fact that somehow a good dog just stands out from the rest; he just looks right. Even someone who does not know about any particular breed can often tell a really nice specimen just by looking at it. The Pekingese should be fairly compact but not too short in the back for that can tend to produce what can only be described as a 'Pomeranian' look. The dog should be of the correct size so that when you are viewing him from above, looking down on the shape, you should see there the correct pear-shaped body formed by a well-barrelled rib-cage. The body should taper neatly at approximately the waist and should be narrower at the rear of the dog than towards the front. Remember this is when you are looking down at the dog.

The dog should give the impression of chunkiness, so therefore one needs good substance and solid bone. When the bone is a little finer than required this look tends to disappear. The dog should also be low to ground, but not so short in leg that the little chap

*Fig 1 Correct overall outline.*

cannot easily carry his weight around. There should be enough length of leg to allow him to move around sedately and unimpeded, but not with so much length of leg that he tends to lose his overall balance and instead gives a lanky appearance.

Set on this nicely shaped and balanced body is the head which should be in equal proportion to the dog and should be wide and shallow.

## Characteristics

The dog should carry himself fearlessly in the ring with an alert, intelligent expression. Good showmen are born and not made; this is true, for some puppies are born with more than their fair share of arrogance. They seem to possess that attitude of 'Hey look at me, I am Number One', and if a dog has that little something extra he really is a pleasure to have. Unfortunately you cannot always guarantee you are going to get this when you most need it – in the show ring. Some dogs are naturally more outgoing than others. If your dog has that little extra something it often has to be worked at to keep it, while for the more reticent dog a little extra training is needed and very often in cases such as this training classes are an absolute boon. Again, this will be covered more fully later.

A dog that is thoroughly enjoying his outing at a show gives that little extra, he has an added sparkle in the eye and is watching what is going on around all the time, as well as being slightly aloof.

## Head and Skull

Much of the beauty of the Pekingese lies in the head. They have been classed as a head breed in the past, and the Standard points, in fact, gave a large proportion of marks to the head properties. The Pekingese is not, of course, just a 'pretty face' and an overall picture is sought. None the less, with a Pekingese the last thing a judge sees is the head especially in view of the way that they are judged in the United Kingdom with the whole class set on the long trestle tables. So, provided that everything else is to the Standard with your little dog, you do have an added advantage if he possesses a lovely head and expression also.

The opening phrase to this section is fairly self-explanatory. We do desire a large head, the skull should be broad and flat and, looking straight at the dog's head face on, the line between the ears should be wide and flat. It should appear as a nice even line and not be domed as that of a King Charles Spaniel. Try to imagine that a

*Fig 2   Correct outline of head.*

*Fig 3  Incorrect head: too deep and narrow, thereby losing the desired envelope shape.*

*Fig 4  Head showing incorrect domed skull instead of the desired flat topskull.*

pencil could be lain on this skull and no daylight would be seen underneath it. The ears should be neatly set on at each end of this flat topline.

The eyes should be set wide apart and looking forward, not at an angle; in between these the nose should be positioned, set well in. The nose should be flat and not protruding so that looking at the dog from the side there will appear a flat profile. The nose itself should be broad and the pigment should be black with no pink smudges. The Standard also calls for wide-open nostrils; they should not be in any way pinched which would, of course, make it difficult for the dog to breathe.

The wrinkle should fall either side of the face, from above the nose and down either side of it, tapering out towards the outer base of the head. A broken wrinkle produces a far better and more attractive picture than an overwrinkle. An overwrinkle is when the wrinkle forms above the nose and then tends to cover the nose slightly, not giving a particularly desirable look. This, as with pinched nostrils, makes it uncomfortable for the dog to breathe. A pronounced stop is where the nose sets into the head and gives an appearance of being flat faced. Now we come to the underjaw which should be firm. One of the easiest ways to explain this is that a weak underjaw will tend to give the dog a 'parrot-like' expression. Invariably this is caused when the top teeth close over the front of

*Fig 5 Head study showing incorrect heavy overwrinkle, thus making breathing through the partially covered nostrils difficult.*

*Fig 6 Head profiles.*

the bottom teeth. On the other hand, one does not require too strong an underjaw as the dog will be inclined to show his bottom set of teeth for all and sundry to admire.

## Eyes

They say that you can see the soul of a Pekingese through his eyes. The correct eyes possess a delightful melting and wondrous look. They should be large, round, clear, dark and lustrous. A small eye in this breed detracts from the other lovely qualities contained in the head. In fact, it tends to give rather a 'piggy' expression and that soulful look tends to be lost. The eye should be round and not almond-shaped and preferably should not show signs of any white between the eye and the lids. Do not panic when taking your youngster out for the first time or when he happens to meet for the first time somebody else apart from the immediate family or friends: wariness can cause them at times such as this to show a little white of eye. Another thing to remember also is that more often than not the eye is the last part of the dog's anatomy to grow, so there is a very good chance that, with time, this earlier fault could disappear. The eye should be dark, giving that really lustrous appearance. A lighter eye, apart from being undesirable, produces a hard appearance compared with the much more attractive velvety look of a dark eye.

## Ears

The ears should be set level with the skull. They should be heart-shaped and set so that they fall against the side of the dog's head. The leathers must not appear longer than the head so that they fall below the muzzle. This must not be confused with the highly desirable feathering that with proper care and attention will be produced as youngster becomes adult. In Chapter 5 we advise on how you can preserve and care for these fringes.

## Mouth

When being judged, Pekingese are not assessed for bite and, as with the Pug, the mouth is not opened. However, for your own

*Fig 7 Head with incorrect wry mouth.*

information it is always a very good idea to look in the mouth yourself. Take a close look and see how many teeth appear in the lower set of teeth. If you see six little teeth in a straight line in a level bite with the top teeth (that is when the top teeth set into the bottom set), or a reverse scissor bite (this is when the top teeth close down just behind the bottom teeth), you have the perfect jaw.

A fault that can occur in this area is a 'wry mouth'. You will discover this if the jaw slopes away at an angle to either side. In a young puppy of approximately five to seven months this could be attributed to a change of teeth. However, if this defect does not right itself as the puppy grows up you could quite possibly have a dog with this defect. As we say, do not panic with a young puppy, for teething can tend to produce some very strange and weird conditions so be patient and wait for the dog's mouth to settle.

The lips should be level which is fairly self-explanatory.

## Neck

This should be very short and thick, producing an impression of the head being set almost straight into the body and enhancing the picture of a well-balanced and thickset dog.

## Forequarters

The front legs should be heavily boned, again contributing towards the thickset appearance, especially with the short legs that are desired. They should also be slightly bowed outwards at the elbow but, at the same time, the shoulders must be tight at the point of contact, where the leg sets into the body itself. The feet should turn slightly outwards. There is a tendency for some dogs to be slightly

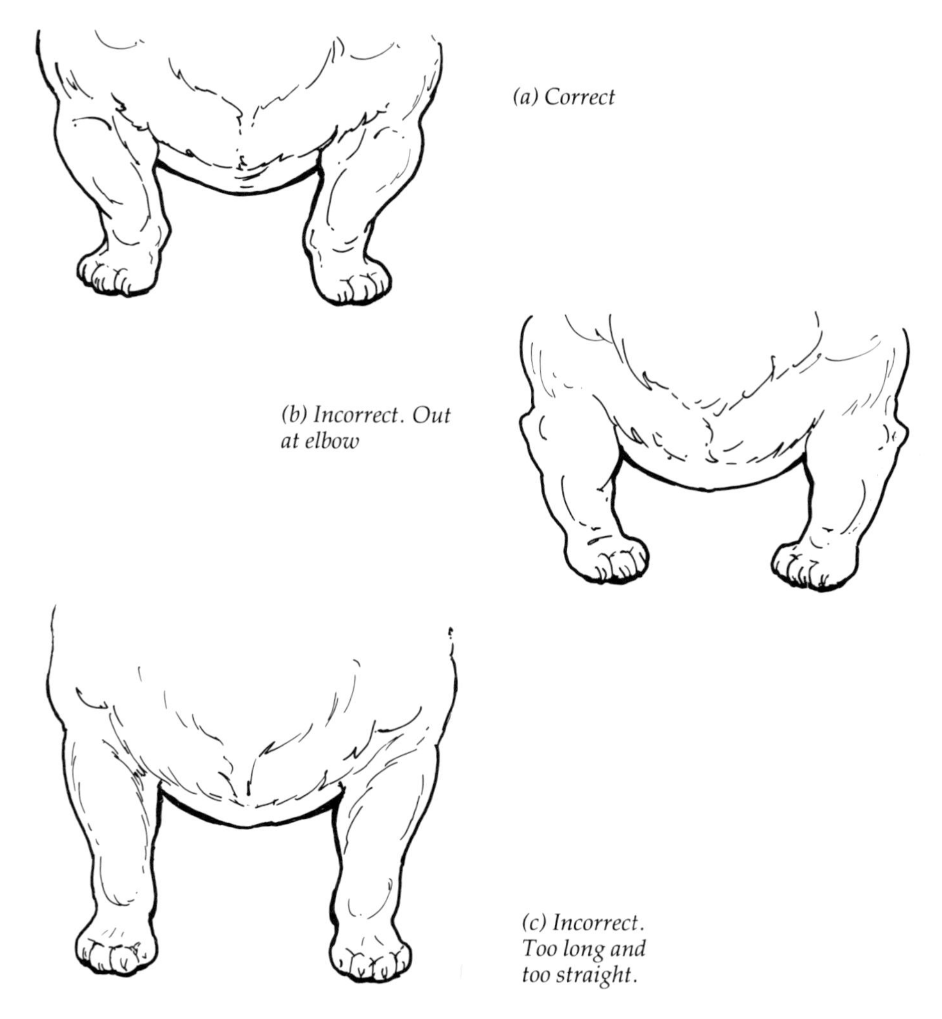


*Fig 8 Forequarters.*

straight in front, possessing the same thick bone as previously mentioned. In many cases they are also tight in shoulder, but the Standard does not wish that any straightness in leg should be present. Needless to say, soundness is desired.

## Body

The body should be short, with a broad chest. The rib-cage should be well barrelled or rounded so that there is plenty of room for the heart and lungs to operate comfortably. The body should be slightly slung between the front legs, so that when you handle the dog from this angle you should be able to place a hand beneath the chest and between the two front legs. The body should not be set on top of the legs but be more set into them. This helps create a low-to-ground impression. Sometimes, when young, a dog is perhaps a little higher on the leg than you would like but, as he matures, this could possibly right itself as the dog will often settle down onto his legs. Very often this can make a difference to a bitch after she has had a litter. Possibly the bone formation at this earlier age is that little bit more pliable and allows for skeletal change.

The back should and must be level; a bad topline or roach back is highly undesirable and is often accompanied by another constructional fault, for instance a bad front. There is a simple way to test for both of these malformations. Very often a young dog can tend to hunch himself when placed on the judge's table for assessment, thereby giving the impression of having a roach back. This may not always be the case, however. Stand your dog on the table in the show position and gently lift him up from the front so that he is leaning against you with his back legs still on the table. Now gently run your hand down his spine; if it was a pure case of nerves the back will feel quite smooth, but, unfortunately, if a roach back is present the symptom will persist.

In order to test your dog's front, once again position him on the table in the show position. Place one hand on the dog's back, at a point at the base of the neck and over the front legs. Now gently rock the dog from side to side, pressing lightly down at the same time. If a fault is present in the front, either one or both of the shoulders will slip out of place.

The Pekingese shape is an unusual one, being pear-shaped. When you work your way from the front of the dog to the rear the

*(a) Incorrect. Bad topline or roachback.*

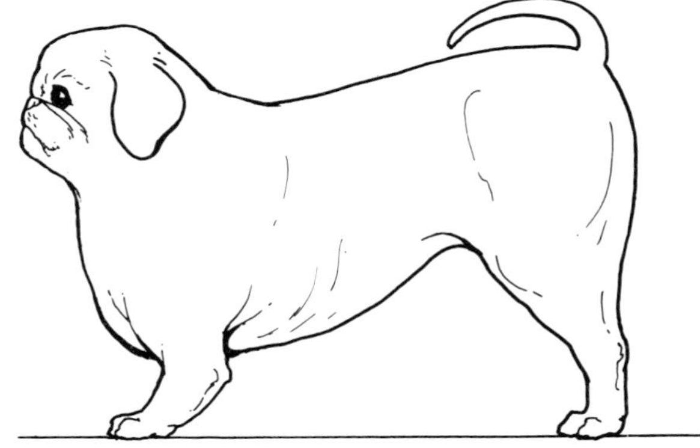

*(b) Incorrect. Bad topline due to straight hocks and bad front*

*(c) Incorrect. Too cobby, lacking the desired defined waist*

*Fig 9 Body Shape.*

rounded rib-cage should neatly taper at the area of the waist so that the dog's shape is lighter behind. Very often because of this shape, a correctly proportioned young puppy will tend literally to 'tip up' when feeding from a saucer. Because of the balance of the dog, it is important that the forequarters are strong enough to be able to contain this weight and carry their burden around.

## Hindquarters

The hind legs can be a little lighter than the front ones, but must be firm and well shaped. From the rear, they appear as being straight but when viewed from the side, a degree of angulation is seen. The upper part of each back leg slopes backwards to meet with the joint of the lower leg which in its turn falls straight to the foot. The back action should be neat and scissor-like. It should not appear to be wide, nor should you be able to see the pads of the feet as in the back action of a Shih Tzu, for instance. The legs must not be cow-hocked (i.e. when viewed from the rear the joints of both legs are close together while the feet are a wider distance apart). Needless to say, soundness is once again essential.

## Feet

Large and flat, but not round. The dog should stand well up on his feet and not the pasterns. To clarify this, the pasterns are set behind the foot and should not be in direct contact with the floor.

## Gait

The true gait of a Pekingese is spectacular for there is nothing more delightful than seeing a lovely exhibit moving in the correct fashion around the ring. This is brought about with a combination of the correctly shaped body, together with the correctly placed legs and neat scissor action from behind, to produce the Pekingese roll. This gait should not be confused with that caused by slackness in shoulder which very often causes a slightly more stilted action but a judge should discover any deformity present on handling. Once again, the Standard stresses the need for absolute soundness.

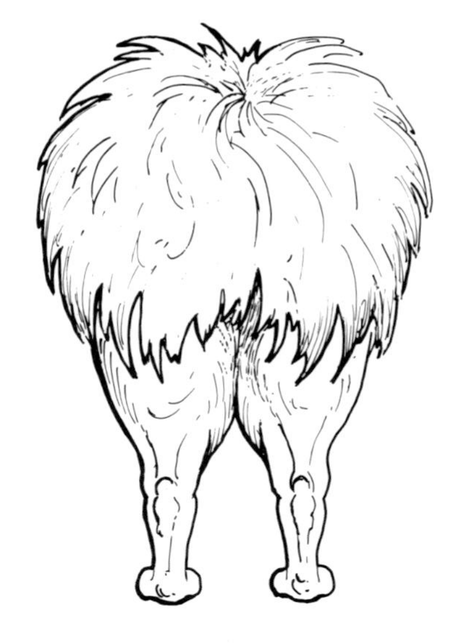

*(a) Correct*

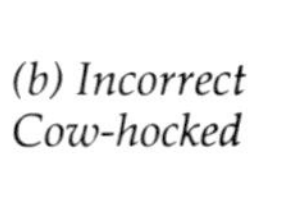

*(b) Incorrect*
*Cow-hocked*

*(c) Incorrect.*
*Weakness in the*
*hocks giving a*
*bandy appearance.*

*Fig 10 Hindquarters.*

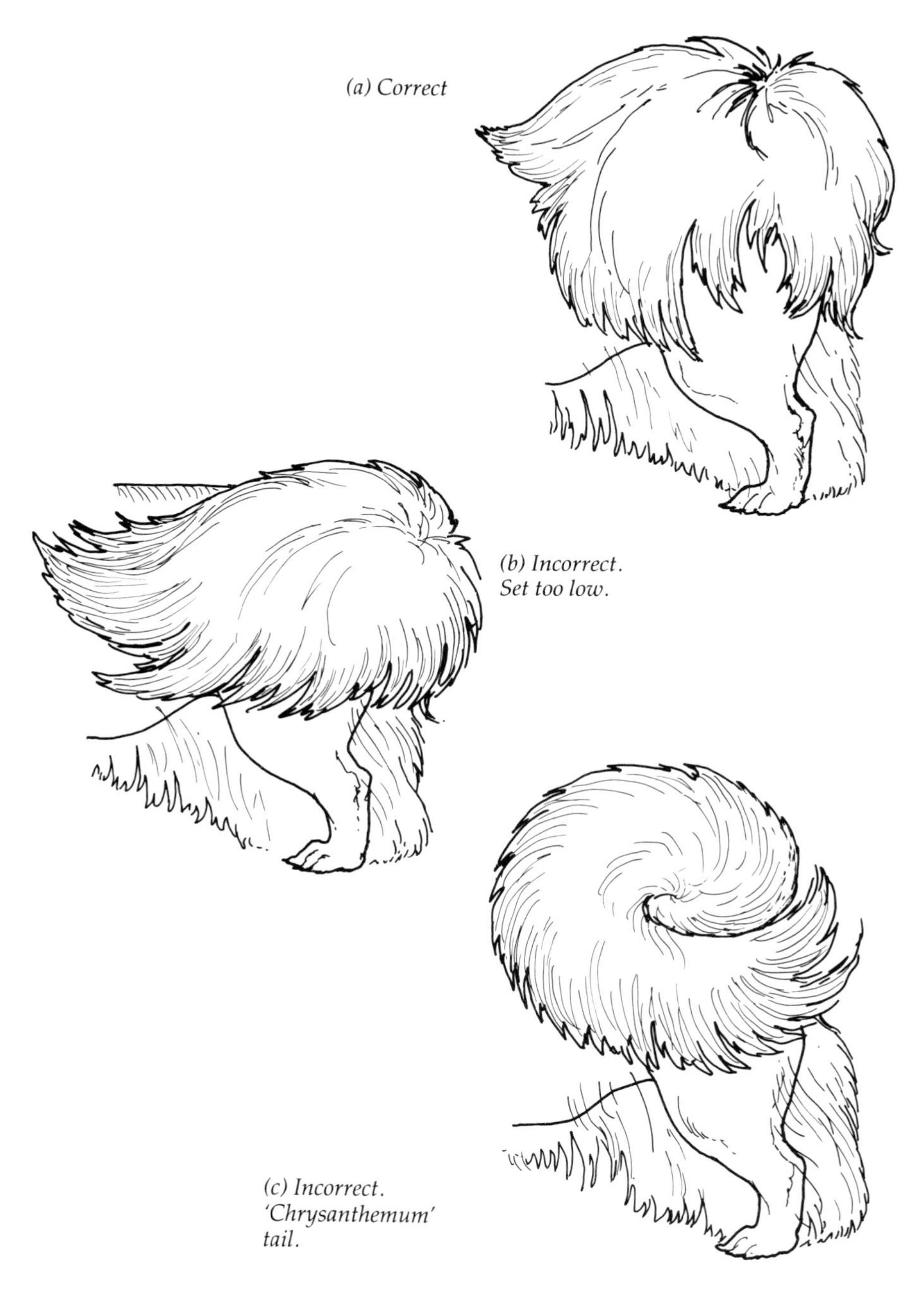


*Fig 11 Tail set.*

## Tail

The tail should be set on high so that when it is slightly curved over the back it will fall gently over the dog's back to either side. A low-set tail will cause it to fall back slightly, especially on the move, and also it will not lie correctly in place. With correct presentation of the tail feathering, the tail will appear to lie flat on the back, and, on some dogs, the long tresses will literally reach up to the back of the head. That of course is no fault, neither is it if the tail falls slightly to the side. It is usually the mastery and expertise of the groomer/ handler which ensure that not a hair moves out of place. A chrysanthemum tail is not desired. This is when the tail bone itself is slightly curved, although as a dog matures and the feathering grows, this is cleverly hidden and would not be seen from the ringside. It would only be discovered upon handling.

## Coat

This is also quite a clear statement. The coat has to be long and straight with obviously no curl in it. The dog should also possess a profuse mane. In Chapter 7 we will attempt to show you how careful presentation of the coat, and the mane in particular, can help to make your dog look that little bit special. The coat should be harsher on top with a slightly softer and woollier undercoat. The undercoat helps to give the top coat a 'stand off' appearance, but it should be stressed that when your dog starts to lose or blow his coat the undercoat must be combed out.

Nothing looks as bad in our opinion than a dog whose undercoat has been left in when it has clearly decided that it wants to part company with its wearer. The coat simply looks dead and out of condition and should not be retained in order to try to make it look as though the dog is still in full coat. When it has reached this stage the skin cannot breathe through this fine woolliness and it must be distinctly unpleasant for the poor animal. Profuse feathering on ears, legs, thighs, tail and toes are called for and again this is fairly self-explanatory, but will be covered a little further on in the book regarding the presentation of these features.

## Colours

We are very lucky that almost all colours and markings are permissable and are equally good. Therefore there should never be the need when, hopefully, it comes to the time that you are asked or wish to judge, for you to decide not to put a particular dog up for an honour for the simple reason that its colour does not personally please you. Provided that as a specimen it is a good one, colour should not make any difference whatsoever.

There are two exceptions, however, that are not allowed, one being albino and the other liver. Another colour that has been known to appear occasionally is blue. This colour on its own does not as such constitute a fault according to the Standard. Unfortunately, though, the pigmentation that seems to accompany this colour is a fault. Usually the nose leather, eye rims and lips will appear as a slate-grey colour. Blue-coloured puppies are often enchanting, the coat is literally a smoky, hazy blue. If you are ever unsure about the colour of your puppy, and should you suspect that he is blue, the pigment is a good guide. Do not confuse this greyish pigment with the pale pigment often found on a puppy of perhaps a few days old. Very often a puppy is born with a portion of his nose paler than the rest, but over the first few days this will gradually fill in and should after a while appear to be black. If you are not sure, do not panic for often an experienced breeder, if asked, will happily give you his or her advice or help in this matter.

Parti-colours are very attractive and come in various colours. There are the black and whites, the red and whites, grey brindle and white or fawn and white. The Standard stipulates, however, that the markings should be evenly broken.

## Weight and Size

This is also fairly self-explanatory. In this country we very rarely use the scales in the general classes. The exception to this is the Special Weight Class in which the exhibits have to be under a certain weight. In the United States, though, it is not an uncommon occurrence for the scales to be called into the ring, the reason being that if one exhibitor feels that another exhibitor's dog exceeds the recognised weight they are within their rights to take this step. Failure to make the right weight can lead to disqualification.

*Fig 12 Outline of Pekingese.*

## The American Pekingese Breed Standard

### *Expression*

Must suggest the Chinese origin of the Pekingese in its quaintness and individuality, resemblance to the lion in directions and independence and should imply courage, boldness, self-esteem and combativeness rather than prettiness, daintiness or delicacy.

### *Skull*

Massive, broad, wide and flat between the ears (not dome-shaped), wide between the eyes. *Nose* – Black, broad, very short and flat. *Eyes* – Large, dark, prominent, round, lustrous. *Stop* – Deep. *Ears* – Heart-shaped, not set too high, leather never long enough to come below the muzzle, nor carried erect, but rather drooping, long feather. *Muzzle* – Wrinkled, very short and broad, not overshot nor pointed. Strong, broad underjaw, teeth not to show.

## *Shape of Body*

Heavy in front, well-sprung ribs, broad chest, falling away lighter behind, lionlike. Back level. Not too long in body; allowance made for longer body in bitch. *Legs* – Short forelegs, bones of forearm bowed, firm at shoulder; hind legs lighter but firm and well shaped. *Feet* – Flat, toes turned out, not round, should stand well up on feet, not on ankles.

## *Action*

Fearless, free and strong, with slight roll.

## *Coat, Feather and Condition*

Long, with thick undercoat, straight and flat, not curly nor wavy, rather coarse, but soft; feather on thighs, legs, tail and toes long and profuse. *Mane* – Profuse, extending beyond the shoulder blades, forming ruff or frill round the neck.

## *Color*

All colors are allowable. Red, fawn, black, black and tan, sable, brindle, white and parti-color well defined: black masks and spectacles around the eyes, with lines to ears are desirable. *Definition of a Parti-Color Pekingese* – The coloring of a parti-colored dog must be broken on the body. No large portion of any one color should exist. White should be shown on the saddle. A dog of any solid color with white feet and chest is not a parti-color.

## *Tail*

Set high; lying well over back to either side; long, profuse, straight feather.

## *Size*

Being a toy dog, medium size preferred, providing type and points are not sacrificed; extreme limit 14 pounds.

### *Scale of Points*

| | |
|---|---|
| Expression | 5 |
| Skull | 10 |
| Nose | 5 |
| Eyes | 5 |
| Stop | 5 |
| Ears | 5 |
| Muzzle | 5 |
| Shape of body | 15 |
| Legs and feet | 15 |
| Coat, feather and condition | 15 |
| Tail | 5 |
| Action | 10 |
| TOTAL | 100 |

### *Faults*

Protruding tongue, badly blemished eye, overshot, wry mouth.

### *Disqualifications*

Weight – over 14 pounds.
Dudley nose.

(Copyright: The American Kennel Club)

## Line-Breeding

Let us now look at the various aspects of applying the Breed Standard in the practice of line-breeding, pedigrees and the choosing of a stud dog for your bitch.

Without wishing to blow our own trumpets too much, we have been complimented on being clever breeders and experts, which is very nice and kind of people, to say the least. However, in planning and breeding, there is a fair proportion of luck, some of it excellent and some of it not so good. For instance, you may think that you have found the perfect match but for one reason or another the two prospective parents simply do not click! On another occasion, everything is right and that future Champion is produced. So having acknowledged the luck element, let us look and see how this can be reduced a little (on the negative side of course) in order to make the odds appear slightly more attractive.

When the time is nearing for your future mother to come into season, look at her critically and also study her pedigree. Now what would you like to change about her; for instance, could she have better substance and bone, could she be shorter or perhaps there is something about the head that could be better? Whichever dog you choose to use cannot improve this or that particular fault on command. Try not to use a dog, however, that perhaps for this reason will not suit your bitch. Have a look around and try to assess what the progeny of that particular dog are like. There are some highly successful and prepotent stud dogs in this country alone who have several successful offspring in the ring. If your bitch is not good enough, though, you really cannot expect the dog in question to be able to place all his qualities into the puppies – it is just impossible. We personally advocate breeding only from a bitch that can happily hold her own at a Championship Show up to Post Graduate, perhaps not to win the class but at least be consistently in the first three in good competition.

Conformation is another important factor. Structurally the bitch should be correct and sound. If she possesses a solid body, moves well and is sound, these are three major factors and something to build upon.

You probably have some idea at this stage of which dog you wish to use or even which particular strain you wish your bitch to go to. Look at her pedigree and, if possible, look at a copy of the prospective sire's pedigree. Try to see if there is any connection through parentage that could provide a common bond. This does not mean, though, that if their great great grandfather is the only tie-up it is just cause to rush off and use that particular dog.

Another point to consider is the progeny of the dog himself. As we have just mentioned, there are some dominant stud dogs in this country, two in particular in the last few years having sired between them over twenty Champions in the United Kingdom alone.

When looking at the bitch's pedigree, consider her father and try to find out whether he has any winning children or a son who is siring well or a daughter who has perhaps acquitted herself well in reproducing her qualities. Of course, her sire could be a relatively young dog, so then look further back and try to see if there is any dog or bitch behind there that has produced any conformity of type.

Obviously her dam's breeding has to be equally good for if your bitch possesses a higgledy-piggledy pedigree the chances of her producing a puppy to carry your banner prestigiously in the show ring are minimal.

Do not be tempted to use Mrs Bloggs' dog for the simple reason that she lives just around the corner or for some other obscure reason. If you are not sure which dog to choose, one of the best ideas is to attend a few shows and see which particular dogs you like. Whether they win one day and are only placed the next should not be a reason to put you off that particular line. Good dogs always come through if they are bred correctly. Compare the dogs that you like: do they tie up in their pedigrees, do you keep admiring stock sired by one particular dog?

When you have decided which dog you think you might wish to use, one of the first steps is to contact the owner of the stud dog and enquire whether or not you would be permitted to use the dog in question. Every kennel has different methods and ideas and some dogs are only available at stud to strictly approved bitches. Do not approach the owner of the sire with the attitude that you are doing them a favour by bringing your little girl to their male. Through their stock and their stud dog or dogs, they have already proved what they can offer the breed and you are still at this stage finding your feet, so to speak.

When this enquiry proves positive, you may be permitted, depending on the owner, to have a copy of the stud dog's pedigree. Compare this with your own and see if there is any common link running through both copies. With any luck there could be two lines running concurrently. This is line-breeding (definitely not to be confused with in-breeding).

The pedigree of our own Champion Toydom Modesty Forbids is shown in Fig 14; he is a Toy Group winner and a sire of three Champions. His son, Champion Toydom Modesty Permits (*see* Fig 32, page 82) is the winner of seven Challenge Certificates and has twice been Reserve in the Toy Group. He is fast proving to be a prolific sire.

From this you can see our own Toydom No Secrets (*see* Fig 83, page 172) who won one Challenge Certificate and two Reserves. However, when she dropped her coat after a successful show season we decided that we would breed from her. She was approximately two years old at this time. She was the full litter sister to Toydom Trump Card (*see* Fig 77, page 162) who sired Champion Jay

*Fig 13 Champion Toydom Modesty Forbids. Owned and bred by Miss A. Summers and Miss V. Williams.*

| Parents | Grand Parents | G G Parents |
|---|---|---|
| Sire Champion Belknap El Dorado. Reg. No. | Sire Belknap King Bee. R.C.C. & J.W. | Sire Champion Yu Yang of Jamestown. |
| | | Dam Belknap Volksmana Queen Bee. R.C.C. |
| | Dam Belknap Ma Tong. | Sire Belknap Tin Song of Jamestown. |
| | | Dam Belknap Myriad of Coughton. |
| Dam Toydom No Secrets. 1 CC. 2 R.CC's. Reg. No. | Sire Sungarth Kanga of Toydom. 3 R.CC's. | Sire Champion Singlewell Wee Sedso. |
| | | Dam Sungarth Anchusa |
| | Dam Dorothello Gay Loretta Wong. | Sire Chophoi Yuan Mei. |
| | | Dam Dorothello Gay Anna Mai Wong. |

*Fig 14 Pedigree of Champion Toydom Modesty Forbids.*

Trump of Sunsalve. Her dam was Dorothello Gay Loretta Wong who was what we would describe as a good, honest, sound and solid bitch. No Secrets' father was Sungarth Kanga of Toydom who possessed all the required virtues, plus glamour and quality.

Going further along you will see Champion Singlewell Wee Sedso (*see* Fig 96, page 217), an amazingly handsome dog with tremendous bone and substance, while Kanga's mother Sungarth Anchusa, a stunning quality bitch, goes back immediately to Champion Yu Yang of Jamestown, one of the breed's great sires.

From Dorothello Gay Loretta Wong, we also get substance and soundness which come down from Sadie Stagg's Chophoi kennel, together with a daughter of Champion Chyanchy Ah Yang of Jamestown, a son of Champion Yu Yang of Jamestown.

We had decided that the dog for this bitch was Antonia Horn's lovely Champion Belknap El Dorado (*see* Fig 98, page 218), and his owner kindly allowed us to use him. This dog combined all his qualities with great dignity, he had a short and tremendous body with a wide shallow head. He was low to ground and has passed on his many virtues down through his children. He encompasses the Belknap qualities which go back to the Jamestowns, to Champion Yu Yang of Jamestown on his sire's side and Jamestown Jin Chi of Caversham on the dam's.

*Fig 15 Champion Yu Yang of Jamestown.*

Obviously everyone has their own theories on pedigrees and breeding programmes but we feel that you have to like the dog as well as the pedigree. You really have to have the 'right feeling' that the male and female are going to go well together. Another factor to take into consideration is that there should be solid breeding in the pedigree that you can reasonably follow. You need only go three or four generations back, no further, for if there is no continuity in these first few lines the breeding will dilute.

Going back to the term 'in-breeding', this is usually the combination of father to daughter, mother to son or brother to sister. This has been used successfully in some cases, disastrously in others and it is one method that we do not recommend. You stand a very good chance of doubling the good points of the partnership but of course it can also go the other way with all the bad faults manifesting themselves.

Also, we feel that, especially when you have been breeding for some while, the time comes when you have to go out and use another line or strain, and in doing this hopefully find a dog that will help enhance your breeding programme. By in-breeding, you are only putting off the day when you will eventually have to find another stud dog or line. By this stage, you could have encountered more problems than you bargained for.

When you choose an 'outcross' you need to go to a stud dog who is likely to produce good solid lines that pass on his good points. The blood lines that he carries should not be carried in the bitch that you intend to breed from but, if they are, they should only be there in minimal amount. But, as we have already stated, this position should only be reached when you have been breeding for some time.

Another pitfall to avoid is that of running out to use the latest made-up champion in the breed. This is perfectly acceptable if he has lovely breeding behind him, but think about this and find out who that dog's sire was. Sometimes it is far better to go to the fountainhead itself until you have seen what the son is going to produce at a later date.

We are extremely fortunate in this country for when we decide on the stud dog we wish to use, invariably it will mean no more than a day's drive for most of us to reach him. Of course, there is the railway or, if we are feeling more than a little affluent and depending on the location, we have the option of travelling by air.

In the United States the distances are so vast that in many cases the bitch has to be shipped by air to reach her prospective husband.

The expense must be more than a little off-putting. If you feel that the dog you wish to use is really ideal for your bitch, then, providing you are not 'breaking the bank', make the effort and do so. Do not be tempted to use another male who is closer at hand just for the convenience. Remember that this is your future kennel and breeding programme you are trifling with.

Over the years, there have been several stud dogs that have helped to produce the lovely breed we have in our homes today. The pioneers of this we have mentioned in Chapter 1. Others that readily spring to mind are Champion Puffball of Chungking and his illustrious son Champion Ku-Chi of Caversham; Champion Chu-Erh of Alderbourne and Champion Tulyar of Alderbourne; Champion Samotha Gay Lad of Beaupres (*see* Fig 101, page 222); the already mentioned Champion Yu Yang of Jamestown; The Honourable Mr Twee of Kanghe and his son Champion Mr Redcoat; our own Sungarth Kanga of Toydom (*see* Fig 97, page 218). These are just a handful of famous sires.

This brings us down to the two great sires of this decade, Terry Nethercott's Champion Jay Trump of Sunsalve and Liz and Paul Stannard's Champion Shiarita Cassidy.

Champion Jay Trump of Sunsalve has sired fourteen English Champions and forty-six overseas Champions to date. The Sunsalves own their home-bred Champion Sunsalve My Love (*see* Fig 62, page 122) and Champion Josto Madam Gaye of Sunsalve, who was bred by Joan Stokoe. Another Josto winner, Champion Josto Royal Flush, is himself the sire of Champions. Although owned by and campaigned to her title by Leonie Rolfe Hazell, Champion Sunsalve Queen Bee of Lejervis was bred by Terry Nethercott. Lilian Snook's latest Champion was Champion Laparata Regal Star. Eileen Newman's home-bred Champion Rosayleen Casino Royale, another dog fast proving his worth as a stud dog, for his son Champion Rosayleen The Gaffer at Sunsalve (*see* Fig 39, page 94) was the top winning Pekingese male 1986 and is now carrying on his illustrious career in the United States for his new owners Don Sutton and Steve Keating. Sue Mannering, who died so tragically at an early age, had made up her first Champion in the breed, Champion Cambaluc Songbird, a pretty bitch bred by Anne Keylock. Our own brother and sister combination both gained their titles, Champion Toydom's Quite Outrageous and Champion Toydom The Drama Queen (*see* Figs 44 and 45, page 105). Champion Pendenrah Lynett was the first female Champion for Liz and Tim Evans and

*Fig 16 Champion Jay Trump of Sunsalve. Owned and bred by Mr T. Nethercott.*

| Parents | Grand Parents | G G Parents |
|---|---|---|
| Sire Toydom Trump Card. (sire of Crufts Reg. No. B.o.B. 1982) | Sire Sungarth Kanga of Toydom 3 C.C.s. | Sire Ch. Singlewell Wee Sedso. |
| | | Dam Sungarth Anchusa. |
| | Dam Dorothello Gay Loretta Wong. | Sire Chophoi Yuan Wei. |
| | | Dam Dorothello Gay Anna Mai Wong. |
| Dam China Bird of Courthill. 1 C.C. Reg. No. | Sire Wuffahoo Wolfstan. | Sire Prince Piers of Changte. |
| | | Dam Sukie Belle of Wuffahoo. |
| | Dam See Lovely of Hills. | Sire Moondust of Dorodea. |
| | | Dam Tra-Lee of Hills. |

*Fig 17 Pedigree of Champion Jay Trump of Sunsalve.*

was also home-bred. Pam Edmonds' Singlewell kennel has been a dominant force for many years, producing a galaxy of stars. Three of these were sired by Jay Trump and were coincidentally all bitches. They were Champion Singlewell Sensation, Champion Singlewell Magic Charm and Champion Singlewell Jay's Dream. The latest to be made up was Maurice and Sheila Smith's Champion Shobris Toyboy.

Also a legend in his own lifetime is Champion Shiarita Cassidy, sire of thirteen English Champions to date and numerous overseas ones. Cassidy is owned and bred by Liz and Paul Stannard and not only is one of our prominent sires, but was also a sensation in the show ring himself, winning a total of twenty-two Challenge Certificates in his show career. He is the sire of the Shiarita's own Champion Shiarita Peter Pan who himself won a total of seventeen Challenge Certificates and was Best in Show at an All Breed Championship Show. Champion Shiarita Fort Lauderdale and Champion Shiarita Diamond Lil are also both home-bred, the latter being the recipient of twenty tickets. Another home-bred Champion came in Champion Shiarita Bobby Dazzler.

Other top winning offspring of this dog are Champion Trentpeke Dreamer, owned and bred by Barbara Wild; Champion Penbi My Fair Lady, bred and owned by Pauline Alcock; Barbara and John McNulty's Champion Silverwillow Gretel; Antonia Horn's Champion Belknap Kalafrana Caspar, bred by Lyn Delaney and now residing in the United States with Mrs Augusta Maynard; and Bert Easdon and Philip Martin's brother and sister dual Champions, who were both awarded the Pekingese Club's Silver Medals for the top winning male and female puppies in 1987. One of them grew up to be Champion Yakee For Your Eyes Only (*see* Fig 68, page 138), the Reserve Best in Show, Cruft's, 1989 and Champion Yakee Gentlemen Prefer. More recently another Yakee-bred dog now owned solely by Liz Stannard quickly gained his title: Champion Yakee Dames Desire of Shiarita. Champion Adlungs My My My is the latest star for May Young, no stranger to success. 'Dames Desire' and 'My My My' both gained their titles in 1989. Last but not least is Champion Royceland Marie, bred by Doug and Joyce Richards. After many years of successful showing and breeding, the summer of 1988 was a year to remember for them when they made up their first Champion.

When you study both of these pedigrees (Figs 17 and 19) you will see that the dam of Jay Trump is China Bird of Courthill who was

*Fig 18 Champion Shiarita Cassidy. Owned and bred by Mr and Mrs P. Stannard.*

| Parents | Grand Parents | G G Parents |
|---|---|---|
| Sire<br>Champion Shiarita Lingsam. | Sire<br>Sungarth Echo of Jamestown. | Sire Ch. Chyanchy Ah Yang of Jamestown. |
| | | Dam Sungarth Anchusa. |
| | Dam<br>Jamestown Yu Darling of Lotusgrange | Sire Ch. Yu Yang of Jamestown. |
| Reg. No. | | Dam Kabrina of Lotusgrange. |
| Dam<br>Champion Shiarita Hello Dolly. | Sire<br>Can. Ch. Pathways Sams Legacy of Jamestown. | Sire Ch. Yu Yang of Jamestown. |
| | | Dam Peek-A-Boo of Pathways. |
| | Dam<br>Ch. Swallowdale Ladybird of Dawoo | Sire Dawoo Prince Orsil. |
| Reg. No. | | Dam Swallowdale Kittens. |

*Fig 19 Pedigree of Champion Shiarita Cassidy.*

the winner of a Challenge Certificate, coincidentally at the same show as Champion Shiarita Cassidy won one of his. The sire is Toydom Trump Card who, is the full brother to Toydom No Secrets, so obviously carries the same blood lines. When breeders first study the pedigree on the bitch's side, they are always surprised that, considering the relatively unknown breeding on the immediate parents of China Bird, so many top winning dogs and bitches have been produced by this incredible dog. But this is where continuity comes in, for behind these initial relatives the breeding is anchored to some solid and world famous blood lines, the Changtes of Pauline Bull and Dorothy Dearn and Heather Beard's Dorodeas.

So through Trump Card comes his father Sungarth Kanga of Toydom. As you will see, behind this dog is the prolific and dominant sire Champion Singlewell Wee Sedso. On the dam's side the strength of the Jamestowns is present, coming down through Dorothello Gay Loretta Wong, a granddaughter of Champion Chyanchy Ah Yang of Jamestown, who is in turn a son of Champion Yu Yang of Jamestown. The combination of Ah Yang and Yu Yang appears behind Sungarth Anchusa who is their daughter and granddaughter respectively.

*Fig 20 Champion Chyanchy Ah Yang of Jamestown.*

It can therefore be seen that these good solid blood lines which have all acquitted themselves equally in the show ring and through their progeny, have all been brought together through Jay Trump and passed on once again to his many winning children.

Looking to the next pedigree, that of Champion Shiarita Cassidy (Fig 19), it will be noticed that both his parents are home-bred Champions. Both Champion Shiarita Lingsam and Champion Shiarita Hello Dolly are the result of discriminate breeding and go back to generations of Jamestown breeding.

Sungarth Echo of Jamestown is a son of Champion Chyanchy Ah Yang of Jamestown and Sungarth Anchusa (the same dam as Sungarth Kanga of Toydom). Jamestown Yu Darling of Lotusgrange is a daughter of Champion Yu Yang. Hello Dolly's two parents, as you will see, are Canadian Champion Pathways Sams Legacy of Jamestown and Champion Swallowdale Ladybird of Dawoo. Sams Legacy's sire is once again Champion Yu Yang. Thus, solid and prolific ancestors have also culminated in this second eminent sire.

# 3

# Buying your Puppy or Dog

The initial question here is, of course, why do you desire to own (or be owned by) a Pekingese? We will not be so presumptuous as to assume that this is the first book that you have picked up on dogs. However, if the answer to this is in the affirmative you are now about to learn the drawbacks, which it has to be said are minimal, as well as the advantages of owning a proud little oriental friend.

Why choose this breed? Usually we find that people have known a Pekingese or have long admired them. They are probably not a breed that somebody merely thumbing through a magazine on the canine world and finding a picture of one would decide that they would like to own. The desire to own one of these delightful dogs, in the vast majority of cases, comes from some association with them. Their beauty literally comes from within, via their personality. Knowing the history of the breed one can always see why the Empress Tzu Hsi was so delighted by them as their genuine devotion, their antics and their 'personality plus' keep one enraptured for a lifetime.

So you have decided that a Pekingese is the dog for you. In this day and age the general idea that they are old ladies' dogs or lap dogs is becoming a fallacy that belongs to the distant past. Even from the showing side of this breed, the exhibitors are fast becoming a younger set. And as for being lap dogs, well they do, of course, like to be treated with a certain amount of fuss – what dog does not? We find, however, that ours seem to be more intent on seeing what is going on around them than simply waiting to be cuddled.

The Pekingese is known as a Toy Dog which means that it comes within the group of dogs known as Toy Breeds, as set by the Kennel Club. Also within this group of dogs come such breeds as Maltese, Pomeranians, Chihuahuas, Cavalier King Charles Spaniels and King Charles Spaniels, to name just a few. As you will probably have realised they are all small dogs, from the tiny Chihuahua to the medium-sized Cavalier King Charles Spaniel. In each show there

*Fig 21 Puppy Pagoda, Toydom Puppies (taken 1957).*

are six groups of dogs altogether. There is the Working Group which includes such breeds as German Shepherds, Great Danes, Rough Collies, and Dobermanns. The Terrier Group has amongst it dogs such as Airedale and Lakeland Terriers, Border Terriers and the distinctive Bedlington Terrier. The Gundog Group includes the ever-popular Labrador, Golden Retriever and Cocker Spaniel. Next we come to the Hound Group which includes dogs such as the glamorous Afghan, the Basset Hound and the Beagle. Last but not least is the unusually titled Utility Group. In this group comes the great British Bulldog, the glamorous Shih Tzu, all three sizes of Poodle (Standard, Miniature and Toy) and the Tibetan Spaniel.

If you want a dog that will happily go for a five-mile hike with you every day, running and catching sticks and balls along the way, diving into the muddy river and swimming to the other side, we really feel that a Pekingese is not for you. This does not mean that you cannot take one for a walk for they will happily trot along beside you, especially if they have been used to it from puppyhood. They will also run happily over the fields and a fair way at that, having a thoroughly fantastic time. However, do take the greatest care should your daily walk take you anywhere near a pond or river for with their heavy coats the sheer weight of it when wet will quickly drag them down.

## Show Dog or Pet?

This brings forth another question, do you wish to have this little dog as a show dog or as a pet? If you want to have a Pekingese for the show ring the preceding paragraph does not wholly apply, and the water aspect is definitely out! This does not mean that Show Pekingese cannot go for walks; in moderation they will help to keep the dog fit. However, if you are hoping to be able to keep any sort of coat on your prospective show dog your little charge flying merrily off over hill and dale, through gorse and brambles is going to set you one gigantic problem when the time comes to groom the dog. So we will treat the two separately here and deal initially with purchasing a pet/companion Pekingese before discussing buying one for the show ring.

First of all you should ask yourself the question as to whether you wish to have a puppy or maybe an older dog. There are advantages to both. With a puppy you do have the opportunity of getting it used to your way of life as they are easily adaptable at an early age. Also, with a little patience they can quite quickly become integrated into your home. With an older dog, it is more often than not that the dog is house- and probably lead-trained which, in the case of an older person perhaps, means that they are easier to manage than a more boisterous pup.

Usually a reputable breeder will not let a puppy go to its new home at under ten weeks of age. However, depending on circumstances, you may be allowed to choose your puppy or be allowed to see it at six weeks. It does, though, need to be with its breeder until it reaches the ten weeks so that it can be regulated onto a manageable and steady diet after it has been weaned away from its mother completely.

If the breeder allows you to come and choose your puppy, or see the puppy that has been offered to you at approximately six weeks of age, however difficult it may be, try to curb your excitement and wait until the time draws near for you to collect your companion. Try not to be tempted to bombard the breeder with requests to visit to see your new acquisition.

Following our current train of thought, this little puppy has been sold to you as a pet, and because of this factor the price you will have paid will be lower than that charged for maybe its show-quality brother or sister. Many people have no desire whatsoever even to attend a dog show let alone show at one. However, there are a few that become tempted when, walking their dearly loved little dog in the park, a passer-by happens to make a comment such as, 'he is beautiful, you really ought to be showing him.' Before you think that is the best idea that you have ever heard, just stop and ponder on this for a moment!

Remember that this little dog who follows you faithfully was sold to you by the breeder as a pet. In their opinion the dog, at the age it was sold to you, was not quite good enough to enter the show ring. Of course, mistakes have been known to be made, and on the odd occasion a puppy sold as a pet has improved enough to be shown. But on the whole this is a very rare occurrence. The breeder has said that this little dog was just what you wanted, a pet and companion, no more or less. So trust the breeder's years of experience in the breed. If you feel though that you have a prospective 'Champion' in your hands, contact the person who sold you the puppy and ask if they would be good enough to appraise this little dog and give their honest opinion.

If you still feel that you definitely would like to show, this is fine but do remember that the little dog you will be taking to the show has been your faithful companion and, despite all else, will still be the same loving little Pekingese when you return home. If the judge does not award him a card, it is not the end of the world; just remember that this little dog will follow you through thick and thin, and the fact that he has not won at a dog show does not make him a lesser dog or a less devoted pal. Simply put the show down to experience and take your little friend home.

## Rescue Services

We are extremely fortunate as a breed in as far as there are hardly any bad cases of cruelty or neglect that necessitates the Rescue Services stepping in. In the vast majority of cases the Rescue Services are called in to home dogs or care for them due to illness in the family or perhaps the death of the owner. These Rescue Services do a magnificent job, going out and fetching the little dogs and bringing them into their homes and from then on caring for them as one of their own until a suitable owner can be found. Many prospective owners would prefer to give a home to one of these poor little dogs that are in need of resettlement rather than perhaps buying a young puppy, and for this reason at the end of the book (*see* Appendix 3, page 238) we have listed some of these Rescue Services for this breed that do such a worthwhile job, many with little or no reward.

## Male or Female?

Another point to take into consideration before you acquire your Pekingese is whether you would prefer to have a male or a female. There are advantages and disadvantages to having either sex.

With a female you have the problem of her coming into season. This can sometimes be a bit of a nuisance but, being a small breed, the slight mess that is caused by this event is fairly minimal. It is essential to ensure that her private parts are kept clean with a little warm water and cotton wool. Of course, if you are used to taking her for a regular walk, at a time such as this you may find that you acquire a few unwanted friends along the way, so this constitutional should be abandoned at this time if at all possible. The average period of time between oestrus is approximately six months; some bitches can extend this time to anywhere between six and twelve months. If you feel that you are able to cope with this, all well and good, but if this does present a problem it is advisable to consult your veterinary surgeon and discuss the possibility of having her spayed.

When offered a dog as a pet some people inevitably worry that he will spend the day lifting his leg and leaving his mark around the house. Usually when you have had the dog since puppyhood he will be trained to your way of life. This is a problem that is more likely to occur with an older dog than a puppy if he has only been used to kennel life and has perhaps been used at stud. If he has been living in someone else's house as their pet dog then hopefully this will not occur.

However well trained to the house your dog may be, it could happen that when he visits unfamiliar surroundings, to your horror he could be very unsociable on your hostess' lovely settee.

With a dog, there is the option of castration on which your

veterinary surgeon will again advise you. This can be done at a reasonably young age and is sometimes a good idea if you have two dogs of both sexes.

If, however, your dog is not castrated, take heed. Do not be tempted to let Mrs Bloggs bring her bitch to him for the simple reason that you would both like to have some puppies. Apart from the fact that you must be sure that both parents are registered at the Kennel Club before they can be sold as pedigree dogs, this could literally be the rock that you perish on regarding your little male. Fine, they could have puppies but your problems may just be beginning, for what your dog had not had he would not miss, but now he could drive you mad wanting a harem of his own. It is no good thinking that breeders will be flocking from far and wide to use him at stud, for as we have already explained in the preceding chapter, a dog will only be used extensively at stud if he is well bred and has proved his worth in the show ring and through his progeny.

We personally prefer the male of the species to the female on the whole as a companion, though obviously others may feel differently. The male tends to be that little more akin to you and gives himself a little more to you. Having said that, this is only a personal preference. You can be sure that whichever sex you choose you are bound to have a wonderful sweet companion, and what more could you possibly ask for?

## Show Pekingese

Now we come to the other aspect of buying a puppy, this time for the show ring. Do not suddenly decide 'I want to show a Pekingese' because you have heard that our friend Mrs Bloggs from around the corner has a litter and says that they are good enough to be shown. So you, then, rush around and buy one – wrong move!

There are in circulation two reputable weekly journals which your newsagent will stock or order for you: *Our Dogs* and *Dog World*. In both these papers a section is carried that advertises forthcoming dog shows. There are three types of shows: Limited, Open and Championship.

A Limited Show, as the name suggests, is limited to members of the show society only, and also prohibits any dog who has gained a Challenge Certificate. An Open Show is basically open to all, for even Champions can be entered here, and one does not have to be a member either. Both these types of show are ideal training grounds for younger dogs which prepare them for the strong competition of the higher-graded Championship Shows. A Championship Show is the only show whereby a dog can qualify for Cruft's and also be awarded a Challenge Certificate. In order to be made a champion a dog has to win three of these Challenge Certificates or CC's as they are commonly abbreviated. These certificates have to be awarded by three separate judges.

Another type of show we should mention here is the Exemption Show. These once again are ideal training grounds for puppies and young dogs. There are usually four or more pedigree classes for dogs of that ilk. The competition can be really hot at these shows for many people like to bring their dogs out to these at a weekend prior to some of the major shows for that little bit of extra experience. After these pedigree classes follow several novelty classes, for instance for 'the dog that resembles its owner' which can cause a lot of fun!

So, what we would now advise is, study the selection of shows advertised (they vary from week to week) and try to find one in your area. Some of the shows have several breeds scheduled and this will usually be listed under each individual show. There are also Breed Club Shows and, at these shows, it will just be that one particular breed that is entered. So preferably try to find an Open Breed Club Show near you (we have in the United Kingdom eighteen breed clubs in all) or a Championship Show either restricted to Pekingese alone or perhaps an All Breed Championship Show. Go along for the day to one of these and see these dogs in competition with one another. This gives you a chance to see which particular lines appeal to you and also, especially at the All Breed or Club Championship Shows, some of the top winning dogs in the ring.

In fact, before you finally make up your mind we would advise you to attend a few of these shows, buy a catalogue and look at the breeding of the dogs that are winning consistently if that particular type appeals to you. Examine their breeding in the catalogue for there you will find the name of the dog, its owner and breeder, also its sire and dam – it is all there for you to study.

So, after attending some of these shows, you have now decided upon the lines that you like and you hope to be able to purchase a puppy from this breeder. Do not be shy; go and introduce yourself, for people in this breed are more than happy to help a would-be fancier, and most reputable kennels will try to help and advise a novice. One word of warning: when you eagerly rush up to introduce yourself, try not to do so just as that particular person is about to enter the ring, patting the dog at the same time and undoing perhaps all their hard work for presentation. If they are busy on the benches preparing their dog for the show, introduce yourself and enquire when would be a good moment to have a word with them. As with buying a pet, always go to a reputable breeder and not to good old Mrs Bloggs. Devoted breeders have their reputations to think of and are committed to the betterment of the breed.

Most breeders know their own lines and at an early age of approximately six to eight weeks will be able to assess which is the puppy or puppies that show enough promise to stand a chance perhaps of stepping into the show ring. However, puppies can change for, with the change of teeth at around three to six months, they can turn from pretty little puppies into little ugly ducklings. A breeder will then wait for the duckling hopefully to develop into a beautiful swan. So if a puppy is sold at approximately ten weeks of age there can be no guarantee that he will develop into being a certain Champion. When you purchase a dog or bitch at this tender age you are literally taking a chance that it will travel through the 'flapper' stage and emerge from the other side of six months as a promising puppy.

The other alternative is to try to buy a puppy when it has gone through this early transition and is over six months of age. Hopefully by this time the puppy has successfully gone through all these trials and tribulations. Then, of course, you will have to remember that the price for this puppy will for obvious reasons be higher than if you had bought it at a younger age. For at this later stage you have in front of you almost the finished picture. In the case of a prospective new fancier coming into the breed we feel that, finances permitting, this is probably the best course of action to take.

Another question that immediately springs to mind is whether you wish to buy a male or a female Pekingese. The ideal situation is of course to buy a bitch that is suitable to be shown and can also be bred from later on. It has to be said that to find a bitch puppy of this calibre is not the easiest task in the world. A bitch of this quality is worth her weight in gold and most breeders tend to keep these very good bitches in order to procreate.

However, do not despair for in the world of showing and breeding patience is the ultimate virtue. Remember, look ahead all the time. If it is at all possible we would advise the novice to buy a bitch that the breeder feels would do a little bit of winning, one that you would not feel ashamed to take to an Open or Limited Show and that, hopefully, would be placed in the first three consistently. You should look for a bitch that does not have any outstanding fault, for instance a bad front, wry mouth, one that is unsound or has a roach back. This particular bitch may not be a top winner herself but could, sent to the correct dog, possibly produce that winning puppy that you desire.

You have to remember at this stage that you are learning all the time. Learning about the breed, how to show your dog and various aspects pertaining to this. So this will, therefore, be a training period for you both. In Chapters 6 and 8 we discuss the training and showing of your dog in more detail and how you go about entering him for a show.

You may possibly decide that you would prefer to have a dog to show rather than a bitch. There are advantages in this, one of the main ones being the question of coat. Unfortunately bitches tend to cast their coats faster and more frequently than their male counterparts. This invariably occurs at a time when you feel that perhaps one particular judge would have looked favourably on her. In the main, a male carries a heavier and more stable coat than a bitch. It is the age-old story of nature; compare the peacock to the peahen or the male pheasant to its mate. This seems to be the way of the wild, that the male of the species invariably is that little more glamorous than its opposite.

Personally, although the standard in both sexes is particularly high, especially in the United Kingdom, the males' classes seem to be harder fought out, most probably due to the aspect of stud work. A top winning male will be highly sought after as a prospective sire for several bitches. Therefore, it is best to bear in mind that if you are buying a male puppy, with this being possibly your first venture into the show world, you must try to ensure that it is a really nice one. A bitch can be bred from at a later date, as we have already pointed out, but a dog will not be in too much demand at stud, bearing in mind some of the prolific dogs that are standing at stud throughout the country.

It really is a case of patience. Showing and breeding cannot be rushed and you must always keep sight of that goal in front of you. So always plan ahead, think of your next move in advance and set your next course of action.

# 4
# Puppy Management

The time has eventually come round to the day that you are to collect your puppy and bring it back to its new home.

## Inoculations

After collecting it from the breeder, remember that it will be at a very vulnerable age in many ways. Firstly, it will more than likely be at an age whereby it is barely old enough to have been inoculated against the various canine diseases, distemper (hardpad), infectious canine hepatitis and leptospirosis. The puppy may or may not have had an injection at approximately eight weeks to immunise it against parvo-virus; this usually depends on the feelings of that particular breeder or his or her veterinary surgeon on the best age to carry this out.

We personally tend to carry this out at approximately eight weeks of age, initially against parvo-virus. The full course of injections is started when the puppy is around twelve weeks of age. This is for the first part of the immunisation; the second part is repeated a fortnight later. Further protection is usually recommended by the vet and we tend to enforce this when the puppy is nearing six months of age.

Once the puppy has had its first part of the course of injections, your vet will inform you that you will need to return with the puppy after two weeks for the next injection. In between these two inoculations, your puppy must on no account go outside the safe boundary of your home for the simple reason that the disease has been placed inside your puppy through the injection and the next couple of weeks are a high risk period for it. Probably, rather to be safe than sorry, your veterinary surgeon will advise you to refrain from taking your puppy out for a further two weeks after the second injection.

During the first few days after the initial injection it has been known for a slight reaction to occur. Because the disease has been injected into the puppy, although of course in a mild form, you may quite possibly find that at approximately the fifth day after the first injection the puppy may go off its food or show a slight discharge in one or both eyes. It could also have a slight upset stomach and appear generally down and quiet. This is not uncommon, but if it does not seem to be showing a distinct improvement after twenty-four hours, contact your vet immediately.

So, bearing in mind that your young puppy will probably be very susceptible to any form of infection, take it straight from the breeder to your own home. Do not call in to see your friends and let this little puppy run about their place unprotected, especially if they happen to own a dog themselves. Their dog should be immune to these diseases but could easily be a 'carrier' as far as your uninoculated puppy is concerned.

Similarly, if you have another dog or dogs of your own and they are especially used to going for walks in the local park or wherever, try to ensure that they are kept away from the puppy, at least until it has had its first inoculation.

## Diet

Apart from the obvious problem of infection, this little mite will be particularly vulnerable diet-wise. The majority of concerned breeders will issue you with a diet sheet or will at least tell you what to feed it on for the first few weeks of its life. Follow this diet to the very best of your ability because with a change of home, even the change of water in various areas can quickly upset a small puppy's tummy and make it feel quite wretched.

This is a diet sheet that we recommend if we let a young puppy go to a new home at about ten weeks.

**Breakfast** Either a hard boiled egg, or a scrambled egg with a little cheese grated onto it.

**Lunchtime** Either a little raw mince or some finely chopped cooked chicken. A little well-steeped puppy meal or cooked rice can be added.

**Teatime** A little tinned puppy food, once again with a very small helping of well-steeped puppy meal

or

a little finely minced tripe mixed with a portion of raw mince.

**Suppertime** A little finely minced chicken, fish or rabbit. Tinned pilchards are quite a favourite with some puppies as long as they are well 'mushed' up.

**Bedtime** Baby's rusk steeped in milk (goat's milk, if possible) with a little pinch of glucose.

We recommend that the puppy should have these five meals until it is approximately fourteen weeks of age, when we decrease this to four by dropping the suppertime meal. At eighteen weeks of age, we once again decrease this by one meal, having three meals: breakfast, lunch and an earlier supper/bedtime meal.

Once the puppy is coming up for six months these meals can be reduced again to two – breakfast and tea. Our puppies, from about five months, seem to love the various doggy biscuits for small dogs that are on the market and these help promote their new teeth. They also amuse them for ages chasing them around the place. One final word on the diet sheet: as the meals decrease you should obviously increase the amount at each meal.

As we have said, this is our method and everyone has their own ideas and methods of rearing, knowing also, of course, which particular method suits their dogs the best. So always go by the diet sheet that the breeder of your puppy advises you to, for it is this food that the puppy will have been used to and, if you stay with this method, you should not experience too many problems.

There have been occasions when we have heard of people buying a young puppy and taking it home complete with the diet sheet. Unfortunately at that stage they seem to think that they know better. For instance, they decide not to feed the tinned puppy food, being quite sure that 'Junior' would absolutely love some liver or heart. This can cause complete disaster resulting in considerable distress to the poor little animal. All it will do is give the puppy the most terrible diarrhoea and, without proper and immediate veterinary attention, it will quickly dehydrate leaving you with a desperately ill puppy on your hands. So this is why we stress that you should take heed of advice given to you by the breeder of the puppy.

## Settling In

The first night away from its brothers and sisters could be a very traumatic situation for the youngster. Remember, you must look awfully big and strange, and the puppy has just been thrust into a large and strange new wide world. Up until this moment, it has more than likely been used to the comfort and companionship of the rest of the litter.

We have found that the following method can be quite helpful when it is time to put the puppy to bed for the night. If you have an alarm clock that you can spare for a short while, wrap it up in a blanket or something similar as long as it is soft and is comfortable for the puppy to want to cuddle into. Before you put it in the puppy's bed or pen make sure that the clock is wound up, with the alarm out of action, of course, for you may wake up to a more than upset little dog. With luck, the gentle ticking of the clock will soothe the puppy and hopefully it will settle down to a good night's sleep.

### *House-Training*

Another exercise to be tackled is the start of the house-training. Not that we are biased in any way, but Pekingese are quite intelligent little souls and soon pick up the idea that the 'loo' is outside the four walls of the dwelling and not on the new Persian rug. However, to achieve this end a little guidance along the way is necessary.

More than likely, when your puppy was with its brothers and sisters he would have been used to playing in a puppy pen with newspaper down on the floor of it, which would have been used when 'nature called'. As you will very quickly find out, 'nature calls' quite often for a ten-week-old puppy! If your little pet can be confined to the kitchen for the first few weeks in its new home you will probably find it easier for training.

We would suggest that at first you would be best advised to place newspaper strategically around the floor, ensuring that there is always some near the various exits, preferably the back door if that leads out into the garden where your little pup will eventually go to relieve itself. After a few days, start to decrease the amount of papers until you are eventually left with only the ones at the door leading outside. You should then find that, apart from the odd little accident, the puppy will always head straight for this piece of paper.

As time goes on and the puppy becomes used to this method, and providing that you have a garden and do not have to take your puppy out for a walk uninoculated to relieve itself, try to extend this system by allowing your puppy to go outside to the toilet after each meal. If, of course, you are not fortunate enough to have your own garden, this will have to be left until the puppy is protected by vaccinations.

Wait and watch the puppy while it is in the garden and, once it has finished what it went outside to do, make a fuss of it and let it know what a good dog it is. Some puppies are extremely quick at picking this up, while others may take a little longer; you cannot generalise. Just persevere patiently and gently – it should not be too long before the penny drops!

## *Sleeping Quarters*

A puppy at this age needs plenty of good food, moderate exercise and a fair amount of rest. When it was with its litter companions it would have been accustomed to the regular meals that you are going to carry on feeding it and will have been used to playing a fair amount of the time and, when it was tired, sleeping. It is best to carry on trying to perpetuate this way of life for the first few weeks in its new home. Therefore, at some points throughout the day try to ensure that your puppy can go into a basket somewhere that it can sleep. For example, after its first meal of the day let it play and, having been outside to relieve itself, put it into its bed and allow it to rest for an hour or two while you attend to your chores.

If your finances permit, there are some extremely well-made puppy pens on the market. The majority of these come in sections and can be easily assembled and dismantled for your convenience. These can be an extra expense if you intend to have only this one little Pekingese as a pet. Having said that, there are advantages to this. For instance, if there is a reason that you wish your pet to sleep in one particular area at night, this can easily be achieved and a routine established that the puppy can happily become used to. To make sure that it settles down comfortably, place a cosy basket in the pen so that it will happily curl up into it and settle down. Another advantage to a puppy pen is that if you are invited to stay with a relation who is not 'canine orientated', an erectable pen that your little dog will go happily into will invariably make the visit less traumatic all round and will quite possibly ensure that you will be invited back, dog and all.

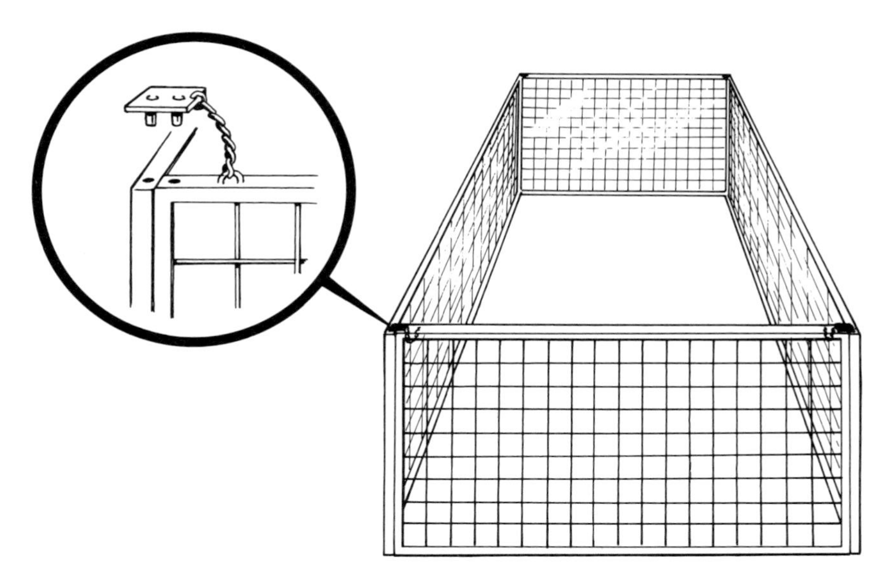

*Fig 22 Puppy pen.*

For those of you wishing to enter the showing and breeding arena, these puppy pens are obviously a necessity, especially when you have your first litter of puppies. Having these pens enables you to keep them under control and out of harm's way.

There are obviously various ways in which you can keep your show dogs. You can, of course, keep them in the house with you or have a kennelled area outside. If you have a couple of dogs only, it is more than likely that you would wish to have them with you in the house. However, we think that a vast majority of breeders and exhibitors alike started off thinking 'I am only going to keep two or three dogs'. This of course just does not happen.

If you think about it practically, of the two that you have, at least one is more than likely to be a female whom of course you will eventually want to breed from. You are breeding hopefully to try to produce a Pekingese that will be superior to its parents. Trying to aim for that better specimen of the breed is one of the main aspects of breeding and showing. So, obviously, if everything works out for the best, you will want to keep at least one from this litter. Presuming that this puppy is a bitch and she turns out to be structurally a good specimen, you will eventually wish to have some puppies from her. Thus, this breeding programme that you have launched into could eventually result in a lot of tiny feet pattering around the house!

Two of the main disadvantages to bear in mind with all these dogs running around the house together are fights and damage to the show coats. There is bound to be at some stage the odd scrap which can result in one at least of your pride and joys suffering a nasty injury. One of the most susceptible parts of the anatomy of this breed are their eyes. Without the protection of an extended muzzle that other breeds have, these marks of combat can lead to some very nasty ulcerations upon the eyeball itself. Another point to consider is that your prospective star, whom you have nurtured in every respect including caring for his coat, will be hard pressed to retain these lovely long fringes that you desire due to the fact that his companions have spent the day swinging and chewing on them. There is nothing more tempting, especially to a young puppy, than these lovely tresses of its older playmate.

It is, therefore, really more sensible to consider instituting a form of routine and kennelling that suits both you, your dogs and your life-style, making it a pleasant way of living for all concerned.

Obviously space is a major factor in deciding on the best way to

*Fig 23 Teijon Tia and Champion Teijon Linetta. Owned and bred by Mrs T. Brickwood.*

keep your dogs. Some breeders convert a spare room in the house, situated downstairs for the convenience of being able to let the dogs out easily, and turn this over to the housing of their dogs. However, the majority are not fortunate enough to be able to do this, and, because of this, many breeders tend to turn to the idea of having a kennel situated in the garden.

There are two distinct types of building that spring to mind, one a brick-built kennel, the other of the wooden variety. Whichever building you decide on, the following points should be taken into consideration. You will have to prepare for the rise in temperature during summer and, in the erection of the kennel, allow for adequate ventilation. These lovely summer days are wonderful for us humans but not so delightful for our Chinese companions who carry such a wealth of coat that the heat is much harder to bear. In the winter months, however, you need to ensure that the kennel is also well insulated so that the damp, cold and draughts are kept well at bay.

There are some extremely well-made sheds around these days that can make a lovely home for your dogs. We would advise you always to go for a shiplap-styled one and not the cheaper variety which in the long run would only bring you problems. A well-made shed that is given careful attention will literally last for years.

Insulation in a wooden kennel, as we will now call it, is even more important than in its brick-built counterpart. The method we have personally opted for is hardboarding the walls and ceiling, with a reputable insulation within the cavity. This helps to ensure a cosy atmosphere in the winter, while in the summer it helps to keep the temperature down a little inside. A brick-built kennel will tend to be that little more weatherproof and is more desirable, once again finances and space permitting. As regards the insulation of this, your builder or hopefully the 'DIY' enthusiast of the family will be able to advise the best method. With our brick-built kennel we tended to use a similar method of insulation to the roof as applied with the wooden kennelling.

If you do not want your little band of dogs running merrily over your recently planted flower bed, it is best to have at least one run sectioned off adjacent to the kennel. This again depends on space and how many dogs you intend to keep. If at all possible, we would recommend that you have more than one run, allowing you to run certain dogs separately for various reasons, one being bitches in season with a male present.

Once you have your kennel built and your runs erected, the subject of heating must be tackled. This really is a matter of personal choice, for some breeders think that heating in the kennel is really quite unnecessary and that, of course, is fine. One of the main arguments for this, apart from the expense, is that some people feel that the growth of the coat is promoted without artificial heat. In fact, we feel that if your dog is bred to have coat in its line this will make no difference at all. If there is no wealth of coat in the line, no amount of the cold weather that we experience at least in the United Kingdom would improve this to a vast extent. But if you decide against installing a heater or whatever, do make quite sure that your kennel is more than adequately insulated.

If, though, you do decide to install some form of heating in your kennels, you will have to decide which method to adopt. We would advise you against the use of paraffin-style heaters for these can easily be knocked over by one of the dogs. Of course, the ideal system is central heating but if your kennel is too far from the house, this is most likely out of the question or may prove to be a very expensive operation.

We personally have installed some very effective slimline electric wall-mounted heaters that have a lower kilowatt rating than some of the larger convectors. These are also fitted with a 24-hour regulator which can be set to come on and go off at whatever times you feel appropriate. You do not need to make your kennel a hot-house; it is enough to set the heaters at a comfortable heat so that the temperature rarely drops much below 50 °F (10 °C). Always keep a wall-mounted thermometer at hand in order that regular checks can be made for the varying seasonal degrees of temperature. It is enough that the heaters merely take the dampness and chill out of the atmosphere.

Electric night-storage heaters are another option and are quite a popular method. These heaters can be operated quite economically as can the previously mentioned ones if incorporated into an Economy Seven electric meter. Both types of heater can be attached to the wall, making sure that they are out of harm's way.

Now we turn to the other end of the scale – those long hot summer days. While these sultry and sunny days are lovely for us, the hot weather is not the most comfortable for Pekingese. Therefore, for this eventuality, we have installed in our kennels large high-powered oscillating electric fans.

These should be strategically placed so that the maximum fresh

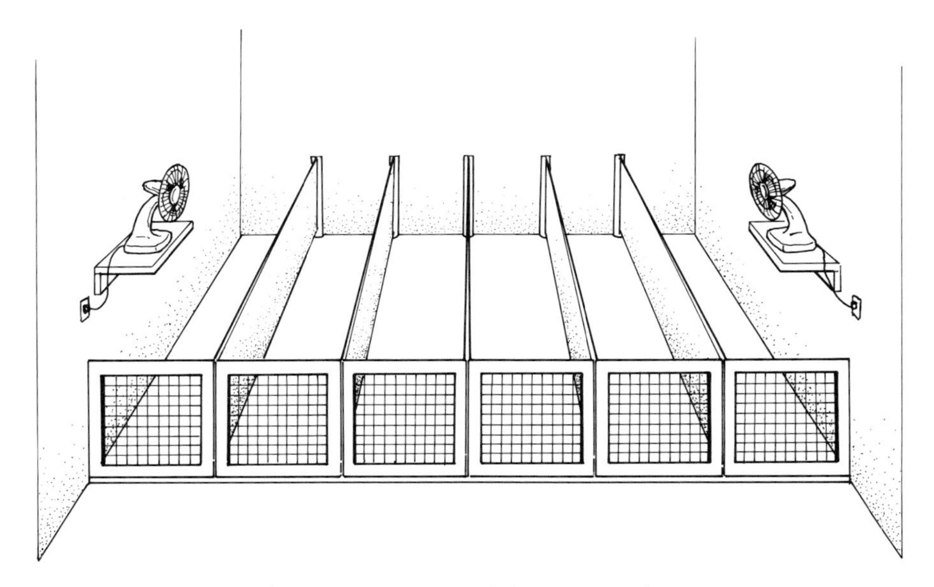

*Fig 24 Kennel with individual runs inside (with fans positioned either side).*

air flow is achieved and your dogs will really appreciate the relief that these create. There are many well-known brands in the shops; do not wait until you are in the midst of a heatwave before you rush out to purchase one for you can be quite sure that at this late stage they will more than likely all have been purchased. Be prepared and buy these aids prior to these hot periods.

Returning to the question of erecting your kennelling, another point that should be carefully considered is the positioning in your garden of the kennel itself. Try to pick a spot that will give a certain amount of shade in the summer but will be protected from the harsher elements in winter. For your own convenience it is always more practical to have it reasonably near the house. One consideration is that the electricity supply does not have so far to go for connection to the main supply and, of course, it does mean that your dogs are always under close supervision.

The best way of keeping your dogs within the confines of the kennel is again a matter of personal preference. You may either decide to keep your dogs in tiered pens or for each dog to have his own individual run on the floor, complete with basket.

Tiered pens have been favoured over the years by breeders and

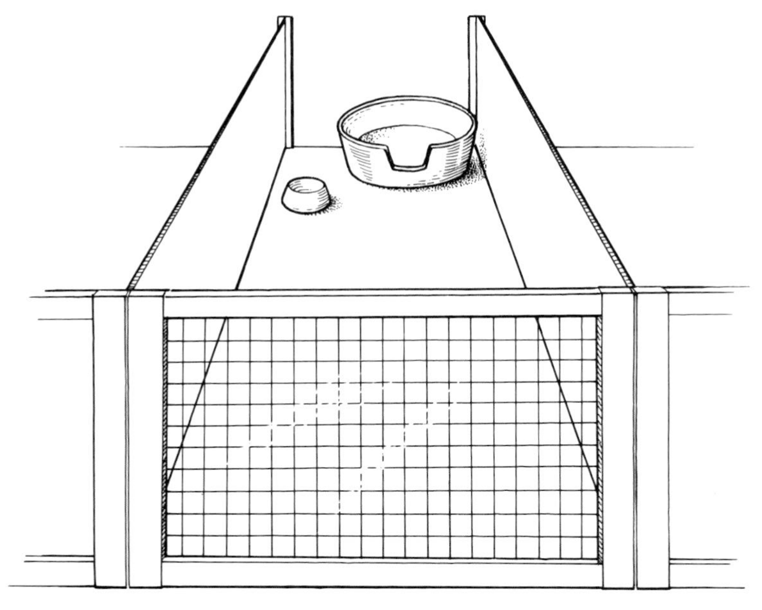

*Fig 25 Individual run with basket.*

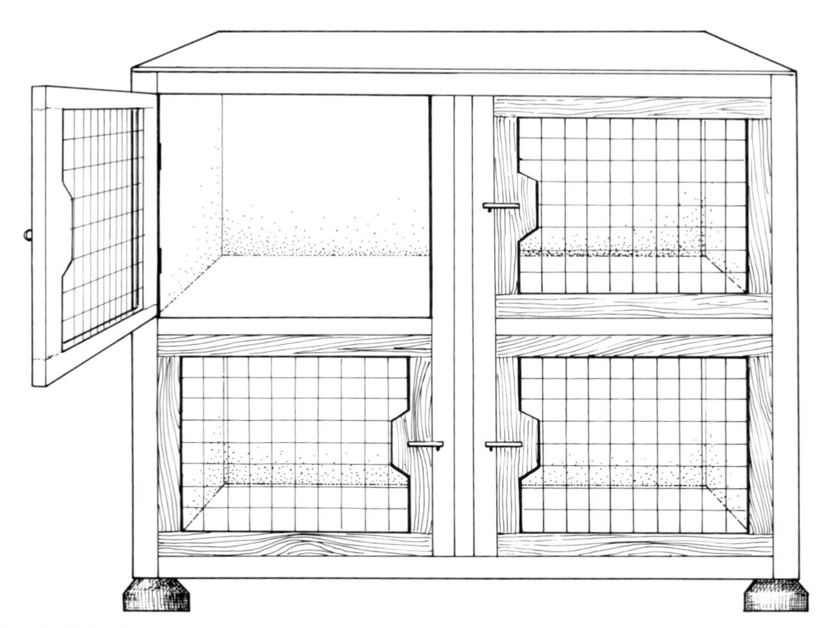

*Fig 26 Tiered pen.*

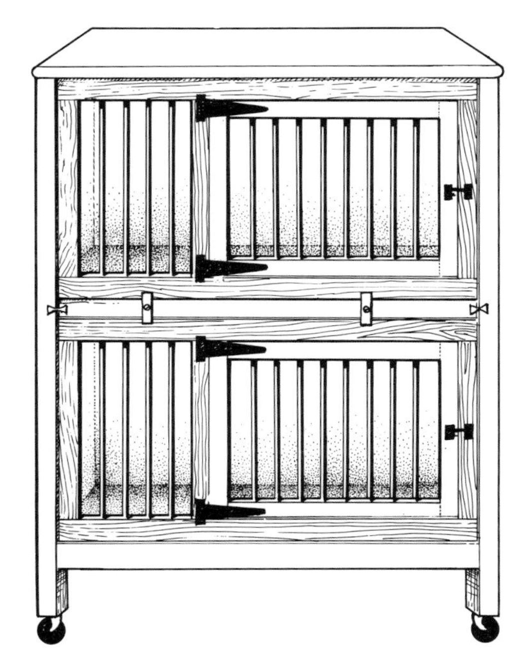

*Fig 27 Tiered pen.*

they are, indeed, an extremely neat way of sleeping your dogs. The dogs are allowed adequate freedom during the daytime and then, when it is time for them to go to bed, they are settled down in their own individual tiered pen for the night. We personally do not like the thought of their being penned up in them indefinitely, with only limited exercise. But again this is really a matter of opinion.

We prefer each dog to have his own separate pen with its own basket, water bowl, etc. The pens are of a sensible size, allowing the dogs to move about in them quite happily when they are not outside, for instance during the long hours of winter when it is too cold and damp for them to be out all the time. This is undoubtedly a harder way of keeping them regarding the work that it entails, but nevertheless we find that our dogs really seem to appreciate this method.

Fig 25 shows one individual run where the sides are hardboarded to avoid any fracas with a neighbour. The front is plastic mesh for visibility. Total height all round is approximately 2 feet 6 inches (75 centimetres).

Fig 26 shows a tiered pen that can be split into four compartments by the use of a middle divider. In Fig 27 we have another type of indoor kennel. The doors are made up with slim metallic bars as compared with the previous illustration where the doors are of a fine wire mesh.

## Day-to-Day Routine

Our daily routine is that first thing in the morning the dogs are all let out to have a run. During this time any soiled newspapers are removed and replaced with clean ones. All the water bowls are washed out, replenished with fresh water and placed back in the pen. In the summer months, if the weather is not too hot outside, the dogs are out for the greater part of the day. If, however, the temperature is very high, we find that the dogs housed in the brick kennel are quite happy to spend the day gently sleeping, with the fans circulating the air around them. Wooden kennels, when the temperature is excessive, tend to hold the heat, and the dogs who are kennelled in these spend their day from morning to sunset, or later sometimes, spread out in the shade of some conveniently placed trees. On these long hot days, water must obviously be easily available and needs to be changed regularly. When evening comes and if, for some reason, the dogs have needed to be in during the day, an evening run is a necessity.

All our dogs are given blankets in their baskets – our favourite kind is the simulated sheepskin variety that is favoured for hospital beds – and underblankets in winter. The baskets themselves are plastic and are easily wiped out for cleanliness. In the winter months it becomes necessary to check daily under each blanket for any condensation that may have formed. Because of this, we also place a sheet of fresh newspaper daily in the bottom of the basket under the blanket. An added bonus of this type of blanketing material is that any condensation present is unable to rise through this particular material. This, of course, makes it an absolute boon for puppies who may wet their bedding at an early age as this will just filter through, leaving the blanketing dry and warm. Older dogs as well appreciate these blankets, especially if one of your 'oldies' begins to suffer from incontinence.

When the dogs have been out for a reasonable run they are brought back into the kennel on wet days and during the winter months. Always ensure that they are thoroughly dried before putting them back into their beds or pens. One particular word of caution here is that when they have been out on a snowy cold morning, make quite sure that the little iceballs that attach themselves quite rigidly to the underneath of the dog, or under the armpits and on the feet themselves, are removed and the coat is dried thoroughly. If these are left they can tend to make a little dog quite ill through rheumatism, chills and cold so always pay a little extra attention on days such as these.

## Grooming

Of course, with a Pekingese the question of caring for a heavy coat is important. When you first get your puppy at ten weeks or after, it will possess a really pretty fluffy coat. As the puppy grows up it will start to cast the vast majority of this from approximately four months or so and the slightly harsher teenage coat will start to grow in.

As your pet, the dog will obviously be living in the house, and the home environment, as compared with that of the kennel, induces the casting of his coat. With central heating, or whatever, a dog living in the house rarely carries the wealth of coat that his kennel counterpart would. Even when the kennels are heated, a show dog housed in a kennel keeps his coat more easily than a house dog can.

So, for your companion, we would advocate a little gentle grooming daily. Just five minutes a day will suffice initially, so that the hair does not become a problem and your puppy gets used to his daily brushing so that when he is older the coat can be managed comfortably. But this we will cover fully in Chapter 7 (*see* page 110).

What we will point out now is that when you have your new puppy try to make sure that you have the following utensils from the outset for the daily routine. You will need a brush and comb; the brush if possible should be a mixture of nylon and bristle while the comb needs to be of the dual-toothed variety (these utensils will be featured in more detail in Chapter 5 (*see* page 86) and will also be illustrated). You will also need a spray made up from either water and bay rum (a hair tonic) with a sprinkling of eau-de-Cologne or there are many prepared dressings, one of which you should find available at your local pet shop. Nail clippers are also a necessity although these, of course, do not need to be used daily.

## Bathing

A question that we are asked a great deal is whether a Pekingese should be bathed or not. Yes, we do believe in bathing, in moderation and at the right time.

We find that at approximately five months of age puppies are inclined to start changing their baby puppy fluff for a slightly more mature coat. It is at this age that we tend to bath them for the first time as we feel that it helps to take out the dead coat and invigorates the skin, encouraging the growth of the new coat. With a show dog, providing that it is groomed regularly and cleansed with the aid of talcum powder, there is no need to keep bathing your dog. If, however, you have bought your little dog purely as a companion, we would advise you to bath the dog as often as you feel is necessary. You can, of course, groom your dog in exactly the same way as a show dog and keep him clean with the use of a coat dressing of some description and talcum powder.

The next time we tend to bath our adults is when they are going through a major cast of coat. In order to be able to do this, you will first need to comb through the dog's coat until you feel that you have managed to relieve it of most of the dead coat. This is most important, and, if the dog is brushed daily anyway, this will not be too major a chore. If you attempt to bath your dog before doing this, it will be most difficult to ensure that you shampoo through the coat right to the skin itself, and the coat will become an uncontrollable mass, making it extremely difficult to dry.

It is also advisable when doing this to use an insecticidal shampoo which we obtain from our veterinary surgery and incorporates an in-built conditioner. We find this extremely effective and, once the coat is dried, it leaves it manageable without being too soft. Once the old coat is out and the skin is clean and healthy, the new coat is free to come through.

## Lead Training and Socialisation

Even though your puppy is unable to go out for a walk on a lead until its second inoculation at about fourteen weeks, this does not mean you should not start a little training indoors. The first lesson is getting it used to having a collar and lead attached to it. You will find that most pet shops will stock a small puppy collar of some type or another. There are some very serviceable nylon ones or the slightly more expensive rolled leather collars. Either will do, although we prefer the second variety. They are a little thinner than the former and are more manageable with the puppy coat of a Pekingese.

It is most advisable really, from almost the first minute you take possession of your little puppy, to let it become acquainted with the following practice. Do allow it of course a few days to become accustomed to its new surroundings and new-found family.

Start by putting the collar on the puppy, making quite sure that it is not so tight that the poor little mite is in danger of being choked, but on the other hand not so loose that it tends to slip and get caught in the mouth almost like a gag!

For these first few lessons, leave the collar on for short periods of approximately thirty minutes or so. During this time never leave the puppy unattended for one minute just in case it panics and manages either to get caught up somewhere or to slip it into its mouth causing it to choke. Now your puppy may love or hate this first little game; if it happens to be the latter you will just have to persevere with this exercise kindly and gently. We have had a puppy who absolutely detested every minute of this particular part of the training process, virtually to the extent that we thought we would never get her on a lead, let alone into the show ring. However, after these initial tantrums, she turned out to be an absolute delight to show.

As the days go by, extend the time that the puppy has the collar on until it seems to be quite at ease with the whole situation. Now comes the time to attach the lead to the collar and this can be the point where the fun really starts. This, of course, can be started before your puppy has its first injection, but stop the training for the few days when we have pointed out that it may be feeling a little under the weather.

Back to the lead! Attach the lead to the collar and for the first day or so simply let the puppy drag this extra encumbrance around for short periods at a time, under close supervision, of course, in case of accidents. When it seems to be quite at ease with this latest stage of the proceedings, take hold of the lead and call the puppy's name to see if it will follow you. You may need to exert a little gentle pressure on the lead to give it the general idea.

With a puppy due to be trained for the show ring, we start by training it to get used to a collar, as already mentioned. When, however, it comes to the point of adjoining the lead, we exchange the collar and lead combination for a nylon show lead, applying the

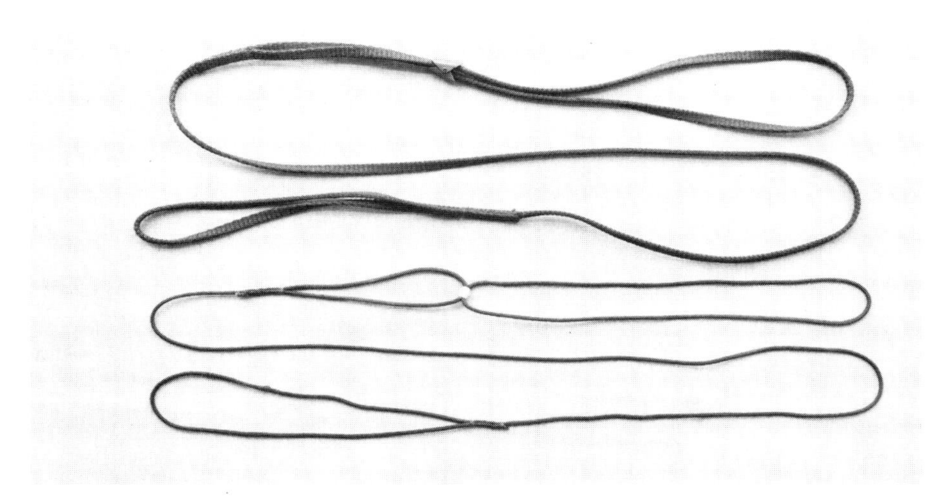

*Fig 28 Leads.*

same principle. There are two types of show lead, a very fine 'shoelace' type or a slightly thicker lead, both with adjustable slip collars. Either type is acceptable in the show ring; it really depends on which type you prefer to use yourself.

Ask any Pekingese breeder and they will tell you that this breed can be, to say the least, very very stubborn, especially when it comes to lead training! So you have to be prepared to persevere. Some puppies never give it a second thought when it comes to this stage, however, and will happily follow you wherever you may lead. There are others, it must be said, who could try the patience of a saint, the word 'patience' being the operative one, and you will need plenty of it. Just practice religiously every day, for it can sometimes be a battle of wills and you have to ensure that with gentle, patient and firm handling you are the one who comes out on top! However close you come to losing your cool, keep calm and persevere, as losing your temper at this stage could set the training back. Eventually, the penny *will* drop and the puppy will more than likely simply set off at the side of you one day as if to say 'Oh, is this all you wanted me to do?'

These early exercises can all be carried out within the confines of the house or garden so that, when your fledgling has had the full course of injections, the training can be carried on outside the comparative safety of home.

When it is safe to do so, start to take your puppy out and about with you as often as possible. A short walk on the lead just down the road initially will help it to get used to new sights and strange noises and is a very good exercise to carry out regularly. Do not overdo this at first, though, and if your puppy shows signs of fright try not to rush and pick it up immediately, short of there being imminent danger close at hand. Bend or kneel down to your puppy and stroke it, reassure it with your voice and stay in that position for a time, until hopefully its fear has abated. If your puppy, however, seems still to be distressed, hold it in your arms and let it see what the cause of the noise or disturbance is. When you are walking your puppy down the street it is advisable to walk so it can see any traffic coming towards it and then it will not be frightened by anything coming up close behind.

Continue these short outings daily until the puppy shows signs of confidence. Do not walk your puppy for miles on end at this early age because, if you wish to show your puppy, this healthy walking tends to lengthen a puppy's legs and, of course, it is preferred that they are low to ground according to the Breed Standard.

If you have a car try to let it get used to short trips out and about in this. Again, if you are hoping to show your youngster it is

*Fig 29 Framptons Tickeroo. Owned and bred by Mr and Mrs D. Lee.*

advisable to let it get used to this form of travelling, preferably in a show basket. If this is not the priority, travel your puppy either on your lap on these first few outings (providing of course that you are not the driver) with a towel on your lap in case these first trips upset your youngster's tummy. It is never advisable to let a young puppy travel loose on the back seat of a car if at all avoidable in case it happens to fall and hurt itself.

In the past, the old adage was to socialise your puppy by taking it around shops such as Woolworths. Nowadays this is not so easy so you have to rely on friends allowing you to take your puppy to see them. If you are a regular visitor to your local pub and they allow dogs in this again is a wonderful training ground, and for some reason a very popular one with husbands! There are also training classes to attend and these we will cover in the following chapter. Basically, you need to let your puppy become accustomed to different people and places, for if it never sees beyond the confines of the garden wall, when the time comes to go to your first show, it will more than likely be overawed by the whole new strange experience.

# 5

# Adolescent and Adult Management

Pekingese, it must be said, are the most affable and easy-going little dogs, even if they are inclined to be stubborn. You might think from the title of this chapter that you are going to encounter problems but, on the whole, they are a breed that just aims to please so we will look at dog management from another angle.

Let us carry on from where we left off with your puppy in the previous chapter. Your youngster is now used to having a collar put around its neck and trots off happily with you at its side on the other end of a lead. You have also accustomed it to the outside world and are now ready to take this training a step further.

## Training Classes

In most areas there are a variety of training classes and very often they will be advertised on the notice-board of a vet's surgery or in a local shop window. These are for show dogs and pet dogs alike and are, apart from the obvious advantages of training your dog, a marvellous place to meet people who love and are interested in dogs of all breeds and types. Many of these classes incorporate two sessions, one for the obedience training fanatics and the other for the show side and general management of a young dog or one that may have behavioural problems.

Let us suppose that you wish to attend these classes in order to begin to train your dog for the show ring. You will find in the majority of cases dogs of all makes, shapes and sizes; they can vary from a Great Dane to a Chihuahua. That is one of the greatest advantages of these classes for your young dog will learn how to go through its paces while surrounded by a variety of dogs that may bark and clatter around on the floor. When the time comes for you

*Fig 30 Champion Findhorn Uffa. Best of Breed, Cruft's, 1981. Owned and bred by Mrs L. Mathieson.*

to go to your first show, which could very well be an all-breed show, your dog will have learnt to take all these different dogs in its stride.

A well-run training club will also help you to handle your charge in the correct manner and instruct you on how to adopt the correct ring procedure. However friendly the atmosphere and chatty your fellow trainees are, never lose sight of the fact that you are there for the purpose of training your dog. That does not mean you have to be unfriendly, just keep alert of the situation in hand. You can learn a lot by watching other people with their dogs and how they handle and show them. In the world of dogs, however experienced you become, there is always something new to be learnt.

At this stage most of your attention should be focused on your puppy. This is its first adventure into a world completely different to the one it has become accustomed to. Therefore, if you notice it becoming a little agitated give the puppy a little confidence by speaking to it just to let it know that it is not alone.

When we decide to take a puppy to our local training class, bearing in mind that this will be its very first outing to such a place, we go with the intention merely of socialising the puppy. We recommend that you just sit with the puppy on your lap or on a chair beside you, letting it see what is going on around.

Usually on this first outing the puppy will be more than a little wary of any sudden noise or movement and once again, the reassurance of your voice, and the realisation that you are close at hand will slowly allay its fears. When your puppy seems a little more relaxed let it sit quietly at your feet on its lead watching all the activity of its more experienced companions. On this initial outing we very rarely join in with the class and would only suggest that you do so if your puppy is ultra-confident. You will probably find that letting the puppy take a leisurely look at all this excitement will ensure that at the following week's class it will slowly become accustomed to all the noise and routine. Try not to let more than a week lapse before you return; once you decide to go to these classes, at least for a few weeks try to attend them regularly, otherwise you may find yourself back to square one.

At the second class, again for the first few minutes just sit with the youngster until you feel that it has recognised and remembered this location. When you feel that it has relaxed and is taking an interest in the other dogs, then you may slowly join in. Stand in line with the dogs that the class teacher has not as yet handled. Just let your puppy stand or sit on the ground without letting it get too close to any over-boisterous neighbouring dog. The presence of such a dog may frighten your youngster and set this training process back a little. Eventually your turn will come to go and place your puppy on the judging table where the teacher or judge will handle your puppy. This is most beneficial to a pet dog as well as a show dog for it learns to accept strangers while at the same time becoming used to different dogs.

The vast majority of people who take these classes are very kind and gentle with their handling of a dog, especially if you point out that this is the first time your puppy has experienced this stage of the training. Their object, through these classes, is to help your little dog learn to accept and enjoy all this, apart from the behaviour training. They will usually do everything possible to help you in any way that they can.

Having had your puppy handled on the table, you will then have the chance to see whether or not it will walk up the hall and back again. When you first try to set off you may feel a little opposition to this exercise. Always remember that you are your puppy's link with security so you will need to keep handing out confidence, and this can be done through your voice. Speak to your puppy all the time, call its name, for this can work wonders, and it may be tempted to

*Fig 31 Champion Royceland Marie. Owned and bred by Mr and Mrs J.D. Richards.*

take a few tentative steps. If, however, at the first attempt it decides to dig in with all four feet do not be disheartened. Quietly pick your puppy up – do not drag it up and down the hall for this can do more harm than good – go back into the line and once again let it sit or stand, whichever it prefers at this early stage, and let it watch all the comings and goings. You will probably find that after a while it will forget all its inhibitions and want to start wandering around a little; within reason, do not check it but let the puppy enjoy itself. Just remember, do not let it get too near any dog that looks as though, by an over-exuberant movement, it might put your puppy off once again. Time and class permitting, if your puppy has now settled down try your walking exercise once again.

If you still have problems do not despair, just remember what we have said, Pekingese can be a very stubborn and obstinate breed. Just return to class again the following week and eventually, with that well of patience that you have managed to muster, and with perseverance, your little puppy will walk up and down as though it has not a care in the world. Try not to persuade it to try and do something at this tender age that it is going to come to detest for then it will associate training and showing with all things nasty! If you let your puppy enjoy itself, and after all it is of course only a baby, eventually it will come to regard these outings as a great enjoyment and a wonderful game.

Of course, in between these weekly classes you are still best advised to continue the basic training of walking your puppy a short way daily (a short distance and no mile-long hikes!). This will help to keep it accustomed to the rigours of having a collar on and will enhance your class training as walking on the lead will become a matter of course to your youngster.

## The Flapper Stage

Your little puppy, who looked absolutely stunning at between eight and twelve weeks, shortly afterwards begins to change, sometimes drastically. This is traditionally known as the flapper stage.

Usually this period starts to manifest itself at the time your puppy's teeth are starting to change. During this stage, the bottom jaw can become quite pronounced and, at the same time, its ears become set at a quite peculiar angle. This is called flying its ears. With these various alterations and the change of its puppy coat, your prospective star seems to be almost disappearing before your very eyes.

It is presumed that if a puppy looks promising at around the six to eight weeks' stage of its life – and still looks very reasonable at approximately eleven to twelve weeks, hopefully it should emerge from this ugly duckling stage as a beautiful swan, or as you wish, of course, a beautiful Pekingese. This is a stage that you have to be prepared for and try not to become disheartened along the way.

On the whole, every breeder knows their particular strain, and the owner of a team of stud dogs will most likely be able to tell you how each dog's progeny will develop. A puppy by, for instance, stud dog X may go through a set pattern of going off at about twelve weeks while the progeny of stud dog Z may not look very promising at an early age but will begin to improve through the first six to eight months of their lives. If you have bought the puppy in and not bred it yourself, the breeder will probably be able to give you a little advice on this stage of development.

Providing your puppy shows no serious structural fault throughout this time, it really is a question of just sitting it out to wait and

*Fig 32 Champion Toydom Modesty Permits. Owned and bred by Miss A. Summers and Miss V. Williams.*

see. One of our own dogs was the most awful disappointment at this age and seemed to go from bad to worse. He looked so dreadful that we really thought we had made the most terrible mistake. We took him to his first show at six months, when he should really have been left at home, a fact that was confirmed by several fellow exhibitors and the judge. The latter, quite rightly, put superior puppies over him and the former agreed with our more recent opinions of him. In actual fact at this stage we thought he had improved. Well, the story had a happy ending! The puppy grew up to be Champion Toydom Modesty Permits and won, in all, seven Challenge Certificates, several Reserves and was on two occasions placed Reserve in the Toy Groups at Championship Shows.

## Diet

As we have mentioned, at this age your puppy will commence to change its baby coat. The coat that will now be growing should, in fact, carry your youngster through all its puppy classes. As with all stages of the coat growth, your dog's coat needs to be nurtured and cared for.

However much you brush and look after the coat, we always feel that the goodness comes from within the dog, and this will reflect itself in the condition and body of your dog. Therefore, a sensible and balanced diet needs to be instituted. Naturally, as your puppy matures into an older dog, the meals you have been feeding will have been decreased although, of course, the quantities will have been stepped up. Feeding is a major and important factor in the care and the health of your dog.

There are many extremely good dog foods on the market nowadays. Whichever one you choose has really to be a matter of preference and one that seems to suit your dog or dogs. Many people in a variety of breeds tend to go for a 'complete food'. This is a food that contains all the essential vitamins and ingredients which are balanced out to the daily requirements of your dog.

Personally we tend to go for the more old-fashioned method and use a balanced biscuit meal full of natural ingredients. This biscuit is steeped for approximately ten minutes and then we add some minced tripe together with either minced beef or ox-cheek, chicken taken off the breast or quarters and chopped up, minced fish or some tinned dog food. The biscuit is soaked either in a little warm water, in some stock from the cooked chicken or beef or in a little gravy, just to add some taste. Once again, your local pet shop will stock several varieties of biscuit meal and many stock a selection of frozen foods that can be purchased in small packs and stacked quite easily in your own freezer.

There is also a variety of vitamin supplements on the market but, before you go mad buying them all up thinking that they will all be good for your little puppy or adult, consult the breeder of your newest acquisition. He or she will advise you on what the puppy has been used to and what would suit it from this moment on. Alternatively, present your diet sheet to your veterinary surgeon and ask for advice on what supplement is needed, if at all. You have to be equally careful for you can over-vitaminise as well as under-vitaminise. We merely sprinkle a little vitamin powder (a pinch at the most) on each dog's meal every day; this seems to suit their diet and life-style.

One thing that should be remembered is that it is inadvisable to change your dog's diet drastically from day to day or even from week to week. When you have a system of feeding do not try to change it suddenly; do not, for instance, keep changing your biscuit meal for the pure and simple reason that you prefer the advertising campaign of one firm against another's. There is a vast variety of brands to choose from so, as we have already stipulated be guided by the breeder, or, alternatively, if you enter shows, discuss this with other exhibitors – you will find there are several favourites.

## Nail Clipping

A practice that you should get your puppy used to is having its nails clipped, and for this it should become accustomed to being lain on its back. If nail clipping is started at a tender age it will save many battle royals in later life. Many people hate this particular chore simply because they are frightened of hurting the dog and making the nails bleed. This is, of course, easy to do and is caused by cutting a nail too high and severing the little vein that runs down through the dog's claw.

*Fig 33 Cutting the nail.*

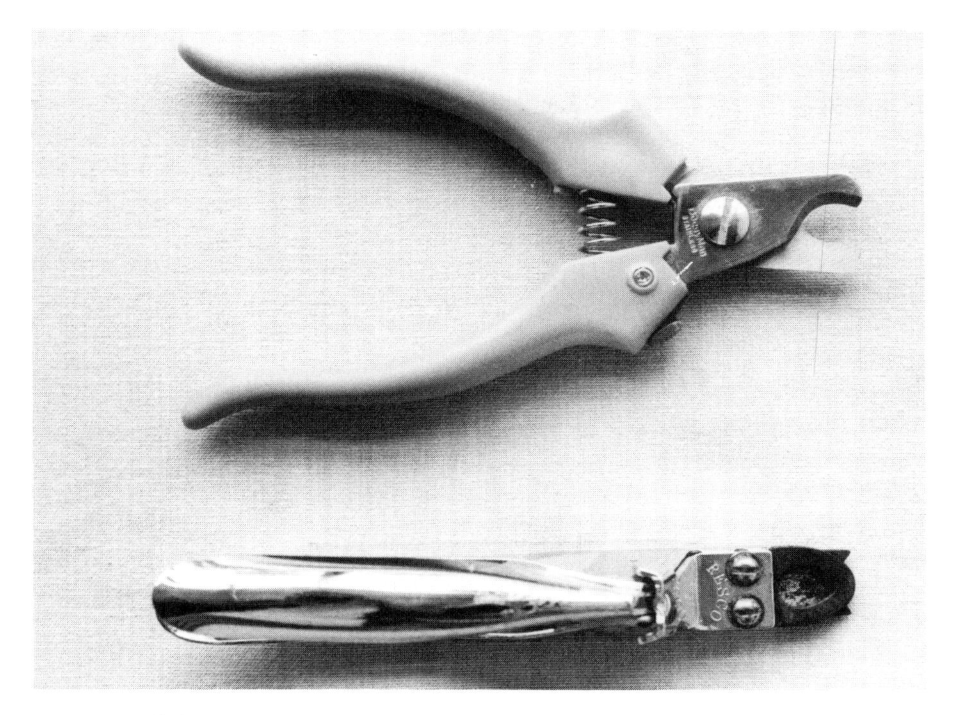


*Fig 34 Nail clippers.*

If you take the dog's paw in your hand and look at the nails or claws they should be a pale clear colour with the vein easily visible. You can, however, get black nails as well; this we discuss below. Your dog should have four main nails on each foot. On the two front feet, though, they have an extra nail on each leg; these are positioned on the inside of the leg marginally above the foot and are known as dew-claws. Always remember to cut these with the others for if left too long they can easily become caught in something and be ripped out; alternatively, they will curl back into the dog's leg causing acute discomfort. Although not a common occurrence, it is possible for dew-claws to appear on one or both back legs so always check for these.

For this part of your dog's care you will need a good pair of clippers and once again, like many grooming aids in the canine world, there are some varying but extremely good makes on the market. The types illustrated in Fig 34 are probably some of the most popular, while for puppies we tend to use a smaller pair designed for use on cats. They are easier to manage when you are manicuring those tiny little nails at approximately four weeks of age.

Let us return to the nails in question. Your dog should have a pale-coloured nail with the vein easily noticeable. You will need to cut this nail a fraction in front of the vein itself; if you are not sure, allow a little extra, rather than make it bleed. Sometimes amidst these lighter-coloured nails appears a dark one where the vein is not visible at all. The only way you can cut one of these is by assessing it against its neighbouring lighter partner. Until you become a veteran at this practice be a shade more generous with this type of nail for it is better to be safe than sorry. Another small word of advice here is, if you are entered at a dog show, carry out this particular part of your dog's toiletry a few days prior to the show. If you should inadvertently cut the nail too far down, it could make your dog limp in the ring if his nails have been clipped the day before.

Should you accidentally sever the vein, the nail will bleed. However experienced we are, this can sometimes happen, if the dog moves at exactly the wrong moment, for instance. As with the Boy Scouts, be prepared!

If you pay a visit to your local chemist you will be able to purchase from there some potassium permanganate. This comes in a small pot and consists of some minute dark crystals; these act as a clotting agent on the nail. Place a little of this on the nail in question and then hold the puppy or dog in your arms for a few minutes until the crystals have had sufficient time to act.

However, if you feel quite unable to undertake this manicure, or if your puppy or dog possesses a large quantity of darker nails, we would recommend that you seek assistance. You will most probably find that the breeder of the puppy or a fellow show-goer and exhibitor will willingly help you in a case such as this. Alternatively, your veterinary surgeon will carry this out for you, obviously for a small fee. Always remember to keep an eye on these nails for if allowed to grow too long they will curl round and embed themselves into the pads of the foot, making the mere act of walking about absolutely excruciating for the dog.

## The Pekingese Coat

With a young puppy's coat (that is, of up to about six months of age), grooming can be easily managed with a brush, comb, a spray dressing and a little talcum powder. There are some very expensive brushes on the market, that will last for years. You may prefer to purchase a cheaper but equally serviceable one, though it will need to be replaced more frequently. We tend to go for a nylon and bristle mixture of the former as this tends to stop the coat splitting at the ends. There is another brush that is very popular at the present time among many of today's exhibitors, and that is a wire pin brush. It must be realised, however, that due to the risk of improper use when in the hands of a novice in the art of brushing a Pekingese, we do not recommend that you immediately go out and buy one of these. In the right hands it can give that finished picture on a show dog, but if used incorrectly it has the opposite effect of taking out too much coat. Another type of brush it is advisable to have is a pure bristle brush which is ideal for the dog's fringes in everyday grooming, being that much gentler on these precious tresses.

The comb should be metal and, if possible, one that incorporates two different widths of teeth: wider at one end and slightly narrower at the other.

There are many different sprays or dressings to choose from, the original recipe that we gave in Chapter 4 (*see* page 71) or one of the ready-mixed varieties that are available at the many trade stands associated with dog shows or at your local pet store. If you are at all unsure ask the assistant for advice as there are different dressings for different breeds which produce the desired effect for that particular type of coat. On a Pekingese coat, for instance, you would not wish to have an oily dressing. We always use babies' talcum powder and a reputable brand of this seems to suit the coat better than some of the cheaper or highly perfumed ones.

You will be able to purchase a spray bottle for the dressing, either from your local garden centre or hardware shop. In the case of wanting to buy your dressing in bulk (in many cases it works out cheaper to buy a gallon can as opposed to the smaller bottles), this can be easily transferred a little at a time and kept in your grooming bag for shows and on hand for your daily grooming sessions.

With the dog lying on his back, spray the coat lightly, brushing it nearly dry and then sprinkle a little talcum powder into the coat and brush all this through. Do not soak the coat with the spray, just dampen it lightly. Try, if possible, to brush as near through to the skin as you can: this is not easy with the thick woolly undercoat, and with a show dog you do not want to lose this as yet. You will find a comprehensive and illustrated guide to grooming your show dog in Chapter 7. Here we give you a guide to grooming for the everyday care of your Pekingese.

While your dog is lying on his back it is possible to wash around the male's sheath, for if left it can become sticky and smelly and there is a strong chance of a mild infection setting in. You will need to have at hand a small bowl of warm water, perhaps with a very mild antiseptic solution (obtainable from your vet) added to it, and also some cotton wool. Soak the cotton wool and gently wipe around this area, drying either with more cotton wool or a small clean towel. A similar practice will need to be carried out with a bitch around her private parts, especially if she is in season.

Once your dog has been brushed underneath and you have checked for any tangles that may have appeared between and around the legs, you are ready to stand your dog upright. If you have detected a mat or tangle, though, do not rush for the scissors! A little judicial grooming and teasing will rid the coat of this unwanted piece of loose hair. Take the offending tangle in one hand and spray it, dampening it thoroughly. Now take your brush and, with even strokes, gently brush through it, extricating it from the rest of the coat. If it is stubborn and will not release, dampen it once again and this time take the comb and gently try to ease it out. Carry

*Fig 35 Champion Singlewell T'Sai Magic. Owned and bred by Mrs P. Edmond.*

*Fig 36 Tirakau the Seductress. Owned and bred by Mrs P. Hunter.*

on in this manner until the coat is free of this mat. Do not be tempted to comb it out roughly for it will cause a certain amount of pain to your dog. Try to imagine how you would feel if someone was trying to rake out a knot in your hair! With puppies, the coat can be inclined to go into woolly mats, particularly at the time of casting, but with this method they are easily managed.

When it does come to the time for your puppy to shed this baby suit, merely comb gently through the coat with the wider toothed comb after dampening and this will extract the dead undercoat.

Now turn your dog back over so that he is standing on his four feet and then brush the trousers, or skirts, as they are known, at the back, after checking first that they are not soiled in any way. If they are, it is best to wash them quickly under a spray or tap, drying with the aid of a towel or a hairdryer. You always have to be careful that the dog's motions do not get caught up in the trousers, especially around the dog's anus, for this can cause immense discomfort if not attended to at once.

From the trousers, work your way through the dog's body coat at the sides and on top, spraying, brushing and talcuming as you go. Always work from the tail forwards until you get to the dog's neck and mane. As a matter of interest, there is no need to complete this grooming practice every day with a show dog, just a little judicial checking of the coat for any tangles, checking and brushing the trousers, tail and ear fringes and a routine daily care of the facial area will suffice. You can in fact overgroom a show dog's coat to the extent that you will remove too much of the dog's undercoat before it is ready to part company with its owner. However, with a house dog, this system carried out each day, or perhaps every other day, will hopefully ensure that any coat loss will be kept strictly to a minimum and keep your house free from too many hairs.

Once you have reached the area of the neck, in a show dog you will find that eventually, as the dog matures, it will carry a huge mane. This is needed to present a picture of wealth and depth of the dog's ear fringing, and we will concentrate on it in Chapter 7 (*see* page 116). Of course, you have to check this area for any undesirable tangles and then carry out the same routine as with the rest of the coat.

You now check behind the ears for any tangles (if done daily they will hardly ever appear). If mats or tangles do happen to appear regularly, turn the ear flap back and check inside to see if there is any waxy substance exuding from the ear canal. If there is, place a few drops of a reputable ear lotion, which can be obtained from your vet, into the ear itself. Make quite sure that this goes right down into the ear by gently rubbing at the base of the ear. If properly administered this will be able to get to work on the cause of the trouble.

Check the progress of this ear condition daily, reapplying the drops as necessary. If, however, you do not start to see a marked improvement after a couple of days, consult your veterinary surgeon as the cause may be more deep-rooted and another form of medication may be needed.

The ear fringes need very careful attention. If these sought-after fringes are allowed to get into a mat and then have to be removed, this will greatly damage future growth. Once these fringes are lost they can never be replaced.

Before we brush the ears, in the case of a show dog, we always dip the ends of them into a small bowl of warm water, thereby washing out any food particles or whatever. The excess water is gently squeezed out with a towel and they are left to dry for a little before brushing them. After checking for these hidden knots behind the aforesaid ears, we spray and gently brush down behind the ears, brushing into the mane itself.

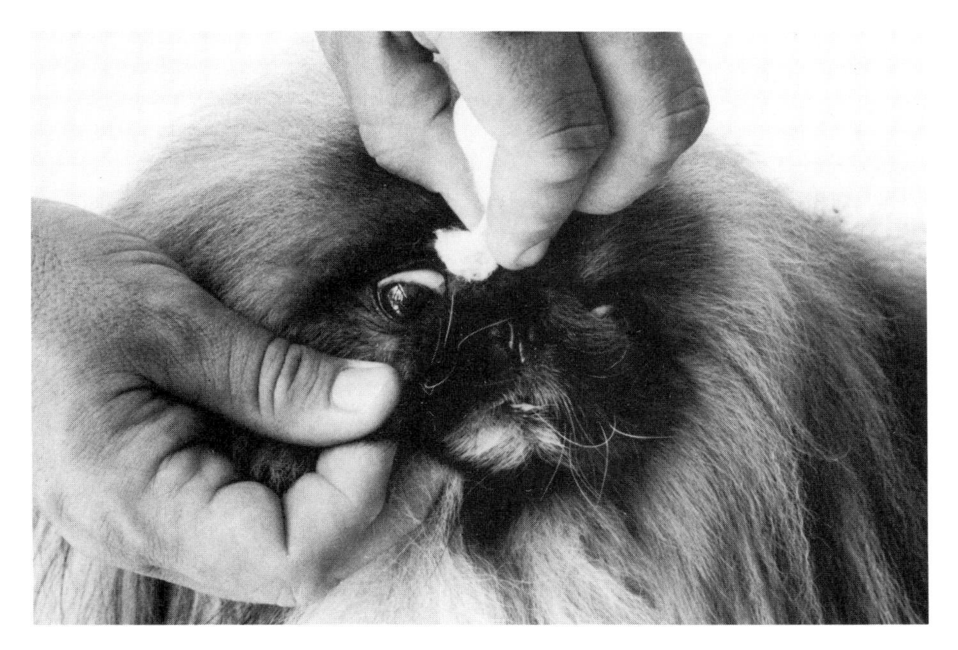

*Fig 37 Wiping the eyes and wiping away any foreign substance.*

While waiting for these to dry, you can be checking the eyes to see if there is any matter or hair in them. If there is, dampen a small piece of cotton wool and wipe around the eye rims to see if this will remove it. If this does not clear the eye, then with a newly dampened piece wipe across the eye area itself without touching the eyeball.

Now you need to make quite sure that the area behind the wrinkle and under each eye is wiped clean with a little warm water and cotton wool. Once this is done, dry this little channel with a dry piece of cotton wool. Now check under the wrinkle and immediately above the nose by gently pulling the wrinkle up from above the nose. This little crevice can get quite wet and dirty and, if you are not careful, a sore spot can easily set in. This is especially likely in the summer months when the weather is hot, so always ensure that this is attended to daily. If for some reason this area does become sore, wash it regularly with warm water and cotton wool, dabbing it dry afterwards with a little swab of cotton wool, and then apply some cream suitable for this purpose (obtainable from your vet).

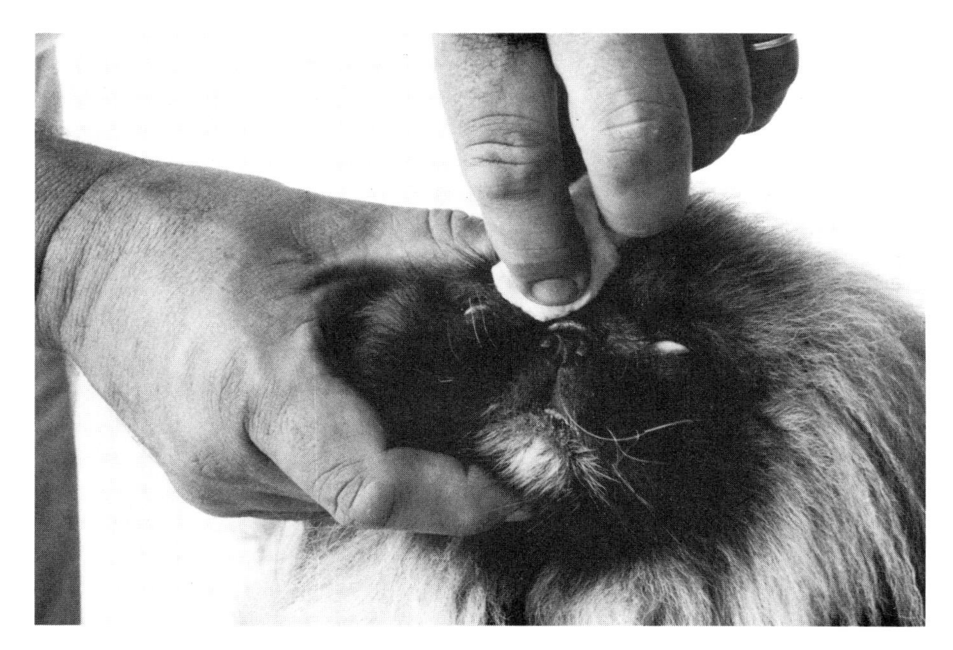

*Fig 38 Checking and wiping out the crevice between the nose and wrinkle.*

By now the ear fringes should be ready to be brushed out. Lay the ear back so that you are exposing the ear canal. Having checked the ear for any substance that may be causing irritation, gently brush the ear fringes out into a fan, and powder and brush until dry. When this is completed, flip the ear flap back to its correct position and spray the fringes from the outside, applying the same process of grooming as before. Turn the ear back over once more, spraying and talcuming the fringes from the inside and brushing and drying as you go. Always brush the fringes out into a fan so that when the ear is returned to normal the fringes have that little extra amount of body in them.

Finally you need to brush out the tail, using the same process. For a show dog that is about to go to a show we will cover this in full detail in Chapter 7 (*see* page 118).

For your house or pet dog, this routine will take only a comparatively short time, possibly fifteen minutes at the most if done daily or at least every other day. Pekingese are dogs that take a pride in their appearance and, if properly cared for, keep themselves clean and relatively tangle free. If you carry out the aforementioned care of the dog's coat, you will have a sweet-smelling, happy little dog of whom you will be immensely proud.

## The Older Dog

If your dog is a house pet, you may decide as he gets older that you wish to have another one to keep him company. If your present dog is a male and has not been castrated, it would be inadvisable to choose a female as his companion unless she is spayed, for this could lead to a load of unwanted problems when she comes into season. Let us assume that you wish this latest addition to be a puppy. If your older dog is nearing the end of his years, we would advise that you let him live out the twilight of his life in peace. For him to be suddenly presented with a rather wild, precocious and playful puppy, may lead to this pensioner being thoroughly upset and cause a certain amount of jealousy and distress.

If your 'firstborn', so to speak, is still active and healthy, the introduction of a young puppy can sometimes give your original dog a second lease of life, and very often a great bond will be forged between the two of them.

As your little companion gets older, in many cases he will be liable to suffer some of the ailments that go with old age and, because of this, he will need a little extra care and attention. Some of these ailments will be dealt with in Chapter 10, but we would advise you always to consult your veterinary surgeon when your dog looks at all off-colour.

Special attention needs to be paid to the older dog's teeth for these are inclined to become caked with tartar. This can in its turn infect the gums through germs, as in the case of humans. If you feel that the teeth are beginning to deteriorate, it would be an idea to consult your vet on this subject. One of the options is to anaesthetise the dog while the vet removes any bad teeth and generally cleans the teeth, but if you can avoid this at all we would advise it. Unfortunately Pekingese are a breed that do not seem to take anaesthetics well and fatalities have been known to occur, so you are best avoiding this course of action unless it is affecting the dog's health.

You can, of course, obtain the necessary instrument that will enable you to scrape the tartar off your dog's teeth as it begins to

*Fig 39 Champion Rosayleen the Gaffer at Sunsalve. Bred by Mrs E. Newman and owned jointly with Mr T. Nethercott. Now owned by Mr D. Sutton and Mr S. Keating, USA.*

build up. These can be purchased from a dog-show stand. However, we do not recommend that you try to become a dentist overnight; do not resort to this until you are at least a little more experienced. There is another more pleasant way to try to keep this tartar at bay, for both you and your dog.

We give our dogs, daily, some of the hard little dog biscuits (not the sweeter human ones) for these help to keep their teeth and gums strong and healthy. Another good idea is a marrowbone; there are some small ones that are individually frozen by a manufacturing company and they are an ideal size for a toy dog. Your pet store may be able to procure some of these for your dog. We would advise that both these biscuits and bones are given individually in the case of several dogs, perhaps in their kennels or baskets in order to avoid the possibility of a nasty fight. You can be assured there is always one little dog who is quite convinced that what is theirs, is his alone!

Veterinary fees can be expensive, especially if your dog is unlucky enough to need a long course of treatment for some particular reason. There are several companies however, that, provide for eventualities such as this, and treatment by the veterinary surgeon can be insured against for a moderately small fee. When you buy your puppy ask the breeder concerned about these schemes, for he or she may very well be able to supply you with the relevant forms or information. Failing this, your vet's surgery will also be able to point you in the right direction, giving you peace of mind and cover for your pet.

You will need to provide the older kennelled dogs with extra comfort, especially in the winter months. A heated pad placed in their beds and an extra blanket will help to ensure that they manage to cope happily with the cold. Many breeders bring their 'oldies ' into the warmth of the house even if it is just to sleep at night. Very often a dog that has been accustomed to the company of his fellow dogs will pine to return to them, detesting the fact that he has been uprooted. Some dogs quite happily take to their new home comforts, while we have had others that literally drive you mad to return to their old quarters.

In the case of a pet dog, old age may mean that some of those lovely walks that it used to enjoy so much need to be restricted a little, especially on a damp and cold winter's day. When returning from such a walk always make quite sure that the dog is thoroughly dried and is not allowed to lie in any draughts afterwards. The age to which a Pekingese can live varies; unfortunately, as a breed they do not have an excessive life span, but, on the other hand, they can live to a reasonably good age. For example, a dog who has become a household name within the breeder's circle, Champion Tuadore Master Bertie, nearly made his twenty-second birthday before his death in the spring of 1989. He was originally owned and bred by George Quinn and Bill Lamb and, after a highly successful career in the show ring, was allowed to go and live with some extremely good married friends of those two gentlemen. The husband, unfortunately, died and Bertie carried on living with his mistress as her devoted companion.

His owner was admitted suddenly to hospital after being taken seriously ill and remained there for several days while Bertie continued to live in his home surroundings cared for by a close relation of his mistress. In the early hours of one spring morning his mistress passed away in her sleep, and that same morning little Bertie was found in his basket where he had peacefully died. They really are a very special breed.

# 6
# Training

We have already touched on the basic principles of training your young puppy. We will now take this training programme one step further. During these formative weeks of its life you will have been slowly and patiently introducing it to house-training, grooming and wearing a collar. Once it has had all its inoculations, you will be also starting to socialise it with the outside world, on shopping trips, visiting friends and the training club.

## The Show Position

You can teach your puppy to stand in the show position at any time of the day and in any location. If persevered with, it will help to make your little dog show himself off to best advantage in the show ring.

You will initially need to stand your puppy on a table; at first it will probably wriggle and more than likely want to be anywhere but the place that it is, so be on your guard and do not, in any circumstances, let it jump off and hurt itself. Speak to the puppy, stroke it and, gently but firmly, make it stand on the table for a few minutes. This is enough at this stage but be sure to continue this exercise for a few days. When it has settled down to the idea of being placed on the table, ensure that it is standing correctly. For instance, make sure that its front legs are in the correct position. They should be placed a short distance apart, not so far that the puppy gives the impression it is doing the splits, just enough so that it is nicely balanced on them. Next, make sure that the back legs are also in the right place; they should be a little closer together than the front ones. While you are doing this, all the time be gentle and reassuring to your puppy; if it decides that it really is not too enamoured of this game you seem to want it to play, keep calm and do not lose your patience. Doing this will only upset the puppy and

*Fig 40 Silverwillow Ku-Jin. Owned and bred by Mr and Mrs J. NcNulty.*

yourself and will put your training programme back a fair way. So if this youngster insists on moving about and wriggling, just take a deep breath and firmly but kindly place it back in the same position.

As with all your training, let your dog or puppy hear your voice and firmly but quietly tell your puppy to *'Stand'*! Repeat this while it is in the correct position. As time goes by and your puppy becomes better accustomed to this new exercise, you should find that it will stand quite happily on the table for a prospective judge to go over.

When your perseverance has paid off and the puppy has grown accustomed to standing in this show position, gently ensure that its tail is placed firmly on its back. If it is inclined to drop back, gently replace it and pat it into the correct position by smoothing it down with your hand. This process will help to make the puppy realise that the tail needs to be in that position. While going through these actions always make sure that you have one hand at the ready in case the puppy suddenly takes it into its head that it is going to try to learn to fly!

Now you have reached the stage whereby your puppy is standing on the table with its tail firmly over its back. The next stage is to

*Fig 41 Champion Adlungs Rah Rah. Owned and bred by Miss M. Young.*

teach it to keep its head in the forward position. Many puppies seem to take more interest in what is going on around them – quite naturally, of course – than in the immediate job in hand. Take your brush and stand behind your puppy while it is in the show position and gently brush its tail over its back. Now brush the coat up either side of the neck, and then brush the topskull gently back. This will get it used to being gently titivated while on the table, and at the same time slowly encourages it to keep its head forward. If it still insists on looking around, place the head with your hands so that the dog is once again looking straight ahead, finally repeating the command *'Stand'*.

Some dogs will take to this training as a duck to water while others can be more than a little obstinate, so repeat the exercise each day and, with time and effort, your labours will be rewarded after not too long.

Having taught your charge to carry this out on a table you will now need to transfer the entire operation to floor level. Therefore, repeat the preceding routine with your puppy now on the ground. While your youngster is still a student of this method, and providing you are physically able, do not be afraid to kneel down to your puppy on the ground while constantly reassuring it and giving the command to stand when needed.

From trying to teach your fledgling the correct method of showing itself off to its best advantage, the next process is to try to get it to do the same while on a lead.

## Showing on the Lead

The basic routine to show your dog off on a lead is as follows. A judge will more than likely request that you walk your dog up the ring, making a triangle of the movement. Then you will most probably be asked to walk straight up and back with your dog. The majority of breed specialist judges ask for this exercise alone, but it is always best to be prepared for the unexpected. If you are being assessed by an all-rounder or an overseas judge, they will invariably expect all the dogs in that class to walk around the ring in a circle following one another before carrying out their own individual walk. In several countries, for example the United States, Pekingese are used to performing this feat quite regularly. However, it has to be said that the Pekingese in the United Kingdom on the whole do not take kindly to this exercise, nor do the owners! Try to teach your dog to walk around with some others, for instance at training club, in order to be prepared for this eventuality.

Teaching your puppy to show should not be too difficult an exercise providing of course that it has been used to having a collar around its neck, and this is where those early exercises will hopefully now make this next stage easier for you both.

The majority of exhibitors show their dogs on a show lead as opposed to a collar and lead (these are illustrated in Chapter 4, page 74). As you can see, the two types of show lead are a thinner nylon one resembling a piece of nylon string or shoe-lace, and a thicker and more substantial one. Both leads possess adjustable necks; on the thinner lead this consists of the small plastic bead through which two strands of the lead are set, while there is a metal clip on the other that can be open and shut in order to set the collar at the desired size. When the lead is in position the clip is merely closed, ensuring that the lead will not slip and you can control your dog without too much bother.

The actual description of the following manoeuvre may not sound very difficult but sometimes it can be hard to be put into practice.

Your little puppy most probably has been used to just wandering around on a lead and has not been actually expected to go in one particular place, in one particular direction.

So let us assume that you are going to set off and walk with your charge in the desired triangle. First of all, get your puppy to stand in a show position, obviously facing the direction you will be going in. When a judge asks you to walk your dog, it is better for you and your dog that you are prepared and the dog is not sitting down. If the dog is set to walk from the show position it presents a far better initial picture to the judge and, in all, looks far more professional. Before you set off, brush its mane at the side of the neck in an upwards motion, thereby lifting the ear fringes at the same time, and gently fluff out these and the chest. Then gently brush the topskull backwards so that it is flat and, finally, brush the dog's tail into position on its back and set off.

Walk straight away from this point with your puppy's lead in your left hand. To perform the perfect triangle, at a moderate distance from your departure point, bear left and walk in a straight line across the 'ring'; once again, after a reasonable distance bear left once more and head directly back to your original position. The whole idea of this exercise is so that the judge can assess your dog's movement and shape from three different angles. The judge will be able to see the dog's hind action as you are moving away, then as you are passing across the ring the dog's topline, overall shape, balance and movement are visible for scrutiny. Finally, as you are returning the front movement can be judged.

What you must remember when moving in a triangle is that your dog must always remain visible to the judge. In other words, when you have your lead in your left hand, always bear left so that the dog remains between you and the judge. If you find it easier to have your dog in your right hand, complete the triangle in the opposite direction, turning right instead of left across the ring.

After you have completed this triangle, your judge will more than likely ask you to walk away from this point and back again in a straight line. When you have returned to the judge (at this time, of course, it will be an imaginary one) teach your puppy to stand for a minute or two, in order that the judge has a moment to assess and take in the full picture of the dog after completing this exercise.

This is the general idea; the next step is getting your puppy to put the theory into practice. As you begin to set off, your puppy may

*Fig 42 Chophoi Silver Dollar. Owned and bred by Mr and Mrs F. Stagg.*

*Fig 43 Dratsum Captain Courageous. Bred by Mrs E. Maycock. Owned by Mrs D. Ballinger, USA.*

decide either that it is not going to walk in the direction that you wish it to or not to walk at all. If it is the former, once again a little gentle persuasion is called for. Give a light tug on the lead, calling your puppy's name and try to get it to follow you up this imaginary ring. Do not drag the puppy for this will not get any good results at this early stage.

You will be quite amazed by the acrobatics a Pekingese can perform when the fancy takes him. There is the 'back feet dug in so that they can touch the front feet' pose, leading to the 'bucking bronco' position and finishing up with the 'I can throw myself onto my back, so there!' manoeuvre. Patience, patience, patience!

Set the little dear back on all its four feet and slide the lead around so that it extends from underneath its chin. You have a little more control if the lead is in this position, for if the puppy decides to give a repeat performance of the aforementioned tricks, there is less likelihood of its managing to choke itself in the process. Once more calling the puppy's name, start to walk slowly away taking a hold of the lead and hopefully it may take a few tentative steps. Initially you may feel a little opposition from the other end of the lead but with a bit of luck and, of course, patience, the puppy may decide it will just humour you after all.

If the worst comes to the worst and you seem to be fighting another pitched battle, do not despair or give in. Just try this exercise everyday for five minutes or so until you do get some favourable reaction. When you do, of course, be quite sure to praise your puppy, for he really will like to please however wilful he may have been. The more the puppy thinks that it has pleased you, the more likely it will eventually walk on the lead as you require.

Another useful tip here, if space permits, is to position an outside mirror on a wall at a height which will allow you to see yourself walking with your dog and will give you the ability to assess it from a judge's point of view. This will also come in very useful when you are standing your dog, for you can see how you can make it look its best. You will also see from the front if you have managed to get it to stand correctly in the show stance.

## Training Classes

It is best to have started to train your puppy for show ring procedure before you attend the first training class. The majority of these classes are held within a hall and very often the surface is inclined to be a slippery wooden floor. In some cases, the caretakers or owners insist that some form of matting be placed on this, and that may come in the form of rubber or canvas. Therefore, if your puppy has not become accustomed to the set show pattern or has not overcome the first lesson of how to walk on a lead, you will find that it may be averse to attempting the same in these strange new conditions.

If a puppy who is already a little nervous is pulled in order to make it walk a few steps, it could easily slip on this shiny surface, thoroughly alarming it in the process. So, bearing this in mind, always make sure that the basic training is completed in more acceptable surroundings.

The great advantage of attending one of these classes as we have already mentioned is the presence of other breeds apart from Pekingese. Another point in its favour is that it gives both you and your puppy the opportunity of being assessed as though a judge is going over your dog. So, if you have never shown a dog before, this will give you a little confidence in ring procedure as well as helping to train your dog.

In the vast majority of cases in the UK, the judge at the show itself will be a breed specialist and in the main will ask you to move your dog before it is handled and assessed for conformation on the table. An all-rounder, however, will want to handle the dogs before assessing them for movement. A training class, therefore, gives you the opportunity to allow your youngster to become used to this method also.

Every teacher at such a class enjoys his or her own favourite method of training, but the same principles apply – letting the dog walk as though it is at a show, handling it on the table and so on. The number of times you will be asked to move your puppy will depend on the individual. Sometimes it is best not to overdo a youngster and if at its first few lessons it walks reasonably well the first time, do not be afraid to say that you do not want to push it in these early stages. As time goes on, of course, it will walk as many times as its older and more experienced class members.

After each dog has been assessed individually you may be required to walk around in a circle, though again with a relative beginner you may be better sitting this one out! Your puppy may become alarmed if another dog gets too close behind it, so join in only when you feel your charge is quite confident with the current situation. Circling the dogs at these classes is of course excellent training for later on. Sometimes in a Variety class at an Open Show, or when you eventually hit the 'big time', you may have to go into a toy group and very often you will be required to circle around with all the other dogs, so this groundwork will hopefully set you in good stead for this eventuality.

There are a few more exercises that come to mind, one of these being weaving in and out between the other dogs. The class will stand around in a circle with enough space in between each handler and dog for another partnership to walk through. In rotation, each dog and owner will then go around the circle, weaving in and out of the dogs until they are eventually back where they started from. Again, this is excellent training, although we would give a word of caution here: always be alert and aware of the various dog's reactions as you approach. A novice handler with a slightly uncontrollable dog may present a problem, so always be prepared to guide your dog away from any trouble should it suddenly arise. Very often at these classes some of the handlers need more training than their dogs.

Another training exercise you may be asked to perform is to walk down the mat or hall side by side with another dog. It is the usual practice for the dogs to be at each other's side and the handlers to be on the outside. A good instructor will match the dogs so that, for instance, you do not have two wild youngsters together; a novice will be asked to walk with a slightly more experienced counterpart.

The majority of clubs will hold a match about once a month. This is usually judged by a guest who has been invited by the club, with all the dogs entering on the night. Each exhibit is issued at that stage with a number, and a knock-out competition then ensues. For instance, in the first round your number will be called out to compete against another number. The winner of this round then goes on to compete in the next round after every dog has been seen. When your dog is more experienced this can be great fun and a happy and light-hearted evening enjoyed by all.

As you will probably have realised if you have attended any dog shows, Pekingese in the United Kingdom are traditionally shown on a table. Once you have been individually assessed both in movement and by handling you are then expected to join the rest of that particular class on the long tables provided for that use. Your little puppy whom you have trained to stand perfectly on a table by itself may be more than a little awkward when asked to stand in the

*Fig 44 Champion Toydom's Quite Outrageous. Owned and bred by Miss A. Summers and Miss V. Williams.*

*Fig 45 Champion Toydom the Drama Queen. Owned and bred by Miss A. Summers and Miss V. Williams. 'Quite Outrageous' and 'Drama Queen' are brother and sister Champions.*

show position on a table with several other dogs. It invariably shows more interest in its neighbouring companions than keeping its mind on the job in hand. This is especially likely when the class is well filled and you are literally all squashed up together. Try not to let your youngster pay undue attention to the puppies on either side for in these conditions it is understandable if one or other of them should become a little aggressive.

This exercise can be carried out at home if you happen to have more than one dog, especially if you are the only Pekingese at training class. Obviously you will need a little assistance from relatives or friends to carry this out. Do not try to do this single-handed as it could end with one or all of them falling off the table causing serious injury. While carrying this out it is always an idea to cajole one of your helpers into 'judging' the puppy while you have it in this position.

The best way to carry out this operation is to stand the puppy on the table and, when it is settled, let one dog be placed alongside of it. If and when your puppy fidgets, quite naturally of course, then replace it in the show position, firmly telling it to stand. When it seems quite at ease with this new situation it has found itself in, ask for another dog to be placed on the other side of it. Once again, if its interest is aroused enough to ruin its concentration, kindly but firmly place it in the show stance, once again repeating the command as often as you feel necessary – *'Stand'*. Remember, after each reasonably successful training session, to praise your puppy. Do not get annoyed and give up if it takes a little while to become used to these routines you are setting it. Pekingese are after all just flesh and blood and high-spirited, loving little dogs at that, not robots. If you try to make these early lessons and its puppyhood as much fun as possible, when you are progressing into the higher classes in its later life, it will not have lost that little bit of sparkle and love of life, while of course still being well behaved.

If your puppy carries out successfully what you have asked of it, do not keep repeating the exercise. All you will succeed in doing is making it thoroughly sick of the whole idea, and this, in fact, could send it completely the other way. Many is the time we have seen people practising their dogs again and again outside the ring at a show, finding that when the time has come to show off their paces under the scrutiny of a judge, they have become completely fed up with the whole idea and refuse to show themselves off to their full advantage. Just remember, all things are best in moderation, for if your little dog enjoys what it is doing it will always aim to please you to the best of its ability.

## Showing Baskets

As we have mentioned in Chapter 4, there is a need to accustom your little dog to the car. When the day comes around that you are travelling off to your first show, you will find the best way of transporting it is in a show basket or pen. It is sometimes a very good idea for you to have let your puppy become acquainted with this form of travel by taking a small drive to your local park or the village green. When you are there you will have an opportunity to let the puppy quickly go through its paces in preparation for the big day. It is advisable to let it get used to walking in this manner in different environments and not restricting this practice to the back garden alone.

There are several makes and shapes of show basket for you to choose from. There are plastic wire baskets, steel-penned baskets, plastic boxes, and the older-fashioned wire baskets. Whichever one you choose, make sure that the puppy is used to being confined to it on short journeys to start with, so that, when it is ready for the longer ones it will have to make to shows, it will take it all in its stride.

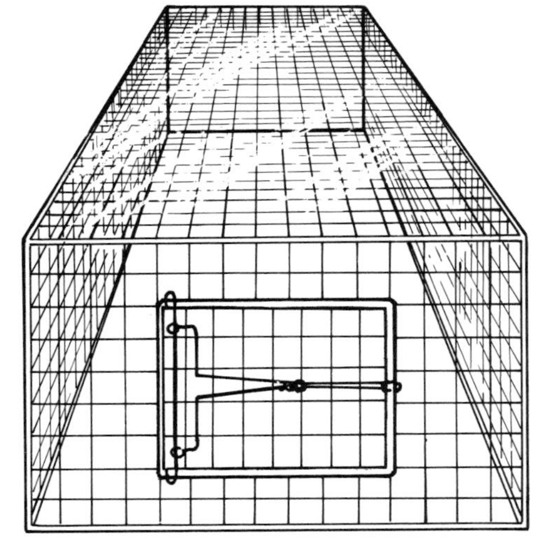

*Fig 46 Steel pen with front-opening door.*

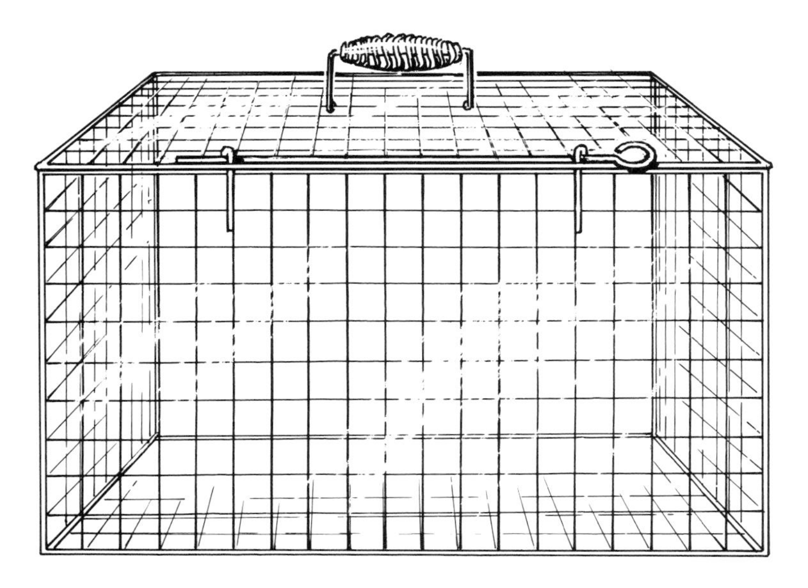

*Fig 47 Wire basket.*

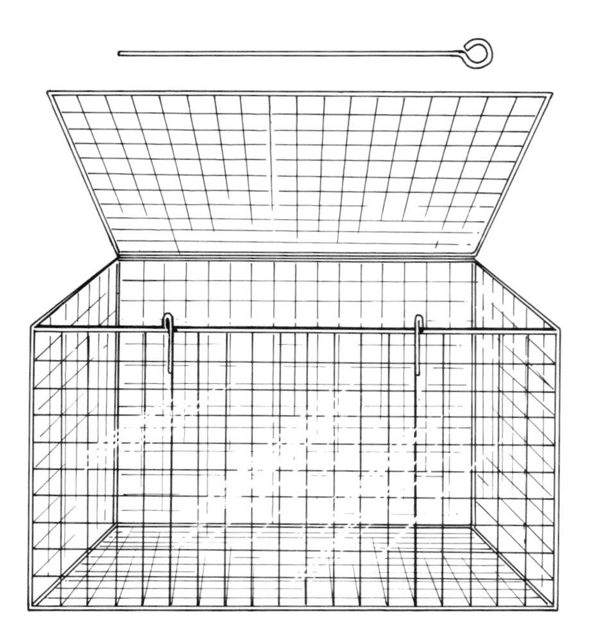

*Fig 48 The opening of a wire basket.*

One very important point here that we must make, is to be very, very careful of transporting your dogs in the car on a warm or hot day. The temperature can shoot up inside the car whether it is stationary or not. Very often, even when the sun is not out, the humidity can be quite oppressive and unbearable, so *never ever* leave your dog in a car unless it is cool, or else the consequences could prove fatal. Because of the heat factor we prefer, for travelling to shows, the steel pens or plastic wire baskets which ensure that there is plenty of all-round ventilation for the dog's comfort. Always keep the windows well open when travelling; remember that the dogs are more important than your windswept hairstyle. For the very sunny days there are now some extremely efficient blinds available which can be easily fitted onto the inside of the car's windows and which help block out the strong sun rays.

Another tip is to travel your dog on ice packs (*see* Chapter 9, page 143). It is better not to let the dog get too hot in the first place. Sometimes when returning from a show on a hot day it is best to have some spare towels in the car with you. These can be soaked in cold water and then squeezed out; one can be placed in the dog's pen and the others draped over the top.

# 7

# Grooming for a Show

As the day of the show is drawing near, you will, of course, have kept up your daily routine of checking closely for any mats that may have formed and also that your pride and joy is smelling sweet and clean underneath. A few days prior to the great event ensure that your dog's nails are of an acceptable length. If they have grown a little, now is the time to cut them, as discussed in Chapter 5 (page 84).

On the eve of the show, you need to start to prepare your dog, grooming him until he looks his best. In Fig 49, you will see the grooming equipment that we take to a show. On the left is a dual purpose comb, the next is a wire-pin brush. We again recommend here that you watch some of the breed's expert presenters at work

*Fig 49 Grooming aids.*

before you rush off and buy one of these. The next brush is the nylon and bristle mixture brush that is perfect for a Pekingese coat. The third brush in the picture is a pure nylon one which we find is extremely good for the very heavy-coated dogs. We would in these early stages advise that you restrict yourself to the use of the last two. Finally, we show here a fine-toothed comb, which is ideal for combing the hairs on the cheeks and on the wrinkle. It can also be useful on the topskull, removing any hair that tends to make the hair on the head stand up too much.

Traditionally, the feet of a Pekingese are supposed to carry long toe feathering. However lovely these may look, we personally feel that they are not very practical. You will find that if allowed to grow too long, when your dog is trying to show himself off at a show which is held on grass (and the 'grass' is more likely to be in a field and in no way resembles your beautifully seeded lawn or park at home) these long fringes will prove an unnecessary burden to him. So, as in Fig 50, when your dog is lying on its back, take its paw and, starting with the two front legs, proceed to trim these a little. You do not have to go completely mad and trim them drastically, just a little trim will suffice. For instance, you do not want the foot resembling that of a cat, a small amount should be left that comfortably covers

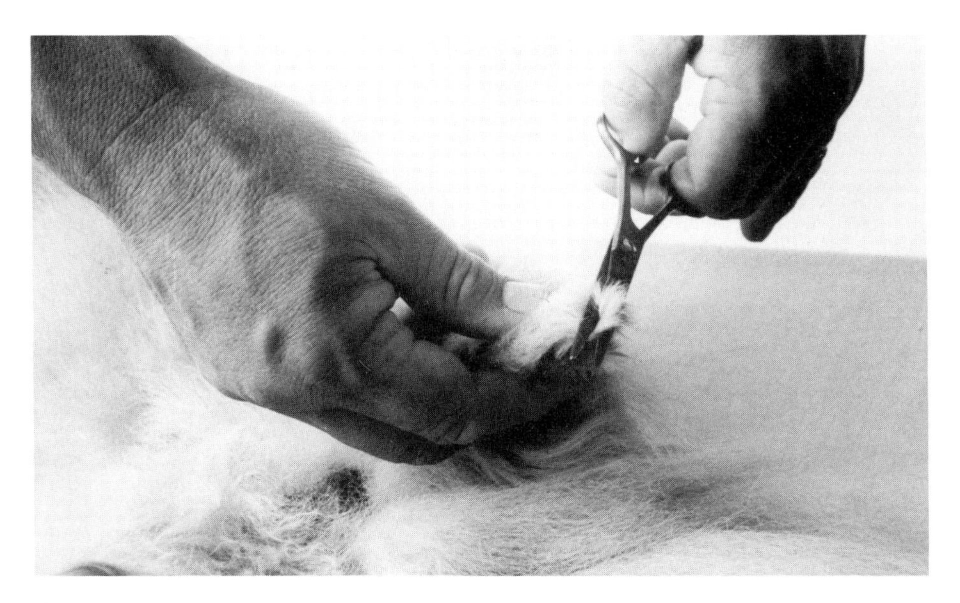

*Fig 50 Trimming of the toe feathering.*

the foot and nails. In other words, when the dog is standing upright there is no visible sign of any nail but there should be no length of toe feathering either.

It must be said here that some of our older breeders will hold their hands up in horror at the mere mention of this practice, but in this day and age there are many of us who adhere to this method. This is a preference and up to each individual.

When you have dealt with the front feet, proceed to the back ones carrying out the same trimming on those also. Remember, do not give your dog's feet a 'short back and sides', just gentle shaping and cutting is enough.

Now stand your dog up on all four feet once again, and, if you look at the back legs, at the rear of these you will most likely see some fairly thick hair growing down (this will become more obvious the older your puppy gets); these are what are commonly known as the bedsocks. We, as many others do, feel that they look untidy and detract from the movement behind. Therefore it is better that they are neatly trimmed off (*see* Fig 51).

You may either use ordinary scissors or, alternatively, thinning scissors (*see* Fig 52), the latter tending to give a more even finish. Once again, it is easier if the dog will lie on his back. Taking one

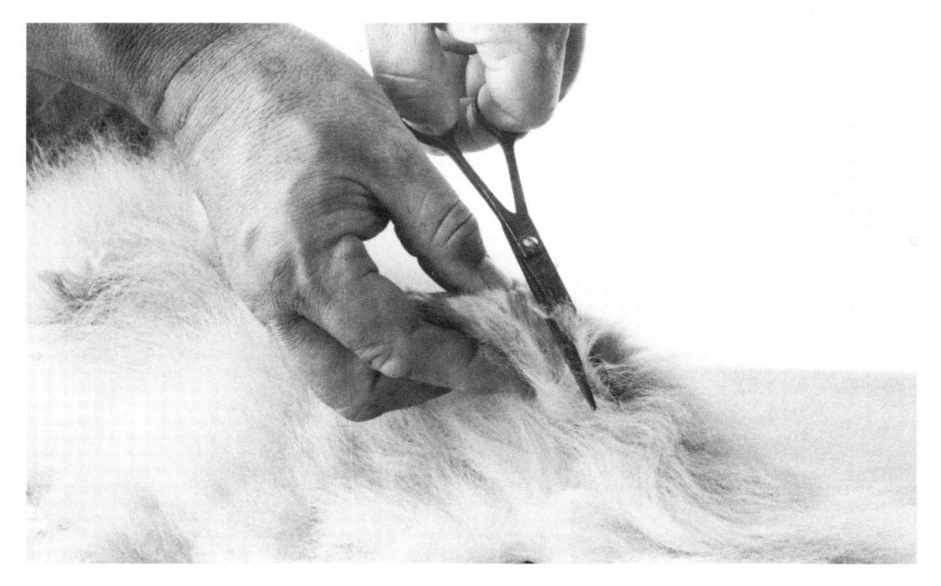

*Fig 51 Trimming the back legs or bedsocks.*

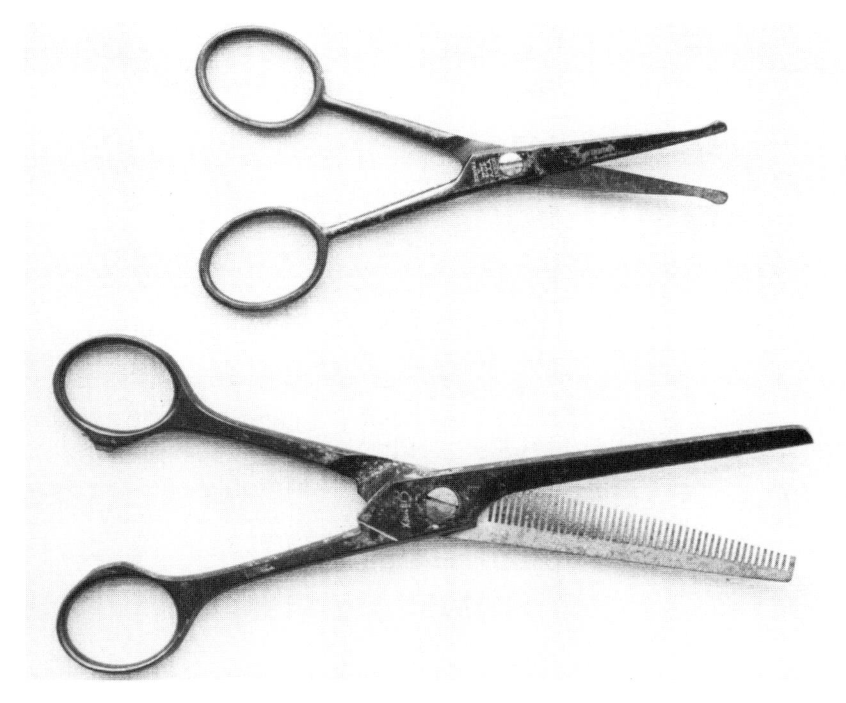

*Fig 52 Small trimming scissors and thinning scissors.*

back leg, gently comb the hair that you need to remove outwards so that you can see the length. Place the thinning scissors parallel to the leg, just a fraction away from the leg itself, and cut once; then remove the scissors. Now comb away the hair that has been severed. You will find that the thinning scissors do not give a clean cut, but remove a little at a time. Comb the hair, this time against the leg to see how it lies; if it is not flat enough, repeat this process again, until you have the desired effect. Always be careful to take a little at a time rather than too much, so do not rush this.

When you have finished the back legs to your satisfaction, they should look neat and not as though they have literally been hacked at. If using ordinary scissors, be even more wary and cut from the outer hair inwards until the legs again look perfectly matched and neat.

A final word regarding the feet. A little further trimming will be necessary on the pads of the dog's feet (*see* Fig 53). While the dog is on his back you will more than likely notice hair growing out from

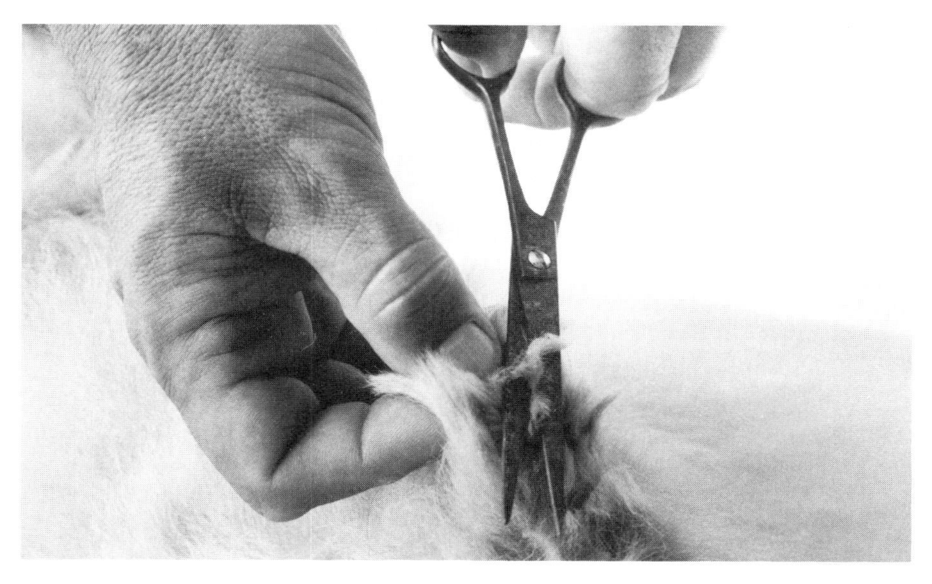

*Fig 53 Trimming the pads of the feet.*

between the pads on his feet which, if allowed to go unchecked, can form a covering over the dog's pad, especially if he is not used to much road work. This time, with the small pair of trimming scissors, trim this hair back to the pad, giving a neat appearance to the underneath of the dog's foot.

Those minor details out of the way, you are now ready to groom your dog for the show. We like to groom our dogs up the day or evening before to the standard of being ready to go into the show ring. The following process is also repeated on the dog once again on the day of the show, excluding the trimming of the feet, of course.

Lay the dog flat on its back and, with warm water, gently wash the area around the sheath or, if she is a female, around the vulva. Dry well afterwards to finish off this part of your dog's personal grooming. This need hardly be attended to the next day, depending on the individual dog and how messy he is inclined to get.

The days of being able to take a dog to a show in this country and liberally sprinkle powder on are gone. This used to help lift the coat apart from cleaning it on the day, but this aspect of the art of grooming has been relegated to the dim and distant past. However, if your dog is groomed regularly and his coat is in good condition, this will not affect you too much. As with many forbidden methods, the few spoilt it for the majority. Venues were being lost due, in many cases, to the inconsiderate actions of others. Very often you would see a dog shake and then literally disappear in a haze of talc!

Any mess that you may make always clear away or take home with you, whether it be at an outdoor or indoor show. Spare a thought for the hard-working committee who, in many cases, have the arduous chore of clearing up after a long day running the show.

The use of talcum powder is restricted to the home, for the Kennel Club categorically state that it must be removed from the coat on the day of the show. So the preparation of your dog on the day of the show will have to exclude the use of this substance. When used on the previous day, always ensure that it is well brushed out. It has happened now on a couple of occasions in our breed that dogs have been tested for illegal substances, so be warned.

While your dog is on his back, spray the coat and brush forward from the stomach towards the chest. Remember always to spray first before brushing, to stop the coat splitting. Once this is brushed and still slightly damp, sprinkle a little powder into the coat and proceed to brush this all out, thus cleaning the coat.

Spray and brush around the dog's back legs, spraying and brushing and, once again, powdering. While the dog is still in this position, spray and brush the trousers from underneath using the above-mentioned process. With the short hairs on the back legs, use a comb and then spray and brush the hair as usual, finally combing out any powder that may still remain on the legs.

On the front legs a certain amount of feathering on the side of the leg itself will be noticed. If these seem over-profuse and tend to make the dog look a little out in the shoulder, thinning scissors may be needed. A little thinning here will help the hair lie back. Do not take it too close to the leg, gently taper it from the top of the leg down and, in the process, leave a reasonable amount of feathering.

The next step is to section your dog's coat, so start by laying the dog on his side and, working from the back, part the coat as illustrated in Fig 54. Spray and brush each section and, while barely damp, clean with the powder. Once you have completed this section, move along a little further forwards, form another parting and then repeat this process. When you reach the area near the front legs, turn the dog over on his other side and repeat this along there. Always work from the rear of the dog forward, brushing the coat forward and back to give body.

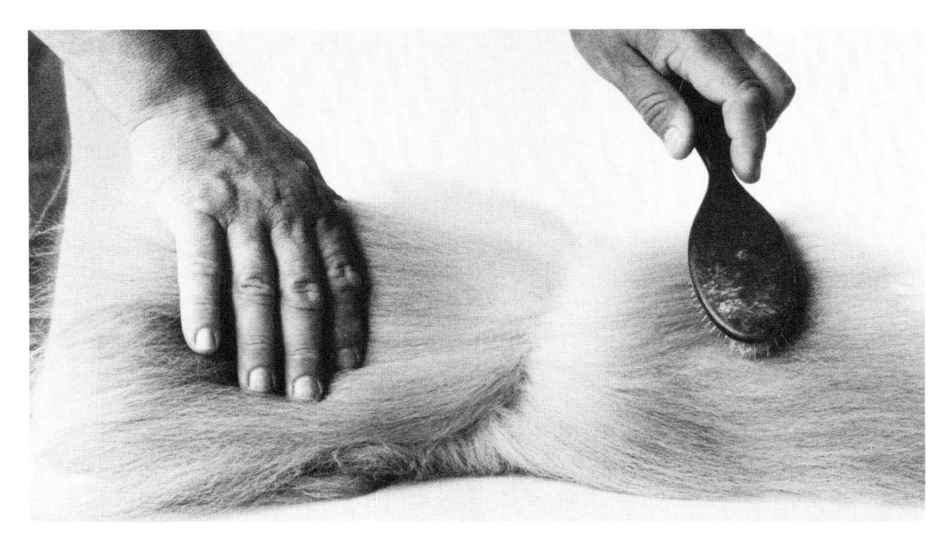

*Fig 54 Sectioning the coat.*

Having completed the work on the sides, stand the dog up and repeat this along his back up to the mane. When you have finished this, complete this part of the grooming by brushing all the coat along the body towards the rear. You will now need to concentrate on the mane, ears and chest.

Providing, of course, that the rest of the dog is presented well, careful grooming of the mane will help to present a picture of profuse ear fringing and to lift the ears and mane, enhancing the topskull to make it appear as flat as possible.

So you now need to brush the mane forward as in Fig 55, spraying and brushing and, of course, finishing off with a little talcum powder. Keep doing this until you ensure that there is plenty of body in this area of the coat, making it almost stand up on end. This will be accomplished by applying short, gentle swift strokes and need not be a heavy-handed exercise. Once this is done, lightly brush the coat backward from the top of the head so that it almost falls into place with a lift to it. Do not flatten the mane, for you need as much volume as possible in this part of the dog's coat to give the desired impression.

With the dog in the standing or sitting position, take one of his ear fringes in your hand and lightly spray the feathering. Ensure before you do this that there are no traces of food in these; if there is,

*Fig 55 The dog's body coat groomed and brushed back, and the mane brushed forward.*

*Fig 56 Brushing the mane back.*

*Fig 57 Brushing the inside of the ear fringes.*

quickly wash them beforehand. Having sprayed them, brush through and, before they dry, flip the ear back across the dog's head. Once again, spray the feathering; this time, of course, it will be the underside of the ear and the fringes that will be getting the benefit of this brushing (*see* Fig 57). After dusting with a little powder and brushing all this out, flip the ear back over again into the normal position. Repeat the same process with the other ear.

The dog's bib and chest is the next priority and so, spraying and brushing as you go, start at the bottom and work up. Lift the coat up with one hand and work up in layers until you reach under the chin. When you have finished this and the whole area is thoroughly dry, run a wide-toothed comb through the mane. This will automatically make it fluff out.

The final part of the coat needing attention is the feathering on the dog's tail, and, if done carefully, this can present a beautiful finish to your well-groomed little dog. Obviously, a young puppy will not have the furnishings of our 'model' until it has fully matured, but careful grooming of the baby coat can encourage and train the coat for later on.

Hold the tail in one hand. Once again you need to brush this in sections, working from the base up to the tip (*see* Fig 58). Groom each small section carefully so that when you have finished, the tail can be brushed to fan out over the dog's back (*see* Fig 59). A little tip

*Fig 58 Sectioning and brushing the tail.*

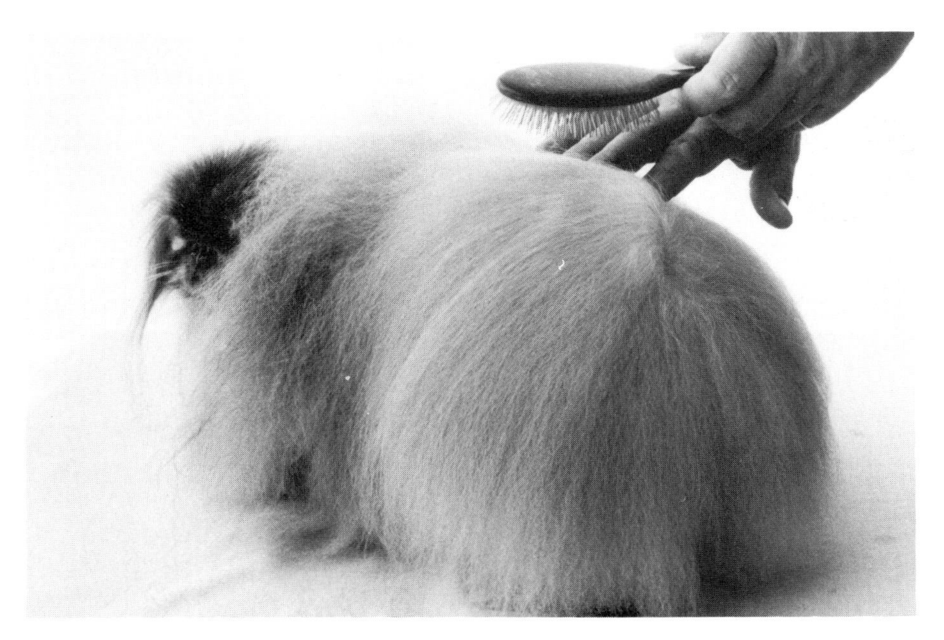

*Fig 59 Finished picture of the tail fanned over the back.*

here is, as with the rest of the coat, a short while before you are due to go into the ring, give a very, very light spray over the coat, especially over the mane and tail. You will see that the dampness will gently lift the coat, holding it in place at the same time.

Before you put the finishing touches to your dog to make him quite ready for the ring, make quite sure that his face is clean and dry. Your everyday routine will have included this facial cleansing so, in fact, this should be just a matter of quickly wiping it dry. Check the eyes and also wipe the wrinkle if needed. If this is wet and sticky – this can be brought on by dust or hot weather – it will completely ruin the picture you are presenting to the judge, apart from being extremely unpleasant for the dog. Do not forget to check in that little spot above the nose, making sure that it is clean and dry.

Again, a little judicial trimming can improve the face, but do not attempt to use the scissors here until your dog is used to the daily care of his face and you are quite proficient with a brush and a comb. For any light trimming around the face, you are best advised to use a pair of blunt-ended scissors for safety. As well as the eyes, also, when working in this area, be especially careful of the dog's tongue. It is very easy to snip at the precise moment he decides to

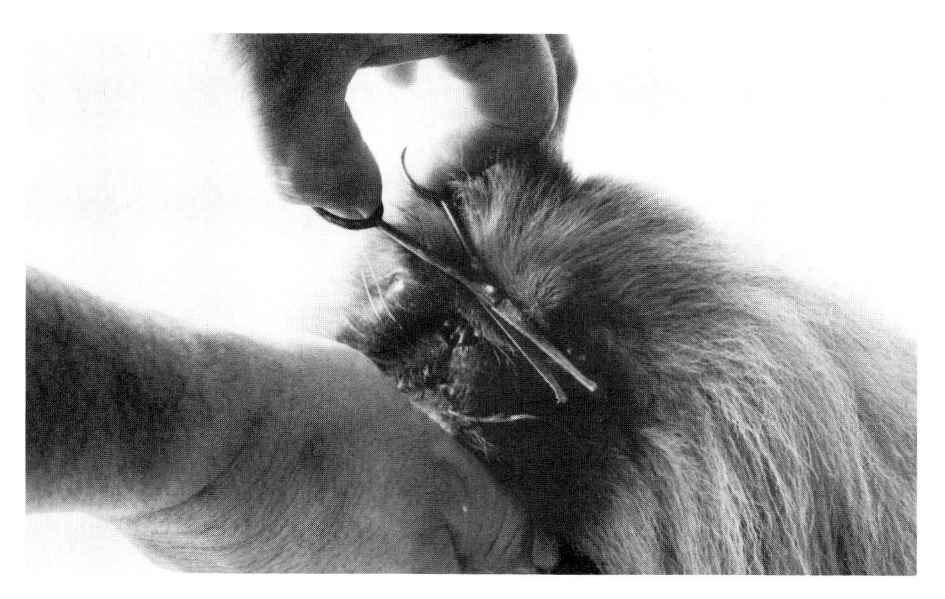

*Fig 60 Preparing to trim the wrinkle and whiskers.*

*Fig 61 Lifting the ear fringes.*

stick his tongue out. So please do not attempt any of this at least until you have seen someone else do it, or are fully capable yourself.

Some dogs are inclined to get a heavy growth of hair off the wrinkle and this starts to grow over the nose. This looks unsightly and, if trimmed, can make the face look totally different. Take the blunt-ended scissors and, from above the nose cut a little of the offending hair away, following the line of the wrinkle (*see* Fig 60). Do not take it so close that it gives an appearance of being shaved, but just close enough to dispose of those straggly, unwanted hairs.

Also, a little trimming on the wrinkle itself can make the head appear wider, because the eyes become that much more obvious. Once again, if you comb the wrinkle from below the eye outwards you may see a few odd hairs that could be neatly snipped off. You are just basically tipping the ends of the hair here; do not go too close or you will ruin the whole appearance of your dog's face. You may not need to touch either of these two places; it depends on each individual dog.

We also take the whiskers off, for we feel that it gives a neater, cleaner picture and again gives the illusion of the face being wider than it is.

Now you are ready to give your dog that last little finishing touch. Gently lift the ear fringes both sides from just below the line of the ear (*see* Fig 61), then very very lightly spray, just giving a little

*Fig 62 Champion Sunsalve My Love. Owned and bred by Mr T. Nethercott and Mr E. Hurdle.*

dampness to the hair. Spray a little dressing out onto your brush and brush the topskull from the front towards the mane, flattening it as you go. This only needs to be a light movement of the hand, in order to coax it to lie flat. That last fine little spray will hold this down in place at the same time.

Finally, make quite sure that the tail is sitting correctly and, as with the ears, gently spray it. Brush the sides of the mane lightly forward, brush the trousers down and the bib up and your dog is ready for the ring.

# 8

# Entering a Show – the Preliminaries

Dog showing should always be taken and kept in perspective. If this is done, many a happy hour or day can be spent enjoying this totally absorbing hobby. Even so, dog showing is extremely competitive. The major kennels and many of the up and coming ones as well go to a show with one object in mind, and that is to win. After all, this is the culmination of all your breeding plans and hopes, for here, so to speak, is the proof of the pudding. Here is where all your months of choosing and studying pedigrees of prospective sires for your bitch, together with whelping, weaning, rearing and training come to fruition.

Having said that, while competition is fierce in the ring, especially at the Championship Shows, outside the ring there is a great deal of camaraderie. Some extremely pleasant hours can be spent with fellow exhibitors. After battle has been done within the confines of the ring, those in opposition there can be seen afterwards chatting away quite happily with one another, the greatest of friends.

It would be naive of us to suggest that all is wine and roses, however, for unfortunately on some occasions you do need to possess a thick skin to withstand the rather barbed comments of the odd jealous exhibitor. Their remarks are often aimed at you or, even worse, your dog and, in cases like this, you really have to learn to keep your own counsel and shrug these stupid little occurrences off to the best of your ability. Do not be disheartened, though, for these incidents are very few and far between and always remember, whatever happens, at the end of the day the little dog whom you love and who reciprocates those feelings will be returning home with you.

What we would suggest is that you start at the smaller types of show; do not be tempted to go straight to a Championship Show and enter every class scheduled.

## Exemption Shows

These shows are held within the rules laid down by the dog world's governing body, the Kennel Club. We have covered the classes available in Chapter 3 (*see* page 55) and we will briefly reiterate that there are classes for pedigree dogs as well as novelty classes. You will generally find these shows advertised in the local paper or the village store. Alternatively, they are likely to appear in one of the weekly dog journals. These shows are ideal training grounds for both you and your dog before you progress to more serious things.

At these shows, entries are taken on the day of the show. In the advertisement the commencement of judging will be stated, probably with the name of the judge. Usually the show itself opens approximately one hour before the first class. It is quite normal for the pedigree classes to precede the novelty ones so always allow yourself plenty of time to get there, settle your dog down and have your entries taken. You can, of course, enter both the pedigree and novelty classes if you so desire. It is most advisable to enter the pedigree ones rather than solely entering the novelty ones. In the classes for pedigree dogs you will be assessed as though you are at a larger show.

Make no mistake in these early days and think that a smaller show such as this will be a walk-over for your 'future Champion'. This could be the first of many hard lessons you will learn along the way, for at these shows many top winning young dogs have been seen getting a little extra practice in. Look on these expeditions as well-needed experience, and if in the due course of events you have a successful day, jolly well done – enjoy these successes. As a highly revered breeder said to us many years ago after we had had a particularly successful day: 'Well done, enjoy your success and your day. Remember this on maybe not such a successful occasion.' This is what keeps you going and what showing is all about.

## Limited, Open and Championship Shows

There are three other standard types of show: Limited, Open and Championship. Limited Shows can be entered only by members of the show society; Open Shows are open to all exhibitors with registered dogs, as are Championship Shows unless a qualification for entry is prescribed by the Kennel Club, for example Cruft's Dog Show. These three types of show can fall into two categories: All Breed and Breed Club Shows.

## *All Breed Shows*

An All Breed Show is for dogs of any breed type, as the name suggests. When you have an All Breed Show schedule in front of you, look through it so you can see if there is a classification for Pekingese. If there is, the various classes available will be outlined here. You may find, for instance, that there will be classes for Puppy, Dog or Bitch; Novice, Dog or Bitch; Graduate, Dog or Bitch; Open, Dog or Bitch. Sometimes you may find that there is an extended classification of possibly eight classes, therefore allowing the sexes to be split.

On the other hand, there may not be any classes for Pekingese on offer, in which case you will usually have the following classes to choose from: Any Variety Toy (usually abbreviated to AV Toy), or Any Variety Not Separately Classified (AVNSC in its shortened state). There will also be variety classes to choose from, for example: Any Variety Minor Puppy Dog, Any Variety Puppy Dog, with, of course, the corresponding classes for the females. So, as you see, there is quite a choice for you to study.

Let us look into these various classes. The Any Variety Toy classes are available for any dog within the toy group to enter, which of course includes the Pekingese. You will probably notice in the schedule that other groups have their own special classes, for gun dogs, terriers, hounds and those that fall within the two categories of working and utility dogs.

Within the AV Toy classes you will come up against other breeds that may or may not have their own breed classes scheduled. If there are classes for Pekingese scheduled at the show, you may, if you so wish, still enter into the AV Toy class.

With the Any Variety Not Separately Classified classes, dogs from any group are entitled to enter, providing of course there are no classes scheduled for them at this particular show.

If you win a Pekingese class with your puppy you will be entitled to challenge in the unbeaten dogs and bitches line-up. This is when the judge chooses his or her Best of Breed. At the same time, the judge will also be required to nominate a Best Puppy. If you were the only unbeaten puppy your dog would automatically be pronounced Best

*Fig 63 Champion Bramblefields Berangaria. Owned and bred by Mr and Mrs P. Jones.*

Puppy. However, there is nothing to stop another puppy being entered in any of the other breed classes, for instance the Novice class. It may not have been entered in the Puppy class for a variety of reasons so, if unbeaten, it can challenge for the puppy honour. This sounds quite complex, but it is possible that it may not even have won the Novice class and may only have been placed second, shall we say. Provided, though, that the dog or bitch that beat it was not itself a puppy, then that same dog is still eligible to compete against the winner of the Puppy class.

Let us now assume that there are no breed classes for you to enter. You can of course then opt to go into the Any Variety Toy classes or, alternatively those for the Any Variety Not Separately Classified.

If you win the AV Toy Puppy class the same principle applies as before, but this time the judge will be choosing a Best AV Toy and the corresponding Best Puppy.

With the AVNSC winners, once again the same system is undertaken with the appropriate awards and titles. At the end of the day, though, when Best in Show comes to be judged, you will need to discover if the finals will be done on a group system or *en masse*. For instance, there could be six different groups judged, with all the relative Best of Breeds and Best Puppies judged within their respective sections. The winner of each of those separate groups will compete at the end for Best in Show and Best Puppy in Show. If this system is not implemented, however, all the dogs meet together in the ring at the end of the day to compete against each other for one or other award.

Let us assume that classes are scheduled for Pekingese and for AV Toy. As we have already pointed out, you are perfectly entitled to enter in both, but take heed. You may, for example, win your class in the breed and have been declared Best Puppy. With that win alone you are eligible to go forward into the final for Best Puppy in Show. If, however, you are also entered in the same class under the heading of AV Toy, and in the process are beaten by another puppy, be it a Pekingese or one from another breed, you are automatically disqualified from challenging at the end of the show. It is quite possible that you could even be beaten by another Pekingese if it is a different judge, perhaps reversing the former judge's decision.

In the case of being made Best Puppy from the AVNSC classes, provided you are not beaten at any time by another puppy, get your little dog ready for the Best Puppy in Show challenge. If the finals are judged on a group system, you would have to compete against all the other unbeaten toy puppies.

You may have entered in the Pekingese Puppy class and also in one of the Any Variety Puppy classes. If you have won your breed Puppy class you are entitled to withdraw from the latter class if you so wish. Due to a Kennel Club ruling, you are allowed to forgo this class in order for you to remain an unbeaten puppy at the end of the day. A win in one of these Variety classes alone does not entitle you to compete for the Best Puppy award at the very end.

## *Breed Club Shows*

In the United Kingdom alone we have eighteen breed clubs in existence, each of them on average holding two shows a year. Some of these clubs have championship status granted annually, by permission of the Kennel Club. In other words, the Kennel Club entitles these clubs to hold a show where Kennel Club Challenge

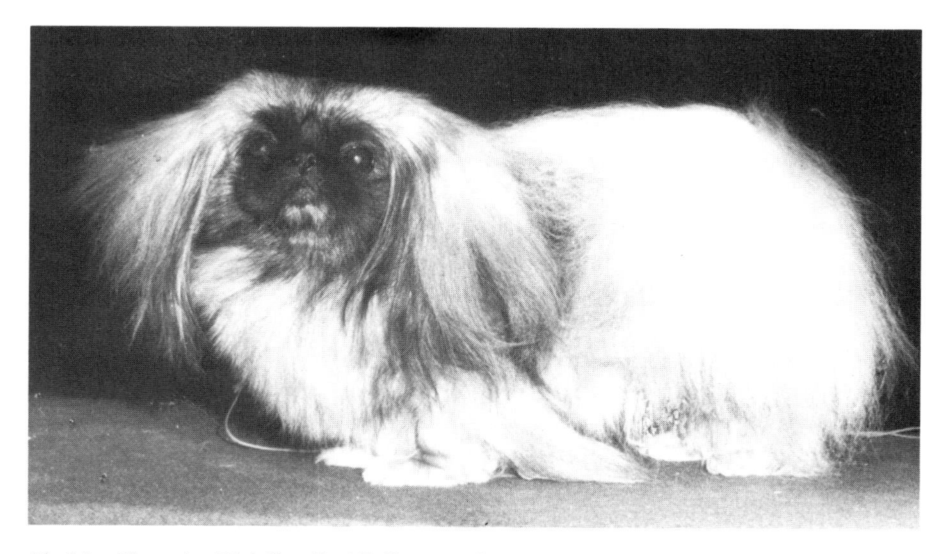

*Fig 64 Champion Wei Sing Prai Pollyanna. Owned and bred by Mrs N. Kerkin.*

Certificates may be offered. The remaining clubs take this privilege in rotation, usually every two years. In recent times, several sets of tickets have been taken away from this breed from All Breed Championship Shows, due to a directive from the Kennel Club.

Breed Club Shows, whether Limited, Open or Championship, host on average twenty-four classes. The majority of these are split between the sexes with, invariably, Mixed Colour classes towards the end of the show (there are classes for Whites, Blacks, Parti-Colours, Reds and Red Brindles, etc.).

## *The Schedule*

To give you an idea of the classes available we will go through a typical schedule, listing the classification and the stipulations on each class.

**Minor Puppy** For dogs of six and not exceeding nine calendar months of age on the first day of the show.

**Puppy** For dogs of six and not exceeding twelve calendar months of age on the first day of the show.

**Junior** For dogs of six and not exceeding eighteen calendar months of age on the first day of the show.

**Maiden** For dogs which have not won a Challenge Certificate or a first prize at an Open or Championship Show (Puppy, Special Puppy, Minor Puppy and Special Minor Puppy classes excepted) whether restricted or not.

**Novice** For dogs which have not won a Challenge Certificate or three or more first prizes at Open and Championship Shows (Puppy, Special Puppy, Minor Puppy and Special Minor Puppy classes excepted) whether restricted or not.

**Tyro** For dogs which have not won a Challenge Certificate or five or more first prizes at Open and Championship Shows (Puppy, Special Puppy, Minor Puppy and Special Minor Puppy classes excepted) whether restricted or not.

**Debutant** For dogs which have not won a Challenge Certificate or a first prize at a Championship Show (Puppy, Special Puppy, Minor Puppy and Special Minor Puppy classes excepted) whether restricted or not.

**Undergraduate** For dogs which have not won a Challenge Certificate or three or more first prizes at Championship Shows (Puppy, Special Puppy, Minor Puppy and Special Minor Puppy classes excepted) whether restricted or not.

**Graduate** For dogs which have not won a Challenge Certificate or four or more first prizes at Championship Shows in Graduate, Post Graduate Minor Limit, Mid Limit, Limit and Open classes, whether restricted or not.

**Post Graduate** For dogs which have not won a Challenge Certificate or five or more first prizes at Championship Shows in Post Graduate, Minor Limit, Mid Limit, Limit and Open classes, whether restricted or not.

**Limit** For dogs which have not won three Challenge Certificates under three different judges or seven or more first prizes in all at Championship Shows in Limit and Open classes confined to the breed, whether restricted or not, at shows where Challenge Certificates were offered for the breed.

**Open** For all dogs of the breeds or varieties for which the class is provided and eligible for entry at the show.

**Veteran** For dogs of not less than seven years of age on the first day of the show.

**Progeny** For a dog or bitch, accompanied by at least three of its registered progeny, the dog or bitch not necessarily entered in another class, however, but all progeny having been entered and exhibited in another class. The dog or bitch and the progeny need not be registered in the same ownership.

**Brace** For two exhibits (either sex or mixed) of one breed belonging to the same exhibitor, each exhibit having been entered in some class other than Brace or Team.

**Team** For three or more exhibits (either sex or mixed) of one breed belonging to the same exhibitor, each exhibit having been entered in some other class other than Brace or Team.

**Special Yearling** For dogs of six and not exceeding twenty-four calendar months of age on the first day of the show.

**Special Open** Similar to Open class except that it is restricted as to weight, height, colour, etc. (For instance, classes expressly designated for black, white or parti-colour dogs or the weight classes for sleeve dogs, etc.)

**Special Beginners** (This definition may vary from society to society: some request the exhibitor not to have won a high award, while others may request that the handler – who may be a different person from the exhibitor – also be a novice to such awards. Some others specify that the owner or handler must not have won a Junior Warrant.) In this case, however, it appears to be for dogs handled by the exhibitor, and neither dog nor exhibitor should have won a Challenge Certificate in the breed at a Championship Show. It should be noted that both dog and exhibitor have to qualify for the class.

*Fig 65 Champion Genisim Charlot the Harlot. Owned and bred by Mrs J. Sims.*

# Advancing your Show Career

## *All Breed Open Shows*

We have recommended Exemption Shows as good practice early on. To start your show career properly we would advise you perhaps to enter one of your local Open Shows; these will hopefully list classes of Pekingese. We tend to go to these shows ourselves with young dogs especially. It gives us a chance to see how a young puppy or dog is going to behave or react. It is a very strange thing, for however much you train your puppies at home, or in the park or at training classes, the atmosphere at shows seems to be totally different. Because of this, we find that they are an ideal settling-in ground and are also of enormous benefit to the novice exhibitor.

At the local Open Shows you also get a chance to know your local fellow breed fanciers, nearly all of whom will be most helpful and friendly. They will, in most cases, take a lost novice exhibitor under their wing.

With your schedule in front of you, you are now deciding where to enter your young seven-month-old puppy. As defined earlier, there will probably be at the least a Mixed Puppy class, plus three others. Do not get too over-enthusiastic and enter your young hopeful in every single class, although the plus side of this would be the extra experience for you and a lovely entry for the judge and society. When you think about it logically, your baby, barely out of the puppy pen, is going to be hard pressed to beat a mature two-year-old from the Open class with a lot of experience and success behind it.

Due to this fact we would recommend that you limit yourself to the Puppy class alone at this stage. When your youngster has a few more months behind it then consider entering the Novice class as well. Remember, be critical and see how your puppy is compared with some of the other younger dogs around at the time. If you enter a slightly harder class with a baby of this age, it can look comparatively raw at this tender stage when seen with the other competitors.

Another point to consider is that, when classes are mixed, sometimes a male puppy can look that little more finished than a female of around the same age. We would think twice about

*Fig 66 Champion Jonsville Daytime Lover. Top winning toy dog, 1988. Owned and bred by Mr and Mrs J. Thomas and Mr G. Thomas.*

entering a bitch puppy at this age into a Novice class. Again, very often it comes down to different lines and different progeny from various stud dogs. Some females or even males are barely ready at six to seven months, while others can present almost a finished picture. These are all facts that need to be considered.

If you are lucky enough to win your Puppy class at an Open Show, apart from winning a lovely red prize card and, possibly, a rosette, you may also be fortunate enough to win some prize money if it is on offer, although this is usually only a couple of pounds. Together with the aforementioned spoils you will also have won a Junior Warrant Point.

A Junior Warrant is an award granted by the Kennel Club for a dog or bitch gaining the required twenty-five points. In the past, these points have been accredited from the outset of a puppy's career, that is six months, and they had until eighteen months of age to accrue them. This has recently been changed to an age limit of twelve months, thus making it harder to achieve and thus more desirable.

Wins at Exemption or Limited Shows do not get credited with any points, nor do wins in Variety classes. A win at an Open Show is, of course, one point, while one attained at a Championship Show is worth a princely three points. These points are awarded at these levels whether the show is confined purely to the breed or open to all breeds.

When you have added your points up (of which, of course, you have kept a record) and found that you have amassed the required twenty-five, your next step is to apply to the Kennel Club on the relevant form (obtainable from them). In return, you will receive a certificate acknowledging your achievement.

## *Breed Club Open Shows*

The breed clubs in Great Britain hold their shows throughout the country at a point central to each individual club. A list of these various clubs appears in Appendix 1, together with details of the present secretaries. Do not be too shy to get in contact with any of these clubs for you will find that the secretary concerned will be only too pleased to help welcome you into the fold. You will be issued during the year with schedules and notice of any forthcoming events, and any matter regarding the process of membership.

If you enter a Breed Club Open Show, you will notice from the classification that there is much more variety of classes than in an All Breed Show of the same standing. For instance, apart from the classes being split for both dogs and bitches, you have the choice of a Minor or Puppy class. Obviously your seven-month-old puppy would be entered in the lesser class, the Minor. Whether or not you decide to enter in the next class also, which is for puppies of less than twelve months of age, is a matter for you to decide. If you feel that your little one could hold its own against the slightly more mature pups, by all means enter this class too. Always bear in mind the fact that there may be puppies of nearly twelve months of age in here, so take a good long look at your youngster and make the appropriate decision. Five months can make quite a lot of difference, especially in these earlier classes.

If your puppy is eleven months old, obviously it is too old for the Minor Puppy class but, of course, is still eligible for the Puppy class. At this stage you could also enter it in the Maiden or Novice class, or perhaps both. Always remember before you enter to check the class definitions carefully – even after all these years we have to double-check on some of them.

Your entries have been written out, signed and sealed with the relevant entry fee enclosed with them. On the bottom of the schedule it will give the closing date for entries. The postmark on your entry envelope will be checked; if it shows a date later than the closing date, the envelope will be refused by the club or society so try to send your entries off well in advance. As a safeguard, it is a good idea to apply at the Post Office for 'proof of posting'. The clerk at the Post Office will give you a pink slip on which you have to list the name and address of the recipient of the letter. You then hand this back across the counter, complete with the stamped letter and the assistant will then hand you back the slip, date stamped. This service is offered, unbelievably, free of charge. This will be accepted as proof by the society and, in turn, the Kennel Club should your entries go astray.

## *Championship Shows*

The day has dawned that you have decided to enter your first Championship Show. You are probably wondering how you find out about the location and time these shows will be held. Once again we would advise that you order either one or both of the weekly dog papers, *Our Dogs* or *Dog World*. In each of these there is a weekly listing of forthcoming shows. Also, the parent club for our breed, The Pekingese Club, annually publish their *Yearbook* in which they list the Championship Shows held throughout the United Kingdom, together with the names of the judges. The Pekin Palace, another of the breed's oldest clubs, also issue their handbook once a year. Of course, once you have become a member of any club or society you will receive all the relevant information. This also applies if you have entered a show, for automatically most societies will forward a schedule for their next event. The same principles apply regarding entering your puppy at a Championship Show as would with an Open Show. What you have to take into account is, of course, the possible strength of competition at a show of this stature. For the dogs that are shown at these higher-graded shows will invariably be of a higher quality overall.

If you have a minor puppy, you will have to decide on whether to take a chance on entering in a higher class or not. We would advise at this stage to restrict it to The Minor class alone. If you are fortunate enough to win this one class, you can, of course, go into the line-up for unbeaten dogs or bitches, whichever is relevant. If you try at this point to upgrade yourself you may be beaten by a more experienced puppy that may have been winning consistently all over the country.

If you are showing a male and you win your class, make quite sure that you keep an eye on the judging and the progress being made. Do not disappear to wander around the show stands for too long, for after the Open dog class the unbeaten dogs will be called into the ring for the challenge. Always make sure that you have your puppy ready, that it has had time to relieve itself and has had that final brush to make it look its best. The steward will call all those who are unbeaten into the ring, and although with a minor puppy in a strong breed such as this it is unlikely that you may receive a CC, it has been known. You are, however, by being in this line-up, in the limelight, and, by showing and producing good dogs and attaining this position, this is how you build up a reputation for showing good dogs. Providing that the CC or RCC is not awarded to another unbeaten puppy dog, you are eligible to challenge with all the other pups for Best Puppy after the Bitch classes. If you have entered more than one class, and perhaps do not win your primary class but win your next one, although you do not qualify as being an unbeaten dog, you still gain three Junior Warrant Points.

## *Cruft's Dog Show*

Once you have trained your youngster and are entering shows, you will inevitably wonder how to enter Cruft's. It has to be said that Cruft's is not just like any other show. As with the other Major Championship Shows, the method of judging is exactly the same, and basically the classification is similar also. The main difference, however, is that you are not able simply to enter your dog for this show without at first qualifying.

At the present time, the qualification for Cruft's is that you need to win either a Junior or Post Graduate class. A win in the Limit or Open classes qualifies a dog, as well as does being placed in the first three in these last two classes mentioned. Winning a Reserve CC or a CC also entitles you to enter.

Up until a short while ago a win in either of the two Puppy classes also guaranteed entry, but this has been recently changed due to lack of space at Earl's Court. A puppy is at the present time ineligible for entry unless it wins a Challenge Certificate or is over twelve months of age on 31st December. As already said, this is not a common occurrence in this country although in 1988 two minor puppies were awarded one CC each, both at the age of six months. One was Brentoy Miramac owned and bred by Ruby and Alan Charlton; the CC was awarded by an American judge, Mrs Martha Olmos-Olivier. This successful youngster now resides with his new owner Mr Robert Marti in Switzerland. The other one was from the Yakee kennel, Yakee Slightly Saucy; she won her ticket under a highly respected breed specialist who has been involved with the breed in the country for many years, Mrs Brabant-Holbrook of the Brabanta Pekingese.

The Yakees in fact have had a Babychamp, a puppy who has won three Challenge Certificates while under the age of twelve months. In order to be declared a Champion one of these had to be won after she was twelve months old. Her title and crown came shortly after her first birthday in the shape of her fourth Challenge Certificate. This was Champion Yakee Gentlemen Prefer, litter sister to the partnership's Champion Yakee For Your Eyes Only, Cruft's Reserve Best in Show winner, in 1989. Unfortunately they lost this young bitch quite suddenly and tragically.

Another 'wonder baby' was Terry Nethercott's Champion Josto Madam Gaye of Sunsalve, who accomplished a similar feat in summer 1981, once again having to wait for the fourth qualifying CC.

Cruft's has always traditionally been held in London. However in 1991, the year of the Kennel Club's centenary, the new venue will be the National Exhibition Centre near Birmingham. Cruft's has always had a dazzling display of trade stands all vying for attention. They cater for virtually every need, and anything pertaining to the canine world can be purchased here. The atmosphere is heightened by the spectacle of some of the *crème de la crème* of winning dogs, and by the various fanciers who come from all four corners of the globe to see dogs that they had previously only read about in dog magazines.

Together with the overseas visitors flock the general public who come to take in the sights and see their favourite breeds all under one roof. As with many of the other All Breed Championship Shows, the number of dogs entered requires that this show be held over four days. So if you are hoping to visit Cruft's, check to see which day you will be able to see your favourite breed.

Apart from dogs being shown, throughout the day in the main arena Obedience Finals are held and these are a great attraction. You can usually purchase tickets for this arena in the foyer, although on the final day the seats for the ultimate spectacle – Best in Show – are generally sold out very quickly.

A Pekingese has not as yet managed to capture that ultimate award, although two have come very, very close to it in the past few years. In 1985, Joyce Mitchell's Champion Micklee Rocs Ru-Ago (*see* Fig 67) was made Reserve Best in Show under an Australian judge Harry Spira, after having won the breed under specialist Dorothy Dearn and being sent through from the group by one of our top all-rounders, Nora Down.

In 1989, another Pekingese made a brave attempt and was also declared Reserve Best in Show; this was Champion Yakee For Your Eyes Only (*see* Fig 68), bred and owned by Bert Easdon and Philip Martin. He won his breed under a specialist judge, George Quinn, won his way through the group under one of the UK's eminent all-round judges, Ellis Hume, and was finally placed on the rostrum by a member of one of the country's dog dynasties, Lionel Hamilton-Renwick.

## The Paperwork

Let us now look at an entry form for a Breed Club Show. You have decided which dog or dogs you are going to enter at this particular

*Fig 67  Champion Micklee Rocs Ru-Ago. Reserve Best in Show, Cruft's, 1985.*

*Fig 68  Champion Yakee For Your Eyes Only. Reserve Best in Show, Cruft's, 1989.*

show. Check which class or classes you are going to enter in. When you have completed the entry form, make a note on the schedule which dogs you have entered or, if you just have the one, which classes. As organisers of one particular breed club's shows, you would be amazed how many people we have ringing us up the night before for the simple reason that they cannot remember which dog they entered.

On the first line you will need to enter your dog's name and in the next box you are required to state whether this exhibit is a dog or a bitch. After this comes the exhibit's date of birth, and then the name of the breeder. If you have bred the dog yourself you would of course write in your own name, or, alternatively, you may just write Owner's. Obviously, if you did not breed this dog, you must then insert the name of the breeder. The following two spaces are for you to insert the sire and dam's names.

Finally you need to enter the number of the class or classes in the box provided; for this you will need to check the class numbers in the schedule. This all seems very basic and simple, but always remember to check your entries before you send them off.

Either on the entry form itself or somewhere within the schedule the entry fees will be printed. There is usually a different rate for members and non-members and this varies from club to club. This fee is for the first class for that particular dog. If you wish to enter extra classes with that same dog the fees for this are reduced. The fee for the first class may be £2, whereas for the following class it may be as low as 75 pence.

At the bottom of the entry form there is a space to fill in your name, address and telephone number. On some of the larger All Breed Championship Show schedules extra spaces are provided for you to include these details again. This is so that your passes and a schedule for next year's show can be sent to you. You are also required by the Kennel Club to sign this form at the bottom, which in essence means that you agree to abide by the rules laid down by this body. This refers also to the fact that your dogs have not suffered from any contagious diseases or been in contact with any that have, for a period prior to the show.

In the case of All Breed Shows especially, there is also a need to check to see if you have to apply for a parking ticket. If so, you will have to include the relevant fee with your entries. Some do provide free parking, but always double-check this point. If you do not apply for the right parking ticket, it could mean that at a large All

Breed Show, you may not be allowed into the exhibitor's car park and find yourself miles away with a long walk ahead of you.

Regarding membership, each society or association has its own methods. Some will require you to complete a membership form, which will be put before the appropriate committee for their approval. Others will simply ask you to pay a membership fee and automatically pass you. In other cases, you may require a proposer and a seconder. Do not be afraid to ask the secretary of whichever club or society you wish to join; he or she will be only too pleased to furnish you with the details that you require.

For the All Breed Championship Shows, your passes will be sent to you nearer the date of the show. This is quite a regular occurrence with some of the larger Open Shows of similar classification. A catalogue voucher may also be included if you have paid for one.

These are the shows that continue to send passes through the post. With the rising costs of postage and printing, the breed clubs and most of the smaller Open Shows do not carry out this practice nowadays. You can, however, request that your passes are sent to you by enclosing a stamped addressed envelope with your entry.

## Prefixes/Affixes

When you buy a puppy from a breeder, it will be registered by the breeder at the Kennel Club. Obviously, to have a puppy registered as a pure-bred pedigree dog, both parents have to be fully registered also. The breeder of the puppy is entitled to put his or her kennel name on; in our case it would be Toydom. Therefore, any puppies bred by us would carry the kennel name of Toydom first, followed by the name of the puppy. Other kennels would apply the same method, for instance the Belknaps, the Sunsalves, Micklees and Shiaritas would all register their home-bred puppies with their kennel name as the first part of each puppy's name.

If, once you have a registered prefix, you buy a registered puppy or dog, you can apply to place your kennel name on it also. It would, however, have to be added on to the end. For example, in the case of Pendenrah So Sensuous who was bred by Liz and Tim Evans, a couple noted for breeding some lovely dogs, we had to place Toydom after the name. We are glad to say that he gained his title and now goes by the name of Champion Pendenrah's So Sensuous For Toydom.

If you are going to become interested in showing and breeding, you will more than likely wish to have your own kennel name. Think carefully and choose some names that really appeal to you. Not only must you like the name yourself, it needs to have a certain amount of impact and be easily remembered. You have to submit several to the Kennel Club who will eventually inform you which one they have granted. If you have chosen some that you are not especially keen on, remember this name will carry you through the whole of your breeding and show life, so make it a good one! The names will then have to be submitted to the Kennel Club on the relevant form. Before finally granting you the desired name, the Kennel Club will publish it in their monthly Kennel Gazette in order that any objections can be lodged if so desired. For instance, the name you have chosen may be similar to another one and so on.

There are various ways of choosing a kennel name. Some people take a variation of their family name, for example the Trimbar Pekingese are an anagram of their breeder's name, Bartrim. Jonsville is the combination of two family names, John and Granville. Josto is made up of the first few letters of Joan Stokoe's own name. Again, Tilly Brickwood's famous Teijon came about by her taking the first part of her full name together with her husband's. Dorodea is another well-known name throughout the Pekingese world. It is another name with a lovely ring to it, taken from Dorothy Dearn's own name, once more. Another prevalent name, Ralsham is again an anagram of the family surname Lashmar, a kennel started by Barbara Lashmar and now campaigned by daughter Carole.

Some kennels go for a more regional outlook. Antonia Horn's Belknap prefix was chosen as it was the original name of her present home. Pendenrah is yet another anagram, this time of the town of Harpenden where Liz and Tim Evans used to live. Singlewell is a lovely prefix devised by Pam Edmonds and her mother Mildrid Woolf when they resided at Single Lodge. In the garden, apparently, was the prettiest little well, hence the name Singlewell. Kettlemere is a prefix that has been in existence since 1957, chosen by the late Lilian Shipley. This was the name of a small lake near where she lived in Shropshire. Since her death the kennel has been carried on by her daughter Joyce. In 1981, the Frampton kennel of Pekingese was registered at the Kennel Club, a name decided upon by the husband and wife partnership of Don and Daphne Lee, Frampton being the name of a village where they had lived.

# 9

# At the Show

The night before the show you will have prepared your show equipment and laid it all out ready for a possible early departure the next morning. In your grooming bag you will need your brushes, comb, spray, leads, nail clippers (in case of an emergency), and towels. You will also need water for your dog and a bowl and, if it is a long journey, a little light lunch (for instance, a little cooked chicken). And, of course, in the summer do not forget your cool-box, frozen towels and ice-packs. Also, do not forget your show clip for your ring number. There is nothing worse than getting into the ring and suddenly finding you left it at home on the dressing-table. There you are with a dog and a ring number and nowhere to put it!

You will see that we have advised you to take water for your dog. It is always a good idea to take a small flask of water or bottle with you, for water from a different area may upset your dog's tummy. Also, you will have water on hand should you need to give your dog a drink on the way to the show.

Apart from your table and trolley we would advise you to remember to put a small chair into the car as your legs can become exceptionally tired by late morning at a show and there are not always enough ringside seats to go around, especially at some of the major shows.

On the night before the show, always check what time judging is due to commence. This will be stated in the schedule or, if for some reason the start time has been altered at an All Breed Championship Show, notification will appear in the canine press, so always try to watch out for any changes.

## Travelling to the Show

Always allow yourself ample time to travel to the show, checking whether or not Pekingese are one of the first breeds to be judged or not. Allow plenty of time also to get your dog settled, walked and prepared for the ring.

You should have accustomed your dog to travelling in a show pen. The night before the show make sure that you have everything ready that you need to put into the car the next morning, your show basket for the dog, a small grooming table and a trolley of some description if you have more than one dog to take into the show ground, for this can be a heaven-sent piece of equipment. You will need all your grooming aids as well.

If this show is being held in the summertime, the chances are that the weather could be hot. We have made mention already of the hazards of transporting dogs in cars in these conditions (*see* Chapter 6, page 109); these can be heightened when you are caught up on a motorway in stationary traffic. You can be prepared for this eventuality; before summer gets into full swing and everything is sold out, make a trip to your local hardware or camping store and purchase several ice-packs. These come in varying shapes and sizes and are quite adequate, although the ones that can be bought in the United States are wonderful and seem to last for hours on end. Also purchase, if possible, a small cool-box, or alternatively a good-quality cool-bag; the former is more effective, though. When you get your ice-packs home wrap them up in newspaper and place them in the freezer (the newspaper allows the packs to stay cooler longer). Make sure they are in there for at least twenty-four hours before you are likely to need them. If the morning is warm when you leave home, do not forget to start your dog's journey by putting an ice-pack in the pen with him. It is best not to let your dog get overheated in the first place – prevention is better than the cure.

Another cooling aid to have in your freezer prepared are iced towels. Soak some clean towels and wring them out. Fold them individually and, placing them separately in plastic bags, stack them in your freezer. These can be carried in your cool-box to a show together with the packs, ensuring that you have enough items that are ice-cold to travel your dog home on when there is a heatwave.

A useful little gadget to have at hand is a small battery-operated fan; these are very effective and can be placed in front of the dog's pen, creating a very welcome airflow for your Pekingese. At some of the summer shows, especially the Championship All Breed Shows, the dogs are benched under canvas in a big marquee. These tend to get very hot and humid.

## The Competition

The competition at Championship Shows is very intense indeed. People travel from far and wide to attend these shows. As time passes and your interest in the breed deepens, you will more than likely join this band of exhibitors. The wonderful aspect of showing dogs is that you get a complete cross-section of people from all walks of life and from all four corners of the British Isles who share a common love for one breed.

Distance is no object; one of the country's successful kennels, the Yakee Pekingese of Bert Easdon and Philip Martin, travel down regularly from Glasgow to show throughout the land. Mrs Watters' Yankui Pekingese are quite often over from Ireland competing at shows on this side of the Irish Sea. When you hear the expression, from John o'Groat's to Land's End, spare a thought for two very experienced and respected breeders from Camborne (a stone's throw from Land's End itself), Doug and Joyce Richards of the Royceland Pekingese. This couple have a three-hour drive from their home, up through the West Country before they reach the motorway at Exeter.

When the showbug bites, competitors think nothing of climbing out of their warm beds in the 'wee small hours' and driving for hundreds of miles in order to reach a show in time for commencement of judging; this can vary from any time from 9 a.m. onwards. We are afraid to say that if the desire to show really takes a hold you are likely to become regarded by close friends and family as completely mad!

However, when we talk about vast distances here they are nowhere near the distances travelled by Pekingese fanciers in the United States or on the Continent. For instance, in the state of California alone, any residents of San Francisco who decide to enter their dogs at a show in Los Angeles, will have at least an eight-hour journey to complete. This is probably why professional handlers are extremely popular in that country, the pure convenience of having someone take your dogs around the different show circuits.

Another difference with the show scene there as compared with here is that many of the clubs in America form 'clusters'. In other words, several shows get together and hold their shows in one location over a long weekend. This enables handlers and owner/exhibitors alike to travel the circuit, taking in several of these clusters along the way. For this reason, motor homes are extremely popular there and are a very comfortable way of travelling to these sites. At the major shows there, the sites allotted to these travelling homes almost resemble one of our vast caravan parks.

Unlike the United Kingdom, exhibitors in the USA are only able to enter one dog in one class. They are unable to enter the same dog once more by going into a later class as we can here. The system for making a dog into a champion differs slightly there as well. In the UK you need three Challenge Certificates awarded by the three different judges but in America a points award system is operated. These points are awarded for the Winners Dog and the Winners Bitch. The most points that can be attained are five, and this depends entirely on the numerical strength of the entry on the day. Obviously the stronger the entry, the higher the points. Fifteen points are needed to make a dog into a Champion. Two of these awards, however, must be those classed as 'Majors'. In other words, they were awarded in strong competition and were not single points.

## Arrival

You have reached the show site (let us assume that it is at one of the major All Breed Championship Shows) and you have arrived at the show entrance. You off-load your dog or dogs and their cages, and all the various paraphernalia that goes with dog showing, and at this entrance you will be required to show your pass to the official. It is hoped at this stage that you have them handy, and not in the bottom of a bag somewhere. When the pass is returned, keep it safe because, for security reasons, you will need it again on the outward journey to be able to remove your dog from the show site.

Your next priority is to check where your breed is benched. Now is the time to purchase or claim your catalogue if you so desire and, if the information appears nowhere else, there will be a guide in this. The number of your bench appears on the pass itself or in the catalogue, so find your allotted position and then see about letting your dog relieve himself before settling him down. If it is pouring with rain, find a covered place to let your dog quickly answer the call of nature. Try not to get your dog wet, undoing in the process all your hard work of the day before.

Benching is supplied by the show committee for the dogs to be placed on. They are theoretically only allowed to be absent from this for fifteen minutes at a time or when they are in the ring. With the latest Kennel Club directive, dogs are not allowed to be around the ringside in their pens at any time. There is nothing to stop you having your dog at the ringside ready for the class, providing of course you do not have all your goods and chattels to go with it. All the All Breed Championship Shows are benched, and some of the Breed Club Championship Shows also, although many of these are now seeking from the Kennel Club exemption from this, because of the obvious cost it entails. Very few of the All Breed Open Shows have benching nowadays.

It is always a good idea at this point to try to ascertain exactly where your ring will be; once this is done you can start to prepare your dog for the ring. However tempting it is to go and chat to one of your new-found friends, there is plenty of time for socialising later, now is the time to get down to business, so first things first. Your dog is your main concern, so if you prepare him now ready for the ring, when the class draws near, some last-minute adjustments will give him that finishing touch. Before you start to get the dog ready for the ring, remember to check that his lead is on; there is nothing more annoying than getting the dog to look absolutely stunning, only to find that you have forgotten to put the lead on.

A lot of Championship Shows nowadays place your ring numbers on the bench ready to save time, so just check and see if there are two sets waiting. If this is not the case the number will be handed out by the steward in the ring, so have a final check of your number in order that you can give this out readily.

When it is getting near the time for your class to go in, always keep a check on how the judging is progressing, allowing yourself time to be at the ringside when the class is called. Do not try to stage a dramatic entrance by rushing into the ring at the last minute. If this happens your dog will become unsettled and, even more likely, so will you.

## In the Ring

When you enter the ring the steward will inform you where to stand. It is an idea to ensure that you are not first in line if your puppy or dog has not been to a show previously. Try to place yourself nearer to the middle and far end, in order that your

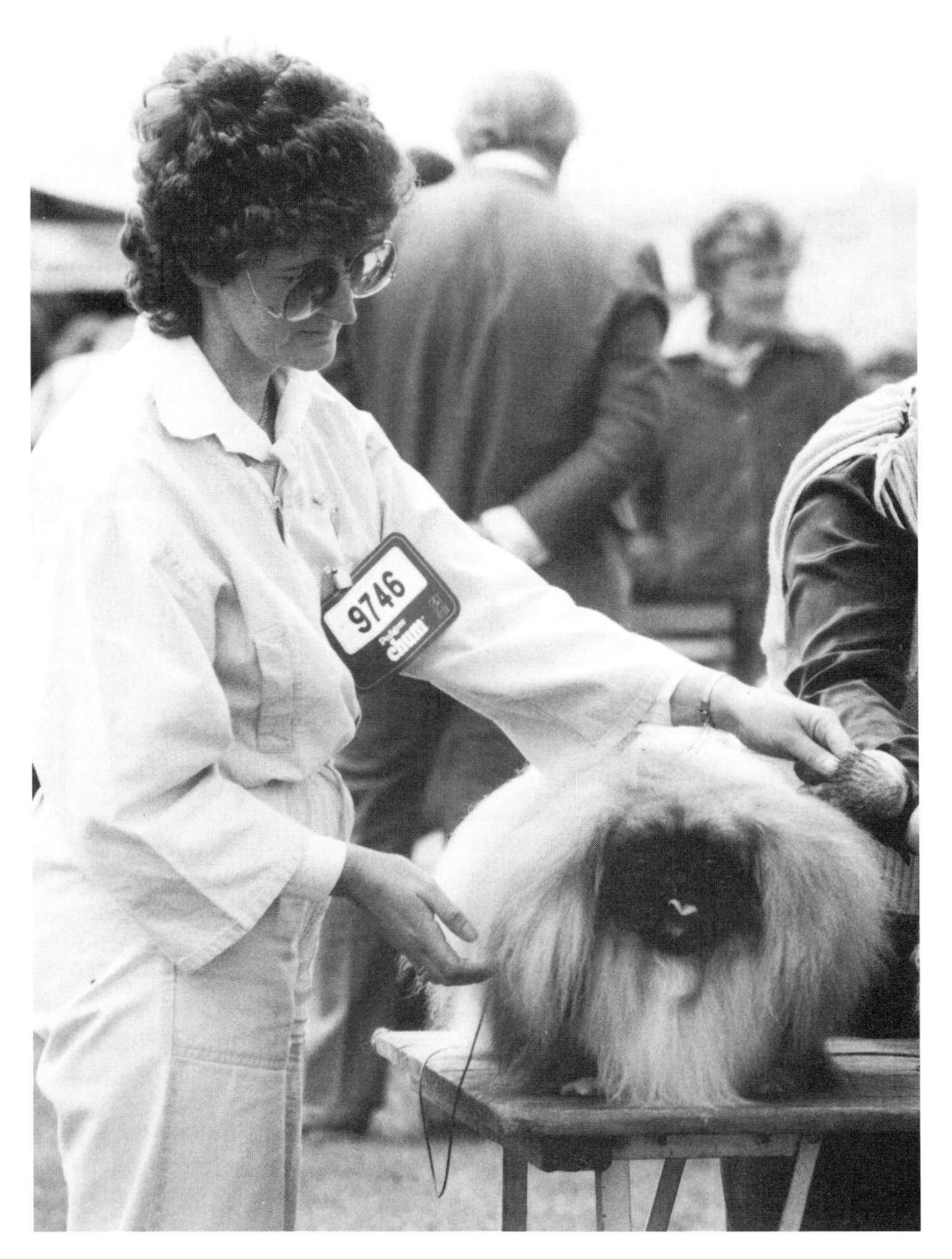


*Fig 69 Adele Summers with Champion Pendenrah's So Sensuous for Toydom. Bred by Mr and Mrs T. Evans, owned by Miss A. Summers and Miss V. Williams.*

youngster has time to become acquainted with the situation. Let the puppy see that there are dogs there that actually look like it and let it take an interest in them without becoming a nuisance. Also, if this particular judge intends to circle the dogs before assessing them each in turn, you most certainly do not want to have to be the one to lead off.

The judge will walk along the line of new dogs in this class appraising them from a distance at this stage, and this is the time your puppy needs to be told to stand in the correct show position. With a gentle flick of the brush, make quite sure that the topskull is flat, the ears are lifted and the coat and tail are looking just right. Once you are satisfied with this result do not keep on brushing the dog; the finished picture makes much more of an impression than an over-enthusiastic groomer constantly rearranging the coat.

When the judge has finished with this part of the assessment let your dog relax a little, but always keep an eye on your dog and the judge. If the puppy wants to sit or lie down at this stage, then fine. Try not to let it walk around with its head and tail down, presenting an appalling picture if the judge should happen to glance over. You may not think it, but these quick impressions can make a difference. Always be attentive to your dog and do not attempt to try to keep up with the latest gossip that may be going on outside the ring.

Before it comes to your turn, check whether the judge is handling prior to walking the dogs or vice versa. Check, too, whether the judge requires a triangle or another movement to be performed.

When the dog in front of you is getting ready to be seen, take a final look at your dog's eyes and wrinkle, making sure everything is in order. If the judge is watching the exhibits move first, then, while the preceding dog is being handled, place your dog in the middle of the ring and once again flatten the topskull, lift the ears, make sure the tail is in place and everything is as you would wish; then wait for the judge to ask you to move. Especially on grass, always watch the previous exhibits, see if they have had trouble with one piece of ground (a large dip or whatever) and try to avoid that area when you set out on the move.

Do not be frightened to check your dog if he is walking too fast or erratically; if he is a little reticent, speak to him calling out his pet name. It is definitely 'not done' to use a dog's full show name while in the middle of the ring.

Another small point to remember is not to chat merrily away to the judge like a long-lost friend. Apart from looking rather peculiar to onlookers at ringside, it is against Kennel Club rules. However, if the judge asks you a question, you are within your rights to answer, albeit as briefly as possible.

In the United States, any conversation whatsoever is frowned upon and judges, unlike here, are not permitted even to ask the age of a puppy or dog. For this they have to consult their steward who will then look up the relevant information in the catalogue.

In the United Kingdom, the dogs are judged finally as a class on the table, as a general rule. When the judge has finished with you, you then join your fellow exhibitors on the table. If it is a blazing hot summer's day and you are being judged outside, particularly if there are several more dogs to be seen, let your dog take advantage of any shade that the table may provide underneath. When there are only a couple of dogs to be seen, finally check the eyes and wrinkle, once again making sure that each part of the coat is brushed into position, and then wait for the judge to come along the table to look at your dog.

After handling each one again, the judge may choose a few dogs to go down on the floor, or, if it is not a very big class, each exhibit may be pulled down onto the ground. Alternatively, the dogs may be placed up on the table into the first five places.

If you are selected in the first group of dogs and the judge has chosen a few to go over again, you may be requested to give another demonstration of your dog's movement, so obviously have your dog looking the part and be prepared for this eventuality. Once this is completed, it generally follows that the dogs are then placed as the judge desires.

## Departure

You will notice in the schedule or perhaps in the catalogue, the time at which early removals are allowed out of the show ground. Always check on this time before you try to get out of the gate, for if you are in contravention of this serious trouble could ensue. Some shows allow you to leave as soon as you have finished your classes while others stipulate a time. At Cruft's, for instance, although this is quite an exception, you are unable to remove your dogs, at the present time, before six o'clock at night. When you have been there from early in the morning you can imagine how long a day it is. In the old days the earliest time of removal was eight o'clock!

If the weather has been warm and the temperature is starting to rise, always make sure that the ice-pack in the dog's pen is remaining cold. If the heat is affecting it a little, be prepared to give the dog another one or a frozen towel. Another handy tip is to get a spare towel and soak it in water, wring it out and place it over the top of the dog's pen; this helps to keep the air around the dog moist, making it more comfortable for him. This is the time that the extra gadget you popped into your show bag – the battery operated fan – will come into its own.

When leaving the show ground on a day like this, try to keep the dog in a shady position near the car while you open all the windows. Once the slightly cooler air is blowing through it, start to load up, placing the dog in last. Then leave as quickly as possible so that your dog will get the benefit of the fresh air blowing in through the still-opened car windows.

# 10
# Judging

There are various reasons that make people wish to judge the breed. One of these is that they wish to take that extra step onwards from showing, and thereby involve themselves more deeply in the breed. Many people feel that they should put back into the breed what they have received in pleasure. You do, of course, get the odd 'glory-seeker' but thankfully they are few and far between. To place yourself in the ring and apply your knowledge to the dogs presented can be a very enjoyable and fulfilling, if not sometimes tiring, experience.

The most important thing to bear in mind if you feel you would like to judge is that you should not try to run before you learn to walk. Think about this seriously before you decide whether or not you wish to undertake a few classes of Pekingese.

## Stewarding

An invaluable way of learning ring procedure, apart from attending dog shows themselves, is to offer your services as a steward to perhaps a local society. If you decide that you would like to steward, it is always best to have a general idea of the basic guides set down by the Kennel Club. We have many highly recognised stewards in the breed, who would, if asked, be only too pleased to pass on a little of their knowledge.

Eddie Hurdle of the Sunsalve Pekingese is a resident steward for several of the London-based Pekingese breed clubs, while Francis Pilgrim, for many many years a devotee of the breed, apart from his skills as a photographer has offered years of stewarding experience to the breed. The former is one of the resident stewards for the breed at Cruft's Dog Show, and the latter also performed this task for many years. Paul Stannard of the Shiarita Pekingese has given his services as well and can often be seen as one of the Group

*Fig 70 Australian Champion Toydom Duper Star. Bred by Miss A. Summers and Miss V. Williams, owned by the late Mr L. Gray and Mr C. Rigg.*

stewards in the Big Ring at Cruft's. A great deal can be learnt from stewarding but it also brings a rewarding day in the form of seeing nice dogs of various breeds, and different people. A good steward is worth his or her weight in gold to a judge so, if you are going to undertake this task, ensure you do it whole-heartedly and efficiently.

When you arrive at a show to carry out a stewarding appointment, make yourself known to the secretary or the chief steward upon your arrival. This official will then inform you which ring or judge you have been assigned to and you will be furnished with the relevant documentation, rosettes, prize cards and a catalogue.

You will also be handed a steward's board which will be marked out with the classes down the left-hand side and the five places across the top, from first place to fifth (Very Highly Commended or VHC). When each class is completed and the judge is satisfied with the placings, you will then write the exhibits' numbers in order across the board. As you become more involved with this new

*Fig 71 South African Champion More Than a Feeling at Toydom. Bred by Miss A. Keylock, owned by Mrs M. Jackson.*

venture, you will possibly find it easier to possess your own board, already marked out.

Your duties as a ring steward will include calling the various classes into the ring. You will, if necessary, hand out the ring numbers to the exhibitors, and, if necessary, make a final call for any latecomers. It is not the steward's duty to have to go and find any stray exhibitors. Having said that, it is always helpful to exhibitors at an All Breed Championship Show if the steward can find time to go to the benching area and inform them that the commencement of the first class is imminent. If the judge has a lunch-break half-way through the classes, once again a brief visit to announce the return of the judge is usually very much appreciated. This is not a duty, however, more a service to the exhibitors. It is always the responsibility of the exhibitors to be at the side of the ring in time for their classes.

When all the exhibitors are in the ring, after first enquiring of the judge where he or she would like the new dogs to stand, it is time to mark down those exhibits present, and it is also equally important to note the numbers of the absentees. The class is then ready to present to the judge.

When the final placings have been made by the judge and, as the steward, you have made a note on your board of the exhibit numbers from one to five, you would then be required to call out the winners of the class. If you are stewarding single-handed, the prize cards and any special prizes that may be on offer would also need to be handed out at this time. If, however, there are two of you, a system can no doubt be devised between you as to who performs which duty.

While the judge is taking down some notes on the winners, you can, at this stage, going through the same basic procedure as before, start to call the next class into the ring. The only difference you may have in this second class is that there may be a dog or dogs in this class who had been entered in the previous one. These dogs can automatically be placed on the table. Then, while ensuring that all is correct with this latest class and informing the judge that it is ready to be examined, you will need to go and place these dogs in the order that they were placed in the preceding class. When the judge has finished judging the newer exhibits, the steward would then inform the judge, when ready, of the placement of the previously judged dogs.

As the classes progress, this is inclined to become more complicated, so this is where the steward's board comes into its own. You can compare, for instance, exhibit A who was placed second in the first class, but may have won the next one. In this class, you may have exhibit A plus a dog who was third to it in the first class and another dog who was second to it in the next class. After consulting your board and noting the numbers, you would then place exhibit A at the top of the table, followed by the dog who was second to it in the last class, followed by the dog who was third in the other class. When relating this information, do so carefully and precisely to the judge, for, especially with a novice judge, this can save a previous decision being reversed.

Let us return to the question of judging. We will of course presume that you are going to be asked and will not tout for classes in the breed. You will probably find that through attending many of your local shows, and perhaps many further afield, you will become noticed and recognised as a familiar figure at the ringside. It is quite likely that you will, through your consistent showing – even with only moderate success – one day stand a very good chance of being invited to judge a few classes at perhaps a Limited or Open Show.

If you really feel that you are capable and are quite happy about the invitation, hopefully you will accept. If, however, you have doubts about your capability at this stage (apart from your obvious slight nervousness at this new aspect of your hobby), and feel that you are not going to enjoy this engagement, then firmly but politely decline. Do not be afraid to make your feelings known, for the society will more than respect you for your honesty. If you feel that you would be happier to undertake this appointment at a later date, mention this also and perhaps another invitation will come in the future.

When you accept an invitation to judge, especially on this first occasion, do limit yourself to judging classes for Pekingese and do not be tempted to accept, for instance, some Any Variety Toys. Try not to see yourself in these infant days as a budding all-rounder; this is something to aspire to later on. In order to take on these Variety classes you would need to be *au fait* with the Standards of other breeds and you will have enough to contend with judging this breed alone.

The Breed Standard for Pekingese, as discussed in Chapter 2, will, of course, be the guide by which you will, or should, judge. This is one of the reasons we feel that it is best to be completely sure

*Fig 72 Sungarth Black Dragon. Bred by the late Mrs B. Prior, owned by Miss A. Hows.*

*Fig 73 Champion Cheryls Atom of Chintoi. Owned and bred by Mrs E. Pilgrim.*

of yourself before you attempt to take on a judging assignment. Everything comes with experience, and just by having been at the ringside and having shown your own dogs with moderate success will have helped your eye become accustomed to what is being sought by the Standard in a Pekingese.

## Interpretation of the Standard

Everyone will interpret the Standard slightly differently, for this is what judging is all about; otherwise, the same dogs would win on every occasion. Each judge has his or her own opinions, and that is what as an exhibitor you are paying for.

For instance, regarding the question of interpretation of the Standard, there is bound at this stage to be the odd voice raised saying that the Standard is the Standard and there can be no deviation. Of course, no serious fault should be forgiven if there is an exhibit of higher quality in the class. But every person has what we will describe as a pet hate and, human nature being what it is, you cannot condemn a judge if a dog is put down for possessing that particular fault. Where it is wrong to do this, however, is when the class is of poor-quality stock and an otherwise exceptionally good dog happens to possess the particular fault that that judge despises. Sometimes you have to forgive a little when you are judging, although not to the detriment of the breed.

Let us say that judge A has two dogs; one is shorter in body but higher on the leg, the other is longer in body but lower to ground. This judge places the first dog higher in the class than the other, forgiving the length of leg because he prefers them to be short in body. Judge B, however, could possibly place the same two dogs the other way around, forgiving the slight length of body because he prefers them to be slightly lower in the leg. We are presuming of course that in every other respect they are equal, so neither judge is wrong since it comes down to a matter of preference or forgiveness of a fault. No dog is perfect, and the fault or faults on each exhibit shown under you have to be assessed by the degree or seriousness of them.

This does not mean that you should fault judge; what we are trying to make clear is that sometimes you may have to put a dog up that does have a fault. You should, of course, realise that the fault is present and know how you came to this decision – this is what judging entails. Always try to take an overall picture of the dog; do not discriminate against a dog for the simple reason that it may have one thing wrong with it which, in your mind, outweighs the loveliness of this exhibit.

Soundness, of course, is imperative, for we do not want to get a breed that cannot walk correctly and soundly. What would you do, though, if you had two dogs in a class under you; one possessed a multitude of faults, for instance its back was roached and the body was too long, as were the legs, the pigment was bad and the mouth was wry, but its redeeming feature was that it was sound; the other exhibit was as near to the Standard in every way and a lovely dog all over, but on this particular occasion it was not going sound? Every person would have their own opinion on this, and it is really only a question that you can answer.

## Invitation to Judge

If you are invited verbally, any secretary of repute will follow this up with an official invitation in writing. Read the letter carefully, for

*Fig 74 International and Nordic Champion Sunsalve Come Play With Me At Toydom. Top winning dog, all breeds, Norway, 1982. Bred by Mr T. Nethercott, owned by Mrs B. Moen (nee Sorenson), Norway.*

each society can sometimes lay down restrictions. For example, you may be asked not to take on another engagement within fifty or one hundred miles of this particular venue for six months prior to the show. Always keep a note of these requirements should you suddenly find yourself in demand! You will then need to accept in writing this invitation as soon as possible if you are willing to take on the engagement.

In most instances, a week or so before you are due to judge, the secretary will write once more informing you of the time that you should be at the show and, in most cases, will give numerical details of your entry.

As with showing your dog, allow yourself plenty of time to arrive at the show to judge so that you can have some coffee perhaps and collect your thoughts. Do not leave it until the last minute, which will then mean that you will have to rush into the ring and will feel completely flustered before you start.

On arriving at the show ground, make yourself known to the secretary to confirm that you are in attendance. You will then be informed at what time your ring will be ready or free, and will be

*Fig 75 Champion Fearnvale Potters Viola. Owned and bred by Mr and Mrs G. Fearn.*

eventually taken there and introduced to your steward. You will also be supplied, at the appropriate time, with your judge's badge, a judging book and two prepaid envelopes addressed to both of the dog papers. These envelopes are for you to send your critique in when you have written it at a later date.

The judging book contains pages marked out for each of the classes that you are about to judge. In the left-hand column will appear the exhibit numbers. The new dogs in the class usually appear written in blue ink, while dogs that have been seen before will appear in red in the ensuing classes. There will be, at the minimum, two more columns: one is for the secretary, the other for the awards board. These will be torn out by the ring steward at the end of, or during, judging, with the judge's book itself retained by you. You are required to write the placings in the spaces provided after each class; if, however, you have a kindly ring steward, he or she will more than likely complete the other columns for you.

Needless to say, it is expected that a judge will not attempt to peruse a catalogue until judging is completed, when one will be presented to the judge by either the ring steward or the secretary.

When you receive your judging book, to save time, it is best to sign each page as many times as required before you commence judging. The slips that are torn out need to have your signature on them, to prove they are a true record.

In the United States, when you receive your judging book you alone are entirely responsible for all entries made in it; the American Kennel Club are most particular on this point. You are required to enter the time that you commence judging, together with the eventual completion time. The book also needs to be signed. Unlike the practice in Britain, your steward is not allowed to mark this book up for you; the judge alone is the only person permitted to complete all the required particulars.

While we are comparing the two countries' regulations, another point of contrast is that, in the United Kingdom, exhibitors are allowed to line up in the ring in any order, whereas, in America, they are placed by the ring steward in numerical order as they appear in the catalogue before they enter the class. Another difference that you would find if you attended one of their shows is that they do not follow our custom of having long tables in the ring for the dogs to be judged on, and are judged on the floor instead. There is, of course, a judge's handling table but, if the judge wants to compare the dogs at a reasonable height, two dogs only are allowed on a table at a time.

Towards Scandinavia and south into Europe, a completely different system is operated. In the majority of these countries, when the dogs are in the ring, they are initially assessed individually by the judge. He or she will handle each one on the table and then ask for the dog to be moved up and down, or whatever. After that particular dog has been seen and handled, the judge is required to give a critique on the dog there and then, in front of the handler. This is achieved with the aid of a ring secretary. If the judge comes from another country, a ring secretary is appointed who is conversant with the native tongue of that particular judge.

These comments are noted down, and the judge has then to make a decision as to what award to present that exhibit with. For instance, the dog might be worthy of being awarded an Excellent or perhaps, if for some reason the judge does not think the dog worthy of such an honour, a lesser prize is given, and so on. After all the dogs in one class have been evaluated, those that were awarded the highest honour are asked to return and are then judged on a similar system to our own and placed in class order.

We have already discussed the method of making a Champion up in this country, and, as we have already mentioned, a dog needs to accrue fifteen points for his crown in the USA. In Scandinavia the system for this honour is similar to the one in the UK. Three CAC's offered in both sexes must be won in order to make a dog or bitch into a Champion.

Exhibitors based in the United Kingdom can make up International Champions by travelling to Southern Ireland. The Irish operate a system whereby they award Green Stars. Their system is similar to that in existence in the United States, as awards are worked out on a points system.

In Scandinavia, up until a few months ago, exhibitors in Norway, Sweden and Finland used to be able to travel freely through each others' countries attending the shows there. Exhibitors in Norway would think nothing of driving through Sweden, picking up a ferry and travelling across to Finland. This crossing involves a journey of several hours and invariably involves further driving at the other side. However, an outbreak of rabies has caused this practice to change, and Finland's borders are now closed to dogs.

Let us return to you, though, the judge elect! Everyone is nervous when undertaking their first judging assignment. If you feel quite confident about your knowledge of the Standard, it will be just a case of butterflies which we have all suffered from on one occasion at least. Just take a deep breath, place the dogs to please yourself and remember that they cannot take you out and shoot you afterwards!

As in the showing of your dogs, with judging you have to keep it all in perspective. You will notice, most probably, that prior to judging you seem to have become a very popular individual indeed. Unfortunately, with human nature being what it is, your final decisions are bound to upset a couple of people on the day. Just remember to do your best and judge the dogs as you see them on the day, and to the very best of your ability. No one can ask for more.

## In the Show Ring

When you eventually get into your ring at an All Breed Show, you may find that, inadvertently, they have forgotten to supply you

*Fig 76 Champion Trimbar Oberon. Owned and bred by the late Mrs K. Bartrim and the Misses S. and E. Bartrim.*

*Fig 77 Toydom Trump Card (at 8 years old). Owned and bred by Miss A. Summers and Miss V. Williams.*

with the tables you need to place the dogs on. Do not be shy; ask your steward if he or she could arrange for these to be made available. Some judges are quite happy to manage without them – it really depends on how you feel on the day. One of the main advantages of the table is having the dogs at a reasonable height, where you can handle them and compare them all together with ease.

Try to appear confident without 'playing to the gallery'. A nervous or unsure judge is not a pleasure to watch and does not inspire anyone with confidence in the final decisions. You almost feel, in cases such as these, that the results were reached more by luck than judgement. On the other hand, try not to rush through the classes, for people will feel that they have not had a fair amount of time spent on their dogs for the money they have paid out in entries.

Another important point, we feel, is how you approach the handling aspect of your assignment. Before you start judging, make it clear to the first exhibitor whether you wish to handle the dog or

*Fig 78 Champion Hidden Talent at Toydom. Bred by Miss A. Keylock, owned by Mrs P. Hunter.*

*Fig 79 Champion Some Man at Lotusgrange. Bred by Mrs Bengough, owned by Mrs M. Robertshaw.*

let it move first. Usually, specialists are inclined to watch the movement before handling.

Assuming that you have opted for the last method, give the exhibitor time to set the dog ready on the table, allowing for that last little all-important flick of the brush. All this, of course, should be done within a reasonable amount of time. You will very often find that any puppy classes you judge are liable to take a little longer than, perhaps, some of the later classes for puppies. Be patient with them, especially babies on their very first outing, for this could make or break them.

Take a look at the head first of all, assess its virtues and make a mental note of anything that perhaps you do not like. In this breed, of course, we do not open the mouth but, if you detect some structural fault in the shape of the jaw, do not be afraid to investigate further.

Place your hand on the back of the dog's neck and feel if there is any length there. The Standard stipulates that it should be very short and thick. From the neck, place your hands either side of the dog's body to feel his shoulders. The description 'well in' aptly describes how they should feel at the point where the shoulder meets the body. Check the shoulders now by placing one hand on the dog's back over the front legs and gently rock the body, pressing down lightly as you do so. If there is any malformation of the joint this will now show up. There is no need to be heavy-handed and literally try to push the dog through the table – any dog would buckle under the strain of that!

Next, place your hands between the dog's front legs; a well-balanced dog will possess enough width of chest for you to do this fairly easily. If it is an effort to be able to do this, the dog may also appear to be a little pigeon-chested and possibly flat-sided as well. From here, run your hands along the dog's sides and hopefully you will feel that required pear-shaped body. At this point, it is also advisable to check for any abnormality of the spine. Run your hands along the dog's back to check for any roaching of the spine. With the correct body it is not very often that this appears.

Now is the time to check the back legs. Lift the dog's skirts up and view the legs from the rear, placing your hand on the dog's back at the base of the tail. As with the front legs, apply the same principle: they should stand firm and there should be no buckling or sign of the patellas slipping out (this is where the joint half-way up the back leg appears to slip out of line).

*Fig 80 Champion Mingulay Seumas of Mathena. Bred by Mrs H. Stephenson and owned by Mrs Y. Hoynck Van Papendrecht.*

*Fig 81 Champion Pekehuis Sir Guy. Bred by the late Mrs Partridge, owned by Miss W. Mee and Mr and Mrs C. Tennant.*

With a male, it is also necessary to check that the dog is entire and that the testicles are both fully descended into the scrotum or sac.

Finally, look down on the dog's back by lifting the tail to see the shape and length of body; the pear-shape of this should be clearly visible. Now lift the dog up to check for weight and feel its legs to see how much substance and bone it possesses, also checking for any malformation of the joints. Finally, either stand back or slightly bend down and view the dog from the side, taking in the overall shape and balance. Regarding the weight of the dog, the Standard asks that it should feel 'surprisingly heavy'; on the other hand, that does not mean that it should weigh 20 pounds (9 kilograms) either!

When judging the exhibits on the move, if a dog does not show itself off well – perhaps it is being a little wilful or, with a puppy, it could be a case of nerves – allow it a further opportunity to try to improve on its first performance.

When you have judged all the dogs in this class and watched them all move, looking for that desired Pekingese roll combined with the neat scissor action behind, you will now need to compare all the dogs on the table with one another. Check the fronts once more as you go along, handling them one at a time and reassessing their virtues and faults if need be. Compare the height of each one along the line; with the dogs standing on the table together, many points become quite noticeable. Do not be afraid to check for weight or anything that you were not particularly happy with the first time around.

If the class is numerically strong, this will be the point where you will need to sort the wheat from the chaff! Most shows call for five placings, although there are the odd few that require only four, so always check with your steward on this point. Pull down, if needed, the minimum of five dogs onto the floor, not necessarily placing them at this stage. If you are undecided, by all means choose more than the required amount. Then politely inform the remaining exhibitors that you have now finished with them. If you so desire, ask these chosen few to walk again before you make your final decision. This is usually more important in a major class than in a puppy class, but you are the judge and you must do what you wish.

It is sometimes beneficial to stand back after you have put these dogs through their paces once more, taking one final look. At this stage, you will have probably chosen your winner and perhaps your second, or possibly you are trying to decide between these two. Once you have made up your mind, be decisive and pull them out as you wish them to be placed. If there are two dogs that you like equally for your class winner, stand them side by side and evaluate one against the other. It is sometimes a kinder method than reversing your places at the last minute, although you are, of course, quite within your rights to do so.

When you are satisfied with these placings, inform your steward who will then carry out his duties while you proceed to fill in the numbers in the first column of your judge's book.

As we said earlier on, you will have been supplied with two envelopes in which you will eventually send your critique to *Our Dogs* and *Dog World*. For an Open Show, these two journals request that you comment only on the first placings, whereas at a Championship Show this is extended to the first two. So, depending on the type of show this is, you will find that the first or perhaps the second as well will remain in the ring for you to make notes on. For this reason, you will need to have at hand a notebook of some description, or a small tape recorder. Note down everything that pleased you about your winners and list also the various faults that may have been present (this is handy for later reference when the dog is not quite so clearly defined in your memory).

Always be courteous and considerate to the exhibitors and, at all costs, try not to let your ego become carried away at the thought of being in charge of the ring. Remember, you may be the judge today, but tomorrow you are back amongst the ranks of the faithful and will not have impressed anyone by having had an overbearing manner.

## Advancing your Judging Career

Providing, of course, that you have enjoyed your first engagement as a judge, inevitably you will be thinking of the days ahead when you will hopefully be asked to dispense the highest award, Challenge Certificates.

Over the years, in the world of dogs you will hear the expression 'having to serve an apprenticeship'. In the case of becoming a Championship Show judge, that is literally what it is. It really is a question of learning and judging over a minimum of five years. This does not automatically mean that at the end of this allotted time there is going to be a show secretary waiting to welcome you with open arms with an invitation to judge a Championship Show. There are several people in this breed who have had to wait quite a while for such an invitation, having served a long apprenticeship.

This does not mean that after having been in the breed for a few months, showing a dog and then fulfilling your first judging engagement in less than a year, you can then sit back and automatically expect to be passed to hand out CC's five years later. Presuming that you are fortunate enough to complete your first engagement quickly, although this is not often the case, it also helps to be seen showing good stock and winning reasonably well.

The qualification needed to be passed to judge at Championship Show level is that you have been judging regularly for at least five years, and that during this time you will have judged on a regular basis and included in your experience two Club Shows.

At the present time, the Kennel Club require each Pekingese breed club to issue a judge's list and send a copy to them. In the vast majority of cases, a copy is also sent to some of the major Championship Shows. Up until recently, several of the clubs chose all their judges from a list compiled by the Breed Council, the format of which is similar to that of the various lists now issued by their member clubs. Let us go through this list and explain how you would expect or hope to be placed upon it.

*Fig 82 A successful group at a Championship Show. From left to right: Erica Crouse with Fonalds Perchance to Dream RCC, Tilly Brickwood with Champion Teijon Shy Won CC, the judge Betty Knowles, Terry Nethercott with Champion Jay Trump of Sunsalve CC, and Eve Brampton-Brown with Sheraton Flashing RCC.*

There are three groups: A, B and C. The A List is for judges who have been passed to award CC's in the breed, while the B List is for those who have satisfied all the requirements and are waiting for such an appointment. The C List is usually for those looking for classes and, because they are on this list, they are automatically supported by the Council or that particular club in their quest for furthering their judging experience. To apply for inclusion on the judge's list, usually a club issues notice in the dog papers or will perhaps include it with material for a forthcoming AGM. You are perfectly within your rights to send in your name with a full list of your judging experience. The committee will then discuss and decide which list you are eligible for.

In order to be placed upon the A list of, say, the Breed Council's list, you have to have completed the desired requirements. It may seem a daunting task to receive invitations for two separate Club Shows. We have, as already discussed, eighteen breed clubs in existence so this is not as impossible as it may seem. When you compare this number with many other breeds who have less than a handful, it does not seem so bad.

When you have completed all the requirements to become a

Championship Show judge, let us assume that there is an invitation for you to award CC's at your first big show. The show society will send you a letter asking if you are available, and your immediate reply is needed. When you write back to accept, you will also notice on the invitation an enquiry as to whether this will be your first appointment at this level. Obviously you will have replied in the affirmative to this question, and in due course a form will be sent to you by the society for you to fill in and return for clearance by the Kennel Club.

Needless to say, you will have needed to keep a clear and concise record of your judging experience. Always keep a note of show dates, the name of the society, how many classes and the entry, etc. You will then easily be able to relate this information when required.

It seems to be the general course of events that when the Kennel Club receive this information, they in turn contact the Breed Council for their agreement or dissent. In some cases, breed club secretaries are also contacted for their comments. If, for some reason, you are turned down (although it must be said here that if all the qualifications you have submitted are correct, you would automatically be sanctioned by the Breed Council) you do have the right to appeal if you feel that this was an unreasonable decision.

When the show society eventually receives a positive reply – and this can take several weeks, so do not start panicking prematurely – the show secretary will let you know that you have been passed, and all you have to do now is look forward to your first Championship Show engagement.

So you are now in line for your first Championship Show appointment after a long period of judging and showing. Are you now thinking, 'When will I be asked to judge Cruft's?' The time-worn remark used to be: you need to have one foot almost in the grave! But for many years now we have become a younger-thinking breed, and, in the world of dogs, the sheer involvement of breeding and showing keeps people young in mind and outlook. Fiona Mirylees of the Beaupres Pekingese must to date be one of the youngest to judge at this prestigious show, having done so in her early thirties, but then she has had a lifetime of experience, having been so involved with dogs with her late mother Betty Mirylees.

Just remember that there are many other people ahead of you who are highly experienced through being involved for a multitude of years in our breed. One day you will be regarded as being one of them too, if your love of Pekingese is as strong as theirs has been.

# 11

# Breeding

Before all else, if you want to become seriously involved in your hobby, breeding will be the foundation of any future top kennel. Breeding can be an expensive, demanding, traumatic (for you usually) and, sometimes, heart-breaking exercise. These are the bad points obviously. On the positive side, it can prove a rewarding (although 'in mind' and not 'in pocket') experience. It can bring you many happy hours of enjoyment, the little puppy that you helped into the world going on possibly to become a Champion one day.

We have discussed in Chapter 2 (*see* page 38) the method of choosing a stud dog and how to book a possible service from his owner for your bitch, so in this chapter we will concentrate on the dam and her puppies and various aspects of rearing and husbandry.

## The Brood Bitch

The bitch that you decide to breed from has to be one that is likely to enhance your breeding programme. We personally feel that it is best to breed from a bitch that you could happily take into a show ring at a Championship Show and consistently be placed in the first three right up possibly to Post Graduate. From bitches of this ilk have come the majority of our Champions. It is also best to try to breed from a bitch who has no particular outstanding fault. Maybe she does not possess the elusive 'it' that thus prevents her from becoming a top-flight show bitch. Nevertheless, if this female is put to the right dog some lovely puppies could result. You must bear in mind that both partners have to be of more or less equal merit, for if the dam is not good enough to breed from, you cannot expect a dog which has stamped his mark on the breed to do all the work.

We strongly recommend that a bitch of less than 7½ pounds (3½ kilograms) is not bred from, although we personally would not consider mating one under 8½ pounds (4 kilograms).

*Fig 83 Toydom No Secrets. Owned and bred by Miss A. Summers and Miss V. Williams.*

Another point to remember here is that it is no good breeding from a bitch that is really not in tip-top condition. When your bitch is mated and is hopefully in whelp, she is going to give everything to the puppies from herself for the duration of approximately nine weeks. You cannot expect the puppies to be in the desired condition if the mother is not in the peak of fitness herself. She will also suffer because of this, and it really is not fair to expect her to mother her offspring in such a condition, further draining her resources.

We prefer to breed our bitches on their third season which would mean that, providing they come in season every six months, they would be approximately eighteen months old. However, some bitches do not always conform to this sequence of events. Some, for instance, extend the time that elapses between each season to nine months.

We personally feel that a bitch mated at around twelve months is still basically a puppy herself and really needs that little extra time to mature. Having said that, it is sometimes unwise to leave your little girl until too late, for instance around four years of age, unless you cannot help it (for such reasons as you may have been showing her, or perhaps family commitments did not allow time for a litter). Bitches can sometimes be that little more difficult to get into whelp the older they are at their first mating. The question of the age at which a bitch should cease to be bred from, once again, is a matter of personal opinion. We never breed from a bitch that is over five years of age, but others may feel differently on this point. Without generalising, sometimes a litter out of a younger bitch is superior than perhaps one out of an older bitch. Of course, as with anything, there is always an exception to every rule.

The number of litters a bitch should have during her breeding career depends a lot on whether the bitch is a natural whelper or not. Pekingese are prone to Caesareans, but it is not a definite rule that this should happen. A good free whelping line is well worth keeping within your kennel, especially if the dam is producing lovely puppies at the same time.

If, for instance, you mated your bitch at eighteen months and, all being well, she had these puppies naturally, you could mate her again on her next season, if you so wished, providing that the litter did not take too much out of her, and she is in good condition. The following season we would recommend that you give her a rest, perhaps mating her on the season after that.

If your bitch has had a litter with the aid of a Caesarean section, however, we strongly recommend, as would anybody, that she be allowed to miss her next season. If all goes well, she could be mated again the following season. Just because she had to have a Caesarean the first time around does not necessarily mean that it may have to be performed the next time. If you are unlucky and once again have to seek the vet's assistance in this manner, we would advise that the bitch is no longer bred from. We always feel that one Caesarean section is bad luck or unfortunate, but for two there has to be a reason.

Before you even mate your bitch, check by means of a gestation chart (*see* Fig 84) when she would be due to have her puppies. If it will coincide with your annual holiday or if it falls at a time of a family event which you cannot miss, either do not mate the bitch then or seek the services of somebody highly competent in the art of whelping Pekingese. Do not be tempted to leave her in the hands of someone not used to performing such a task; it is highly unfair to the bitch and is also unfair on the kind but inexperienced friend.

When the first day of colour is noted, contact the owner of the stud dog, find out whether the dog is available and check on the stud fee. Try to keep a close eye on the progression of your bitch's season. A normal healthy season will probably mean that your bitch will continue to show colour until approximately the tenth day, at which time it will decrease in shade and visibility, until it disappears completely.

| Jan | Mar | Feb | Apr | Mar | May | Apr | June | May | July | June | Aug | July | Sept | Aug | Oct | Sept | Nov | Oct | Dec | Nov | Jan | Dec | Feb |
|---|---|---|---|---|---|---|---|---|---|---|---|---|---|---|---|---|---|---|---|---|---|---|---|
| 1 | 5 | 1 | 5 | 1 | 3 | 1 | 3 | 1 | 3 | 1 | 3 | 1 | 2 | 1 | 3 | 1 | 3 | 1 | 3 | 1 | 3 | 1 | 2 |
| 2 | 6 | 2 | 6 | 2 | 4 | 2 | 4 | 2 | 4 | 2 | 4 | 2 | 3 | 2 | 4 | 2 | 4 | 2 | 4 | 2 | 4 | 2 | 3 |
| 3 | 7 | 3 | 7 | 3 | 5 | 3 | 5 | 3 | 5 | 3 | 5 | 3 | 4 | 3 | 5 | 3 | 5 | 3 | 5 | 3 | 5 | 3 | 4 |
| 4 | 8 | 4 | 8 | 4 | 6 | 4 | 6 | 4 | 6 | 4 | 6 | 4 | 5 | 4 | 6 | 4 | 6 | 4 | 6 | 4 | 6 | 4 | 5 |
| 5 | 9 | 5 | 9 | 5 | 7 | 5 | 7 | 5 | 7 | 5 | 7 | 5 | 6 | 5 | 7 | 5 | 7 | 5 | 7 | 5 | 7 | 5 | 6 |
| 6 | 10 | 6 | 10 | 6 | 8 | 6 | 8 | 6 | 8 | 6 | 8 | 6 | 7 | 6 | 8 | 6 | 8 | 6 | 8 | 6 | 8 | 6 | 7 |
| 7 | 11 | 7 | 11 | 7 | 9 | 7 | 9 | 7 | 9 | 7 | 9 | 7 | 8 | 7 | 9 | 7 | 9 | 7 | 9 | 7 | 9 | 7 | 8 |
| 8 | 12 | 8 | 12 | 8 | 10 | 8 | 10 | 8 | 10 | 8 | 10 | 8 | 9 | 8 | 10 | 8 | 10 | 8 | 10 | 8 | 10 | 8 | 9 |
| 9 | 13 | 9 | 13 | 9 | 11 | 9 | 11 | 9 | 11 | 9 | 11 | 9 | 10 | 9 | 11 | 9 | 11 | 9 | 11 | 9 | 11 | 9 | 10 |
| 10 | 14 | 10 | 14 | 10 | 12 | 10 | 12 | 10 | 12 | 10 | 12 | 10 | 11 | 10 | 12 | 10 | 12 | 10 | 12 | 10 | 12 | 10 | 11 |
| 11 | 15 | 11 | 15 | 11 | 13 | 11 | 13 | 11 | 13 | 11 | 13 | 11 | 12 | 11 | 13 | 11 | 13 | 11 | 13 | 11 | 13 | 11 | 12 |
| 12 | 16 | 12 | 16 | 12 | 14 | 12 | 14 | 12 | 14 | 12 | 14 | 12 | 13 | 12 | 14 | 12 | 14 | 12 | 14 | 12 | 14 | 12 | 13 |
| 13 | 17 | 13 | 17 | 13 | 15 | 13 | 15 | 13 | 15 | 13 | 15 | 13 | 14 | 13 | 15 | 13 | 15 | 13 | 15 | 13 | 15 | 13 | 14 |
| 14 | 18 | 14 | 18 | 14 | 16 | 14 | 16 | 14 | 16 | 14 | 16 | 14 | 15 | 14 | 16 | 14 | 16 | 14 | 16 | 14 | 16 | 14 | 15 |
| 15 | 19 | 15 | 19 | 15 | 17 | 15 | 17 | 15 | 17 | 15 | 17 | 15 | 16 | 15 | 17 | 15 | 17 | 15 | 17 | 15 | 17 | 15 | 16 |
| 16 | 20 | 16 | 20 | 16 | 18 | 16 | 18 | 16 | 18 | 16 | 18 | 16 | 17 | 16 | 18 | 16 | 18 | 16 | 18 | 16 | 18 | 16 | 17 |
| 17 | 21 | 17 | 21 | 17 | 19 | 17 | 19 | 17 | 19 | 17 | 19 | 17 | 18 | 17 | 19 | 17 | 19 | 17 | 19 | 17 | 19 | 17 | 18 |
| 18 | 22 | 18 | 22 | 18 | 20 | 18 | 20 | 18 | 20 | 18 | 20 | 18 | 19 | 18 | 20 | 18 | 20 | 18 | 20 | 18 | 20 | 18 | 19 |
| 19 | 23 | 19 | 23 | 19 | 21 | 19 | 21 | 19 | 21 | 19 | 21 | 19 | 20 | 19 | 21 | 19 | 21 | 19 | 21 | 19 | 21 | 19 | 20 |
| 20 | 24 | 20 | 24 | 20 | 22 | 20 | 22 | 20 | 22 | 20 | 22 | 20 | 21 | 20 | 22 | 20 | 22 | 20 | 22 | 20 | 22 | 20 | 21 |
| 21 | 25 | 21 | 25 | 21 | 23 | 21 | 23 | 21 | 23 | 21 | 23 | 21 | 22 | 21 | 23 | 21 | 23 | 21 | 23 | 21 | 23 | 21 | 22 |
| 22 | 26 | 22 | 26 | 22 | 24 | 22 | 24 | 22 | 24 | 22 | 24 | 22 | 23 | 22 | 24 | 22 | 24 | 22 | 24 | 22 | 24 | 22 | 23 |
| 23 | 27 | 23 | 27 | 23 | 25 | 23 | 25 | 23 | 25 | 23 | 25 | 23 | 24 | 23 | 25 | 23 | 25 | 23 | 25 | 23 | 25 | 23 | 24 |
| 24 | 28 | 24 | 28 | 24 | 26 | 24 | 26 | 24 | 26 | 24 | 26 | 24 | 25 | 24 | 26 | 24 | 26 | 24 | 26 | 24 | 26 | 24 | 25 |
| 25 | 29 | 25 | 29 | 25 | 27 | 25 | 27 | 25 | 27 | 25 | 27 | 25 | 26 | 25 | 27 | 25 | 27 | 25 | 27 | 25 | 27 | 25 | 26 |
| 26 | 30 | 26 | 30 | 26 | 28 | 26 | 28 | 26 | 28 | 26 | 28 | 26 | 27 | 26 | 28 | 26 | 28 | 26 | 28 | 26 | 28 | 26 | 27 |
| 27 | 31 | | | 27 | 29 | 27 | 29 | 27 | 29 | 27 | 29 | 27 | 28 | 27 | 29 | 27 | 29 | 27 | 29 | 27 | 29 | 27 | 28 |
| | | | | 28 | 30 | 28 | 30 | 28 | 30 | 28 | 30 | 28 | 29 | 28 | 30 | 28 | 30 | 28 | 30 | 28 | 30 | | |
| | | | | 29 | 31 | 29 | | 29 | 31 | 29 | 31 | 29 | 30 | 29 | 31 | | | 29 | 31 | 29 | 31 | | |
| | Apr | | May | | June | | July | | Aug | | Sept | | Oct | | Nov | | Dec | | Jan | | Feb | | Mar |
| 28 | 1 | 27 | 1 | 30 | 1 | 29 | 1 | 30 | 1 | 30 | 1 | 30 | 1 | 30 | 1 | 29 | 1 | 30 | 1 | 30 | 1 | 28 | 1 |
| 29 | 2 | 28 | 2 | 31 | 2 | 30 | 2 | 31 | 2 | | | 31 | 2 | 31 | 2 | 30 | 2 | 31 | 2 | | | 29 | 2 |
| 30 | 3 | | | | | | | | | | | | | | | | | | | | | 30 | 3 |
| 31 | 4 | | | | | | | | | | | | | | | | | | | | | 31 | 4 |

*Fig 84 Gestation table. First column lists mating date, second column lists whelping date.*

When this has happened the entrance to the vagina, the vulva, which will have become more swollen as the season has progressed, will be softer to the touch than in the earlier days of her season. Another point to watch for is that, more often than not, when a bitch is ready to be mated she can become a little flirtatious, and may start to 'tail' with one of your other dogs, be it male or female. This is noticeable when she stands poised and swishes her tail to one side or the other of her back.

If you are having to arrange to have her sent to the stud dog of your choice, it is sometimes more prudent if she is sent a day or two prior to the possible day of mating. This arrangement, of course, depends entirely on the owner of the stud dog. We find this beneficial to the bitch herself in many cases, for they can be very wary of being shipped off to a strange place. Allowing them an extra day or so before the service gives them that little extra chance to settle and become used to these new surroundings. This practice is sometimes less traumatic for the bitch and can result in a better mating.

The owner of the stud dog will more than likely offer two services, especially on a maiden bitch (i.e. one which has never been previously mated). It is best to take the bitch to the stud dog a day early rather than a day late. It really depends on the individual bitch. Some are mated on the eleventh and thirteenth day, some earlier and some much later. If, however, you wish to take your bitch to the sire yourself and, for one reason or another, you are to have only one service, it is even more important that you choose the correct day.

If you follow the preceding guide-lines, hopefully the result will be successful. However, if this is your first step into the 'maternity ward' and you are unsure, a brief consultation with one of your newly found breeder friends or your veterinary surgeon (in the latter case obviously a small fee would be liable) would ensure that you had the correct information.

We have presumed that your bitch follows the normal pattern in her season. Sometimes, though, it is not always quite so straightforward, when for instance, you come across a bitch with a *colourless season*. When you think the time is drawing close for your bitch to come into season, monitor her progress closely, checking her daily. More often than not with a colourless season, she will show a slight spot of colour at the outset, but from that moment on all traces of this will disappear. Therefore, you will have to assume that this first show of colour is possibly the very first day of season. But, of course, sometimes this is not quite so simple, so continue to keep a strict watch. A change in her behaviour pattern is a guide; also keep a daily record on how the vulva becomes swollen and eventually softens.

If you have a male dog of your own, he can be a help at a time such as this. When the male starts to show a distinct fancy for this lady, then you will know the time is drawing nigh for you to arrange for transportation to her mate. This is, of course, presuming that you had not intended using your own male on her. It is always a very good idea to inform the owner of the stud dog at the outset that her season is colourless for, if she is being sent away, this gives the owner a little extra information on her progress.

When it is nearing the time that you feel she will be ready for mating, and you will be taking her to the dog yourself, the very moment that you think the time is fast approaching inform the owner of the stud dog, preferably the day before. If she suddenly seems to be ready for mating that day, it is best to try and contact the dog's owner as early as is reasonably possible in the morning.

For example, if you have perceived one morning that she is hardly showing any sign of colour, her vulva is more swollen and softer and that she is beginning to tail, ring the stud dog's owner and ask if it will be convenient to bring her the next day. If it seems that she is suddenly ready then and there, ask if it will be possible to arrange a service for that day. Do not forget that this person has a family or other commitments and will have to rearrange their day to accommodate you. Because of this, therefore, a little advance warning is always appreciated. Do not just turn up on the day without warning as you may find yourself a little unpopular, to say the least.

## The Stud Dog

If you have a dog that you wish to use at stud, he should, of course, possess some very desirable attributes. If you wish to use him with one of your own bitches, you must feel that he would suit your bitch and, in the process, benefit the breed itself. You should not decide to use him for the simple reason that he happens to be close at hand and will save you a journey to a perhaps more suitable dog.

A stud dog is as popular as the number of winning children he sires. Therefore, do not think that just because you possess a male, people are going to come flocking to use him. Any young dog takes a little while to build up a reputation as a dominant stud. Serious breeders will want to know that a dog is bred well to reproduce his qualities; 'breeding will out' is indeed a very apt saying.

Being able to handle a stud dog in order that he will mate a bitch is not the simplest task in the world, and a few breeders have found it an impossible one. We recommend that you have two people for this, one to hold the bitch and make quite sure that she does not turn on the dog, the other to help the dog.

## Mating

The dogs can mate either on the floor, or on a table or wide shelf. It is best to ensure that there is something solid or substantial behind, so that the two have nowhere to go at the point of being tied. We personally find that this task is more conveniently performed on a table, for when the dogs are tied – and this can last for ten minutes to one hour – it is a lot more comfortable being able to stand than having to kneel for that length of time. Some people favour letting the dog and bitch get acquainted on the floor prior to the actual mating. It is a good idea in the respect that, if the bitch is of an affable temperament she will flirt with the dog, making him even more interested in the forthcoming procedure. If, however, she is a little overawed by the whole experience and therefore more than a little tetchy, she could end up attacking the male. An experienced dog most likely would not mind in the least, but a younger and less experienced male could be put off the whole idea completely.

Let us now assume that you are using the table method. Firstly, place the bitch on the table, getting the person present to help you hold her. Make quite sure that she is held firmly so that she is unable to swing round and give the dog a nasty nip at the most crucial moment. The next step is to introduce the dog on to the table, at which point he will most likely start to take a general interest in his new companion. Let him go near her so that he can pursue his interest – he will more than likely sniff at her. A highly experienced male will know whether or not she is ready for mating, while a younger dog would maybe need a little more encouragement.

While he is taking an interest in his new mate, gently part the skirts of the bitch so that it will be easier for him when he comes to mount her. One of the easiest ways of discerning whether everything is happening in the right place with this long-coated breed is by the following process. Place two fingers, one either side of the entrance to the vagina; this will enable you to check quite easily that penetration is taking place.

When the dog is ready, let him climb on to the bitch's back. Hopefully you should feel him start to work. A younger and less experienced dog may need a little aid at this first stage and may have to be lifted on. When the dog is starting to work, you will feel with your hand underneath exactly what is happening. If everything seems to be going off-course, so to speak, you may need to guide the dog's penis with your free hand or, alternatively, guide the bitch's vulva to the dog.

When the dog enters the bitch, you have to remember that because of the formation of the pelvic girdle the angle of penetration is slightly upwards. You will know when the dog is actually in the bitch and beginning to tie for he will literally hunch himself. When you feel him start to go into her, a helpful push with your free hand will ensure that he is well up before he begins to swell. Hold him in that position for a few minutes until you think that he has actually tied with the bitch. At this stage, he is unlikely to fall back out and it then becomes a question of waiting for the parting of the two dogs.

Occasionally a small dog may have trouble with perhaps a bigger bitch at the point of entering her. In cases like this, you may need to offer a little elevation, and telephone directories make ideal steps in such instances! When the two dogs seem to be well tied, you may let the dog down to one side so that there is no constant pressure on the bitch's back. If it appears that the mating has resulted in an 'outside tie', it is sometimes safer to hold him there for the short time this is likely to last. An outside tie is when the dog does not completely penetrate the bitch, but none the less the sperm is still pumped up into the bitch, and puppies will still result from a mating of this type.

When the dog is ready to come away, and the bitch is ready to release him, ensure that the bitch is held on her back with her rear end held slightly higher than her front end. Keep her in this position for a few minutes. Another tip is to place something cold on the bitch's vulva for a split second or two. An ice-pack works wonders and causes the muscles to contract, hopefully holding back inside the bitch all the precious sperm needed for a successful result.

*Fig 85 Champion Attercliffe Cornelien. Owned and bred by Mrs L. Williamson.*

While this is being attended to, make quite sure that the dog's penis returns normally within its sheath. If the bitch has prematurely pushed him out, it may take a little while for this to return to its normal size. In a case like this it is best to hold the dog so that no dirt or particles can be withdrawn into the sheath, as these may cause an irritation or slight infection to set up. When everything has returned to normal, check the entrance to the sheath, ensuring that any of the hairs here have not been drawn inside. There are various creams or antiseptic washes that can be obtained from your veterinary surgeon, which can be inserted into the sheath after the mating and help to reduce the chance of infection.

Returning to the bitch, who has been held on her back for these last few minutes, return her to normality by standing her upright and place her somewhere quiet for at least half an hour. If you have travelled to the stud dog, return her to her travelling basket so that she can recover from the whole experience.

When a bitch is absolutely ready for mating she will usually take everything in her stride. It can, however, be traumatic for a maiden bitch as the hymen will need to be broken down. Usually an experienced stud dog will automatically do this upon entering the bitch. Some stud-dog owners insist that this is done prior to the

*Fig 86 Champion Ralshams Lady Ku-Donna. Owned and bred by Mrs C. Lashmar.*

actual mating and carry this out themselves. It is done by inserting a lubricated finger in the vulva until the task is accomplished. We prefer to let the dog do this himself, as we feel that this lessens the chance of introducing the slightest infection into the bitch. She will most likely show signs of discomfort at this point and will quite possibly cry out, but usually after this she will settle down and accept the male without too much worry.

## Pregnancy

The next few weeks see you debating whether or not your bitch is going to be in whelp. Some breeders like to see a clear, sticky discharge approximately one week after the mating which is, they feel, a sure sign of the bitch being pregnant. We have had some bitches show this sign, while others have not and have still been in whelp. Usually, however, a similar discharge around the fifth week of pregnancy is a healthy sign, should this manifest itself. Another symptom of pregnancy is in the third or possibly fourth week of gestation when the bitch will show a slight loss of appetite. This varies in degrees, for some bitches can go off their food for a week or even a little longer while others will literally fast for a couple of days and then return to their normal eating habits. When the bitch is at this stage she may need tempting a little; a small portion of cooked chicken or rabbit usually does the trick. If she does not feel like anything at all, though, try not to worry too much for eventually she should begin to look interested at meal times.

From about the sixth week, start to split her meals up a little. If she is a bitch that is used to having just one meal a day, divide this meal into two. She may like a boiled egg in the morning with a little grated cheese on it which provides her with an added source of protein. On her evening meal sprinkle a little liquid calcium over her meat and biscuit, or whatever. (Check with your veterinary surgeon the amount required if you are unsure, although the dosages are clearly defined on the side of the bottle.) As the pregnancy wears on you may even prefer to split her meals into three. Little and often is more desirable for a bitch at this stage than one large meal. Some breeders are also great believers in raspberry leaf tablets which are designed to aid a natural birth. Another essential at this time is the required dose of a multi-vitamin powder.

## Preparations for Whelping

As the time draws close for your bitch to produce her litter, make quite sure that you have everything ready and close at hand for when you need them. We always ensure that the whelping box is thoroughly washed out and disinfected so that at least one week before she is due to whelp, you can introduce her to it.

It is wise to have at the ready a good supply of old newspapers, several clean towels and sterilised instruments such as scissors, and a surgical clamp if you can get one. You will also need a jar of Vaseline or similar lubricating jelly, a reel of cotton thread, a heated pad and a hot-water bottle. Have at the ready some bedding or blanketing to place the new-born puppies on and, last but not least, a small cardboard box.

The cotton will be necessary if the birth is natural and the puppy has to have the afterbirth severed from the umbilical cord. The hot-water bottle needs to be filled as soon as the bitch starts to show serious signs of straining. The heated pad should be switched on at approximately the same time as the water bottle is filled, to allow it time to reach the desired temperature. The cardboard box is the

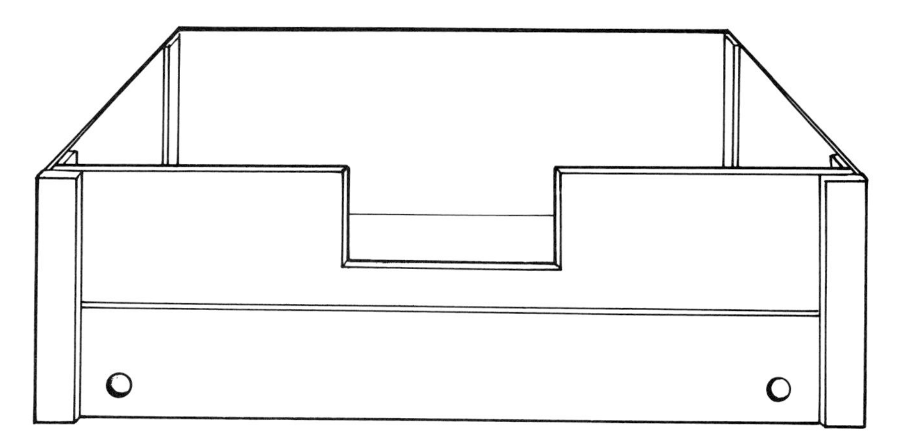

*Fig 87 Whelping box.*

receptable into which the hot-water bottle is to be placed, with one of the blankets over the top. This is for putting a puppy or puppies into when the next one is in the process of being born. For when the bitch is straining and in the throes of bringing her next offspring into the world she will, in most cases, not want to be bothered with the other whelps. There is, though, the slight chance that she may

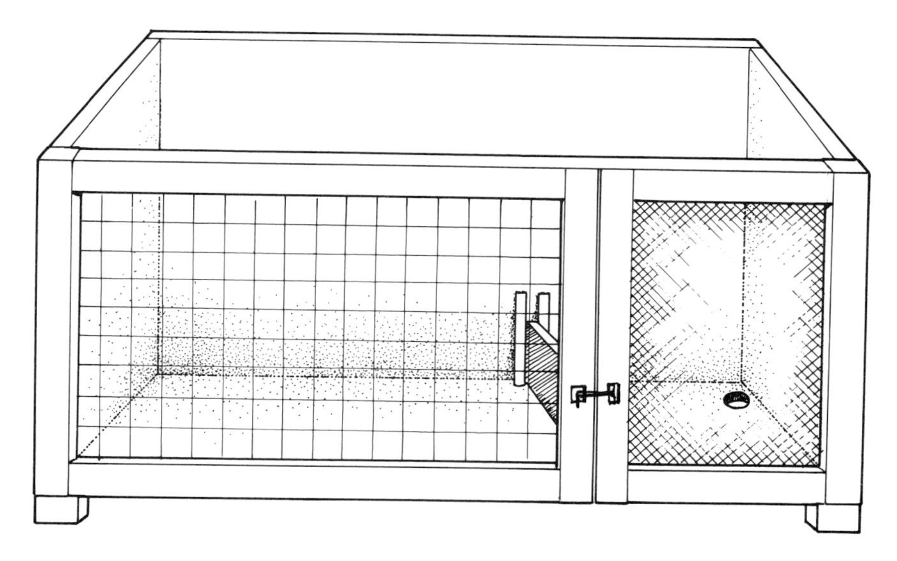

*Fig 88 Larger, sectioned whelping box, enabling the bitch to remove herself from the puppies' quarters for a rest.*

get a little uptight if you try to take the puppies away too soon, so play this part of the midwifery by ear.

We initially set up a small whelping box in our lounge where she is under constant surveillance. Around this we place a pen so that she can step out of it if she so desires. When she has had her puppies and settled down with them, we transfer both the mother and puppies to a large box which is sectioned. This enables her to get away from her fledglings whenever she wants to rest.

Needless to say, as the whelping becomes imminent she should not be left, especially at night. If you are a sound sleeper we would suggest that you set your alarm clock at regular intervals throughout the night, when you feel that the time is drawing near. You will probably find also that it is easier to wake at the slightest sound by sleeping on your settee with the whelping box easily visible, rather than being in bed.

# 12
# Whelping

At this primary stage you will find that a bitch will start to go off her food approximately twenty-four hours before she starts to go into labour. Having said that, though, we have had on the very odd occasion a bitch eat a hearty meal and then settle down to have puppies a few hours later.

Another good guide is to take the bitch's temperature if you feel competent enough to do so. The temperature is taken by inserting the thermometer very gently into the anus. Do not force this action; as the anus relaxes ease it slowly in. We have invested in a digital thermometer which automatically relays the temperature onto its small screen, stopping once the body temperature is reached. The average body heat is 101.5°F (38.6°C). From anything up to about twenty-four hours before whelping begins, the bitch's temperature will slowly start to drop to approximately 99°F (37°C). Generally it will begin to rise again prior to the production of the water bag and the first puppy.

Another sign to look for is a very thick and sticky clear mucous discharge which will appear about twenty-four to forty-eight hours prior to whelping. She will start to become wild-eyed and distressed should you attempt to leave the room for a second.

Always keep a very close eye on her for the first signs of any straining, for when this happens the bitch is entering the Secondary Stage. When doing this, she will appear to be pushing from the shoulders back, resulting in what can only be described as a strong rippling movement running along the body towards her rear. This initial straining should hopefully result in the production of the water bag within a period of two to three hours. These contractions should increase in strength and frequency up to the birth.

The water bag will be presented at the edge of the vulva and appears as a dark shape. Very often a puppy can be right behind this and will be produced shortly after the bag has burst. Do not be tempted to interfere, but let nature take its course.

When the bag eventually bursts, the bitch should continue to strain to bring forth the first puppy. The puppy will be passed through the birth canal until it reaches the head of the uterus, and, with another couple of good, strong, strains, the puppy should appear head first (the normal birth position). The puppy should be expelled from the mother suddenly, and your first priority is to clear the membrane around the puppy's head.

If it has been half presented and there is no obvious sign of imminent release, take one of the clean towels you have prepared and grip the whelp firmly. With each ensuing contraction, pull the puppy away in a downwards direction to help it on its course. Never panic and pull when the bitch is not straining, do so only during her contractions and the puppy should soon be born. Any breeder will tell you how frightened they were on the first few occasions of this happening that they might actually damage the puppy or mother, or both. You have to be prepared to be fairly firm when having to conduct this operation.

Having made sure that the membrane is cleared from the puppy's face and body, the next move is to clear any fluid from its head and lungs. When a puppy is born fairly quickly this does not present so much of a problem.

Wrap the puppy in a towel and ensure that the sac or membrane is also gathered up and rub the puppy dry. Be quite vigorous and quick in this action for it is imperative to ensure that the puppy is made to breathe as quickly as possible. With this brisk rubbing you should soon hear the first 'squawk', and by its healthy crying you will know that all is well. Wipe away any fluid that may appear from its nose and, once you are content that it is breathing quite normally, you may stop rubbing it. The next step is to ensure that the airways are quite free of fluid so, with the puppy still wrapped in the towel and holding it firmly, stand up and with your feet slightly apart swing the puppy down from shoulder height to your knees. Check to see if this action has produced any fluid and, if so, gently wipe it away. Repeat this until you are quite satisfied that there is no congestion. You will be able to detect any 'wheeziness' if you listen carefully.

Before the next puppy is born, you will hopefully have time to cut or sever the umbilical cord. If the bitch quickly starts to strain again keep a careful eye on her in case she needs your assistance once more. Take the cord between your fingers and ease any substance within the cord back toward the puppy. If you have a surgical clamp, place it around the cord approximately two inches from the puppy. If you do not have a clamp, after squeezing the cord as just described, tie a knot in it at approximately the same distance with the cotton you hopefully have remembered to include amongst your surgical aids. Make sure you tie this tightly and securely, and then cut the cord with a pair of sharp scissors on the side of the cotton near the afterbirth or membrane.

Providing the mother is not thinking about carrying on with some more contractions, let the puppy try to feed off one of the teats. The easiest ones to 'plug' it on to are those nearest the back legs. Some puppies can be a little slow on the uptake regarding this essential part of their survival. If need be, hold the puppy on until you are sure that its little mouth is firmly wrapped around the teat and is giving some healthy sucks. When the mother starts her contractions once more, remove the puppy and place it in the cardboard box on the hot-water bottle, covering it with a fine blanket or light towel where hopefully it will settle down and sleep, while you go to the aid of its future brother or sister.

## Complications

We have just covered a whelping that is quite natural where everything is just as you would wish it to be. Unfortunately, you can have the complications of Caesarean sections, lost placentas or afterbirths and there is also the chance of a breech birth.

### *Caesarean Section*

Should the bitch cease straining without producing the water bag, this could be the first sign of problems. If she has been straining constantly for several hours and nothing has actually shown a sign of presenting itself, it will be necessary to consult your veterinary surgeon as professional advice is needed at this stage. As we have already said, when you have decided to enter the realms of breeding you will have realised that Caesarean sections are not an uncommon occurrence in this breed. Inertia is invariably one of the main causes that will necessitate a vet to step in and operate in order to save the litter. Other reasons make it necessary, for instance sometimes the birth channel may have a stricture, thus preventing the puppies to pass through it safely. Alternatively, you may have had the majority of the litter naturally and for some reason the final one just will not come the same way; this again sometimes, but not always, requires surgery.

With inertia, a bitch will proceed to go through all the various initial stages quite normally. She will attempt to make her nest, her abdomen will become as tight as a drum as is normal, her eyes will take on the expected worried expression and the temperature will fall and rise as described on page 184. She may or may not start to strain. It is more than usual at this stage of the proceedings that everything will suddenly stop. She may settle down again, losing that feverish expression and become quite relaxed; even her stomach area will seem softer to the touch, and her temperature, if taken, will be normal. You will, of course, need to consult your vet who will want to see her and decide what course of action is necessary. Unfortunately, whenever this has happened we have found that the only remedy is a Caesarean section.

## *Cleft Palate*

Check the puppy's mouth for any sign of a cleft palate as soon as it is born. Open the puppy's mouth and look at the roof of it as far back as you can see. A cleft palate is literally a split in the roof of the mouth, and there is no other course than to have the puppy humanely put to sleep by your vet. Fortunately, cleft palates are not a regular occurrence.

## *Lost Afterbirth*

Sometimes when a puppy is being born you may have the misfortune to lose the afterbirth. It can be delivered with the next puppy, or the membrane may break with the delivery of the puppy, consequently leaving it retained within the uterus. In a case such as this you may need to sever the cord in the same manner as previously discussed, in order to release the pup.

Always keep a close check on how many afterbirths you manage to get or recover for, however small the piece is, if it is left, it is quite capable of setting up an infection. This in turn will cause a dangerously high temperature and make her very ill. In a case such as this, these symptoms will also be accompanied by an evil-smelling pinkish discharge, so always keep a close observation for any signs of this occurring.

## Breech Birth

This is where the puppy is presented with the posterior first. The bitch will undoubtedly need assistance here. When there is enough of the puppy visible, take a firm hold once more with the towel, trying to ensure that your hand does not slip. Once again, as previously described, with each contraction pull the puppy downwards towards the bitch's head until it is released. Never pull the puppy upwards or away from the back legs for you are going against the formation of the bitch's pelvis and uterus. If you quickly realise that there is no progress being made even with this assistance, it may be that one of its limbs is stuck and consequently you may have to try to extricate it internally. This is where the lubricating gel you have placed ready comes to the rescue. Place a little of the jelly on one finger and slide it into the vulva feeling for anything that may be impeding the passage of this puppy. Perhaps one back leg has become caught; this can be freed with gentle manipulation.

If the membrane should break, which with the aforementioned problems could possibly have happened, you now have added to your worries the thought that the puppy could drown unless it is born quickly. So, as soon as any limb that has caused the hold-up has been released, be ready to pull down firmly at the very next contraction. As soon as the puppy is born, quickly attend to it in the normal fashion, rubbing life into it and dispelling any fluid that may have accumulated.

This probably sounds all very traumatic to a beginner but just remember that however worried you may be, do not panic and start rushing about. Keep calm, for your nerves will transpose themselves to the already rather distressed bitch, who will be quite uptight enough without you panicking too. She really needs your help, and this you must give without any fuss, fluster or histrionics!

## Care of the Bitch and Puppies

When your second puppy has been delivered successfully and checked for the aforementioned problems, and you have fully attended to it, then introduce it to the mother's milk bar and, once this one is firmly implanted and having its first meal, reintroduce its litter companion and let it also have another feed if it so wishes. After each puppy is born, offer the bitch some liquid refreshment. A

*Fig 89 Champion Dorodea Yu Song. Owned and bred by Mrs D. Dearn and Mrs H. Beard.*

drink of milk, or water with a little glucose would be very much appreciated.

When you are quite convinced that there are no further puppies in the womb, you can start to clean up the bitch and the whelping box and then proceed to make the mother comfortable with her little fledglings.

Place the heated pad in the bottom of the clean whelping box together with a blanket over the top of it. It is often a good idea, when switching the pad on to warm up, to wrap it in a blanket. This helps to retain the heat in the pad itself. Place this warm blanket on top of the pad and rehome the puppies and mother on it. When cleaning the bitch up, a gentle wash around her private parts with a little warm water, which are then dabbed dry with a towel, will suffice at this stage. She will be naturally anxious to be with her offspring and also to have a rest. If she would like a light meal, offer her some cooked chicken or a little cooked rabbit, or perhaps even a boiled egg.

Once she is settled down with her babies, try to ensure that they are each feeding off the teats and are quite content before you relax. You can always tell when a puppy is safely 'locked on' and feeding well for there is a gentle silence broken by the occasional slurp!

Their little heads will gently bob backwards as they suck and pull on the teat to draw the milk down. If you hear too much sucking and noisy slurping you can be quite sure that one of them at least has not as yet managed to learn or is maybe not quite strong enough to hold on. This will mean that you will need to keep holding the puppy on as many times as possible, until it has managed to accomplish this feat on its own.

In the case of a natural birth it is advisable to have your vet visit after all is completed to check the mother and, if necessary, give a cleansing injection. This helps to dispel any afterbirth that may have been left behind or even a minute particle that may have lodged itself inside the bitch.

Returning briefly to the question of a cleft palate, your vet will check for this at the same time if requested. The presence of a cleft results in the puppy being unable to feed properly, with the milk constantly coming back down its nose. Sometimes a harelip will accompany this defect. This on its own will not affect the puppy's chances of survival but these two conditions, in the main, go hand in hand. If the harelip is the only defect, the chances are that as the puppy grows up it will eventually heal over if not too prominent.

For the first few days after having the puppies you may find that the mother will become decidedly fussy about her food. A good mother will not want to leave her babies for one minute and will have to be coaxed to go outside to relieve herself. If she will not leave the puppies for one instant, it may be necessary to hand-feed her until she becomes a little less possessive. There is a very good brand of beef essence available from most chemists that is advisable always to have in stock. This can be given to the mother with the aid of a needleless syringe and will keep her strength up and, in most cases, help the appetite to return.

When she is eating normally once again, we like to carry on splitting her meals up throughout the day for the first couple of weeks. It is sometimes better to give her three smaller meals at regular intervals. Always ensure that she has water at hand if your whelping box is of the kind where she can be apart from the puppies to eat and drink. If, however, the puppies are liable to wander anywhere near her dishes, on no account leave any water or food in with her as this could lead to a tragic accident. She may become overly possessive about her food and, without really meaning to, nip one of the puppies should it come too close. Also, a puppy could easily fall in a water bowl and drown.

If you have a puppy that is constantly wailing and gives a thin painful cry, the chances are that there is something radically wrong with it. The dam usually knows and will sometimes have nothing to do with it, pushing this little one away every time you try to make it suck from her. On the other hand, sometimes this crying just means that the puppy is not getting enough food so it will need extra assistance until it gets the strength to hold on for long periods at a time. It will be necessary in a case such as this to hold the puppy on before it gets left behind in relation to its littermates. Once it has built up enough strength you will hopefully find that it will improve and feed confidently on its own.

When the dam is settled down with her newly born litter always make sure that they are somewhere quiet and that she is not in danger of being annoyed by other dogs. This may upset her and the puppies in the process. Try to find a corner of the house where she can turn all her attention to rearing her babies. Also make it an accessible spot where, if possible, you are able to keep an eye on her and their progress.

Warmth is a major factor with puppies, especially in this breed, as many fatalities are caused by hypothermia. If the bed and blanketing are not warm enough or there is a draught, any one of these factors can cause unnecessary problems, so always pay careful attention to where you are going to place your new family. With just a little common sense and good luck you will, all being well, have a happy and healthy mother and litter.

During the period of lactation, there will be a certain amount of dark discharge from the vagina whether the birth was natural or by Caesarean. For purposes of hygiene this will need to be cleaned up daily. This is quite a normal event but, if the discharge should change colour and become pungent, ring your vet for his advice. You can be sure that if the bitch's temperature is taken at this stage it will have a high reading.

Always keep an eye on the bitch's milk glands, particularly during the first few weeks. When a lot of milk is being made, sometimes all the teats are not drained properly by the puppies, especially in the case of a small litter. Puppies tend to have their favourite outlets which are generally the back ones for the obvious reasons that they are easily accessible. The ones nearer the front of the bitch are likely to become overfull and will need to be drained. If you can easily get a puppy to feed off one of these, then all well and good, but if it is not so easy you will need to drain them manually

*Fig 90 Misha of Mathena at Toydom, in a reclining pose. Bred by Mrs Y. Hoynck Van Papendrecht, owned by Miss A. Summers and Miss V. Williams.*

yourself. You will need some warm water and cotton wool. Bathe the affected teats and individually drain the milk off by squeezing gently with the dampened cotton wool. This is obviously a sore process for the dam but, if left, the condition will become worse and result in dire consequences for her.

## *Post-Caesarean Care*

If a Caesarean has been the only solution to the delivery of these puppies, when the bitch comes round she may take a little time to become accustomed to her puppies, who have suddenly appeared – in her mind at least – from nowhere.

After the operation the veterinary surgeon will ensure that the bitch has recovered consciousness sufficiently before being allowed home. When you get her home she will more than likely want to sleep off the after-effects of the anaesthetic for a few hours at least before she sets her mind to maternal duties. It is best at this stage to keep her separate from her babies until she is conscious enough to know what is going on. If at all possible, and her milk has been released, hold each of the puppies on for their first feed as soon as you get them home, staying with them all the time this is happening.

You will then find that you may need to clean them and encourage the puppies to go to the toilet. In order to do this, you just need a little warm water and cotton wool. Dip the cotton wool into the warm water, squeezing the excess out, and gently rub the puppy's tummy with this in a rotating movement. This will automatically make the puppy spend a penny. To make it do a little more, repeat this operation down near the back legs and around the anus, without trying to rub that area itself which would make it sore. Once this has been attended to, place the puppies in the little cardboard box on a freshly filled hot-water bottle and blanket. Cover them over with a lighter blanket and place them somewhere safe out of any draughts. Always beware in cases like this if you happen to possess a cat, for it would not be able to tell the difference between these wriggling little creatures and a mouse!

When the mother is sufficiently *compos mentis*, slowly start to introduce the puppies to her. Try to hold one of the puppies on to her to feed. A maiden bitch may take fright at this new turn of events so do not overdo it at this stage. Get her confidence by slowly trying this once more, stroking her at the same time. Place the puppies on the heated pad in the pen with her, keeping watch on her every move. All being well, after a short time she will take an interest in them and hopefully before too long realise that they are her own flesh and blood, even though she does not remember where they came from! Never leave her alone with them at this stage; if for some reason you need to leave the room even for a second, place them back in their little box warmly tucked up. If she becomes distressed when this happens it is a good sign and means that it will not be too long before she accepts them totally.

Once she has settled down with them and is gently licking them you can relax. Up until that time it is a vigil unfortunately, but is well worthwhile for the good of the mother and her offspring.

## *Hand-feeding*

If the bitch really is averse to letting you hold them on, you will need to supplement them for the first few hours. This you can do with a little boiled water which is allowed to cool, mixed with a small teaspoonful of glucose. If it looks as though this will go on for a longer period, you can either use one of the prepared puppy food powders that your vet will stock, or alternatively the following recipe can be mixed up and used. Do not resort to milky supplements unless the dam shows no signs whatsoever of wanting to mother her babies in the foreseeable future.

This recipe has successfully reared many a puppy for us and others. You will need 2 ounces (55 grams) water, 5 ounces (140 grams) milk (tinned or goat's), 1 teaspoonful glucose, 2 drops cod-liver oil and the strained yolk of an egg. This mixture makes up to approximately half a pint (a third of a litre). Strain enough for each feed and gently warm it in a saucepan. For those of you who possess a microwave, warm it in there enough to take any chill off.

In order to get this mixture inside the puppy you will need either an eye dropper or an orphan puppy baby feeder (which resembles a baby's bottle). Another method is to tube feed. We will not go into long explanations of how to implement that system for it is best to watch someone else carry this out who will teach you. The advantage of this is that the feed goes directly into the stomach so that you know exactly how much the puppy is getting and it is much quicker than the other two methods, but it should only be carried out by somebody experienced and with the correct equipment.

If you need to resort to hand-feeding the litter, in these early days it will need to be carried out every two hours to give the puppies any chance of survival. Take the puppy in one hand and fill the eye dropper. Let the mixture into the puppy's mouth in minute quantities – too much at a time and the liquid will go straight up the puppy's nose or into the lungs, causing further complications and possible fatality. You will need patience with this. Let the puppy take approximately a couple of teaspoonfuls at each feeding time (you will lose a certain amount as it dribbles from the mouth). As the puppy grows increase the amount of its intake.

If you are very unfortunate and are left with an orphan litter, or if the mother for some inexplicable reason becomes aggressive when asked to accept the litter after a long period of time (and by this we mean several days), it will become necessary to try to find a foster mother or prepare yourself for a marathon of hand-feeding.

Foster mothers are not always very easy to come by so we will now presume that you are left to your own devices. For the first ten days of a puppy's life we feed each puppy every two hours, day and night. To say this is an exhausting task is an understatement. It helps if there is another member of your family or a partner who can assist you with this. For the first ten days this regular routine of two-hourly feeds needs to be carried out religiously; after this you can extend the time to every three hours. Continue this for another seven days, lengthening the time between the night-time feeds to every four hours. If you give a feed at or around midnight, that means that another one is given at four, and then not again until eight. It may sound rather shattering but, believe us, after being used to every two and three hours, four hours seems a luxury in comparison!

## *Eclampsia*

Eclampsia is a condition that can occasionally rear its ugly head at any time throughout the lactation period; very often it appears in an exceptionally good mother because of the fact that everything is given by the mother to her puppies. The dam will become very restless and upset and her temperature will rise to a dangerous level, the result being that she will collapse in a state that closely resembles a fit. At this stage, immediate veterinary assistance is needed to save her life.

## *Weaning*

The time of initial weaning will depend on the size of the litter and the amount of milk the mother is producing. At approximately three and a half weeks we try to see if the puppies will take their first solid meal, a little scraped meat. For this you will need a good-quality piece of beef, a little braising steak for instance. Take a knife or a spoon (the instrument does not need to be sharp) and scrape it along the piece of meat. The meat should come away in fine thin pieces so that you can almost see through it. For their very first feed, a piece a little larger than a pea is sufficient. Place the individual portions on a saucer and dampen with a little water. Never feed this dry for it will be inclined to stick in the puppies' mouths and throats; when moistened it can be taken easily by the puppy and made a more enjoyable exercise all round.

Hold the puppy on your lap. A little word of advice is that whenever you handle one of these babies in these first tentative few weeks of their life: always make sure that your hands are warm. If they are not, then ensure that there is a blanket or towel wrapped around the baby before you pick it up. With the puppy held firmly in one hand, place a little of this new diet in its mouth. Either it will take to this new meal like a duck to water or it will literally spit it back out at you. Persevere and at least try to get it to take a little. If not, then try again the next day. You will very often find that the puppy that is always at the milk bar is the hardest to persuade to take this new food.

Once the puppies are happily accepting this new menu, you can progress to supplementing them further with the aid of one of the more popular brands of tinned baby foods that are available. We find the lamb flavour a great favourite! When first weaning with the meat, try to do this daily, increasing after a few days to at least twice and so on, introducing the other meals along the way. How soon you step this up, or start it at all, of course, depends on the flow of milk. Always keep a close eye on this, because it could of course build up again in those higher teats while the puppies are finding another source of food from you.

Some of the milky baby foods are another source that you can resort to especially when mother is not with them so often. Once puppies get to the scrambling around and into everything stage, we start to take the mother away for short periods at a time. As already mentioned, we use a whelping box that has an area for her to get away from the puppies. However, when this private part of the nursery is becoming regularly invaded by her rather demanding litter, she will need to be given some respite. If you have the kind of whelping box where she is unable to get away at all, you must ensure that she is let away from them regularly, for otherwise her health may seriously deteriorate.

The period that she is removed from them is increased, so that when they are between six and seven weeks she is away from them completely. In the week or so up until this time she is allowed in with the litter only at night. We find that, in the majority of cases, the mother will be quite happy to relinquish them completely to your care and be more than happy to return to her pals, leaving the nursery behind.

For the following two weeks at least we would recommend that you regiment a system of five small meals a day. Puppies usually lap up boiled or scrambled egg for one meal. A little finely minced raw beef is another favourite. Very often at this age we also find that they adore very finely minced tripe either on its own or mixed with the raw beef. Goat's milk is usually quite popular with puppies and there is more goodness in this than cow's. This can usually be obtained in your local supermarket in a long-life carton. Babies' rusks soaked in this milk are an ideal bedtime snack as they grow up. Other favourites are minced chicken, fish and rabbit, all checked very carefully of course for the minutest particle of bone. At this time also, it is advisable to institute a daily dosage of liquid calcium, checking the amount to give on the bottle.

Reading through some of the earlier traumas we have described, you are probably thinking that you never, ever want to breed a litter of Pekingese. However, many many whelpings go ahead without any hitches at all. It is always best to be prepared, though, and these rather depressing paragraphs are to prepare you for any eventuality that could arise. Try not to become paranoid and jump at the sign of the bitch even moving but, on the other hand, do not become so complacent that you leave them all to their own devices. Just use a little common sense and this will see you through.

Finally, before we leave this chapter, one or two words of advice that may help you during this time. Before your bitch is due to whelp, always make quite sure that your veterinary surgeon is informed of the event and the date she is due. In this way he or she will be prepared for you ringing up in case of any problems, and this forewarning is usually very much appreciated by these hardworking professionals.

# 13
# Ailments and Diseases

To be able to cover, in depth, the various ailments and diseases that exist in the canine world would mean that we would have to be highly qualified veterinary surgeons, which alas we are not. So we will be content to outline some of the more common complaints together with a few that perhaps pertain more to this breed.

We would most categorically state that whenever you suspect that your Pekingese is feeling off-colour, immediate expert consultation should be sought. Many illnesses show similar symptoms, so do not trust entirely to your own diagnosis as, in doing so, you may cause your little animal unnecessary suffering. There may be certain drugs or antibiotics that only a vet can prescribe for the alleviation of the complaint.

When you have read through this chapter you will probably think that we rush to the vet for the slightest condition. We would argue here that it is better to be safe than sorry. However, as your experience of keeping and breeding dogs during their good and ill-health widens, you will gradually learn to recognise certain symptoms and will know whether or not you need to trouble the vet. In some cases you may be able to administer first aid yourself. But to begin with, we strongly advise that you learn to lean on your vet for help and advice, especially in the formative years of your new hobby.

## Parasites

Parasites can appear internally as well as externally. One of the most common and well-known of the external variety is of course, the flea.

## *Fleas*

Fleas can be one of the more difficult parasites to rid the dog of, for the simple reason that they are quite able to live away from their host, in the carpet, floorboards and furniture of your house or, alternatively, in the kennel. So you have to remember that when you are attempting to exterminate these little devils, you will also have to attend to the surroundings. This is particularly important as it is in the dog's environment that their eggs are laid.

The presence of a flea or fleas can be detected by the faeces or 'droppings' on the skin of the dog. These appear as little black specks, almost similar in type to small particles of coal dust. They will invariably be found along the dog's back, especially near the tail and around the neck.

The regular use of a good-quality insecticidal shampoo or aerosol spray will help to rid him of these unwanted visitors.

One shampooing or spraying is not enough. Treatment needs to be repeated as per the directions on the container; usually a week or ten days later in the case of severe infestation. You must also treat the dog's living quarters: the bedding is best burnt and the basket scrubbed out and sprayed. Also spray the surroundings or, if the dog is living outside, spray the kennel. In cases of severe infestation it may be necessary for professional help to be sought and the house to be fumigated in the process.

## *Lice*

Lice are another highly undesirable parasite, causing the dog to itch. As with the flea, the discomfort that this can bring to your animal hardly bears thinking about, and if they are not treated very quickly the dog's condition and health is bound to suffer.

Unlike a flea, the louse spends its entire life cycle on the dog, but it can reproduce at such an alarming rate that unless dealt with rapidly, control is extremely difficult. Once again, the only alternative is bathing or an insecticidal spray. Shampooing is more efficient and, as with fleas, this will need to be repeated several times until you are absolutely sure that all the lice have been efficiently destroyed along with the eggs that are laid. Always keep a close check on the dogs' companions at a time like this for it is pointless curing one animal to find that the others have also become infested in the meantime.

## *Mites*

By their very name you will realise that mites are tiny but be under no illusions, the suffering they can bring your dog is no small matter. Mange, one of the conditions caused by mites, was quite prevalent in the earlier part of this century although fortunately it is not seen quite so often nowadays.

## *Mange*

There are two forms of this complaint, sarcoptic and demodectic.

**Sarcoptic Mange** With this form, the mite burrows under the skin causing irritation and eventual hair loss. If left unattended this highly contagious condition can progress and cause terrible damage, making the animal extremely ill in the process.

**Demodectic** As with sarcoptic mange, this condition results in hair loss, but it is caused by the presence of a different mite and is accompanied by an unmistakable and foul smell. It is very difficult to cure and it would be advisable to obtain veterinary advice before attempting to treat it.

## *Ear Mites*

If these are allowed to take a hold they can set up quite unnecessary suffering in the shape of *otodetic mange*. These particular mites live in the dog's ear canal, causing the dog to scratch and shake his ears and a waxy substance is visible appearing from within the ear. This can be cured with regular attention and by applying some ear solution that you would need to obtain from your veterinary surgeon.

The presence of parasites can in turn bring other problems. For instance, the presence of fleas could also mean that the dog is suffering from worms. Worms can be highly debilitating and there is no need or excuse for any dog to suffer from them.

## *Worms*

There are two types of these, *roundworms* and *tapeworms*. In the group known as roundworms, fall the highly publicised and undesirable *toxocara canis*. In the unlikely event that a child should come into contact with this worm's larvae, infection is possible and can occasionally cause partial or complete loss of sight. Roundworms can be prevented with the use of worming tablets or paste obtainable from your vet.

Sometimes, in the case of a puppy especially, the stomach being visibly distended can indicate that worms are present, but with medication these can be effectively dealt with.

Tapeworm eggs are carried by fleas. Dogs become infected if they happen to swallow a flea. Segments of the adult tapeworm living in the intestine are passed through the dog's system and appear at the other end. These segments carry the eggs which hatch and begin the cycle again. Because of the relationship between fleas and tapeworms, it is important that a dog which has been suffering from fleas should be checked for worms.

## Diseases

### *Distemper*

Even a person who has never had the pleasure of owning a dog knows this dreaded name. Nowadays, this one-time scourge of dogdom is kept largely under control with the help of vaccines administered to the puppy at around twelve weeks of age. At the same time, immunisation is given against equally lethal diseases such as *hepatitis* and *leptospirosis*. Another complaint that accompanies distemper and is also vaccinated against is *hardpad*, a condition which causes swelling and hardening of the pads of the feet.

The basic symptoms of distemper are a very high fever which is followed closely by a thick yellowy-green discharge from the eyes and nose. Shortly after this a cough is evident and the dog will look and become very ill. Together with these symptoms, the dog will vomit badly, the bowels will become upset and the motions will be loose. One of the last stages is that the dog's central nervous system becomes affected, causing fits.

### *Hepatitis*

The very mention of this disease sent shivers through the spines of many of the breeders of yesteryear. Before immunisation, many kennels were nearly wiped out by this virulent illness that could sweep through a group of dogs like wildfire. Even nowadays, in highly acute cases, this disease can prove fatal if not properly treated. Symptoms are incessant vomiting and diarrhoea together with a very high temperature. As you can see, these symptoms are similar to those of some other illnesses and this is why expert attention is needed to be absolutely sure of hepatitis infection.

## *Leptospirosis*

This disease is transmitted to the dog via the rat or, to be more specific, through the rat's urine. It is therefore always advisable never to leave down any bowls of water in outside runs overnight. Not that you may have rats, but the chance that the odd one may filter in from somewhere, even in built-up areas, is always possible. As with the two preceding conditions, this disease can prove fatal.

## *Parvo-Virus*

This is the modern-day killer disease. Before a suitable vaccine was found many dogs, particularly young puppies and old dogs, lost their lives through this terrible illness.

The frightening aspect of this virus is that a dog may appear to be perfectly healthy in the morning but by the afternoon he could be dead. This is a highly infectious disease causing vomiting and acute gastro-enteritis which in turn can lead to internal bleeding. In puppies especially, the disease is known to attack the heart, causing sudden death.

Thanks to modern technology and drugs, a vaccine has been discovered which is incorporated into the initial course of immunisation given to puppies. Your veterinary surgeon will advise you of the need of and time for boosters to be administered; he or she will probably recommend a parvovirus booster a few weeks after the main combined vaccination. A booster for all these diseases is necessary approximately once every twelve months.

## *Gastro-Enteritis*

This complaint on its own can cause a certain amount of distress to the dog and if not treated quickly can become quite dangerous. It can be caused by a virus or merely by changing the dog's diet. A morsel scavenged by your dog that was perhaps past its 'sell by' date can also cause this nasty stomach upset. The motions become very soft and loose until they are very watery indeed. Dehydration is one of the main complications here, so once again quick and efficient attention is needed. This complaint can accompany several of the dangerous diseases or illnesses so never trifle with this and always seek expert attention. Your vet may inject medication which soothes the lining of the stomach and the bowels. You may possibly be prescribed tablets or a kaolin-type mixture to help ease this condition.

Your vet will probably tell you not to offer the dog any food for at least twenty-four hours and then when the diet is resumed it will need to be very light. A white of an egg may be recommended or a little cooked chicken with some boiled rice. Up until the time the dog is allowed food, you may also be advised to restrict the intake of water by offering him a few sips of boiled water which has been allowed to cool. Never deviate from any advice that your vet gives regarding this until you are given the 'all clear' because the slightest thing may trigger the condition off again, making the dog miserably ill.

## Other Ailments

### *Eyes*

**Ulceration** One of the weakest and most vulnerable spots on a Pekingese is its eyes, and if care is not taken ulceration can quickly set in. A simple draught, for instance, can make the eye start to turn blue; a speck of dust on a windy day, once again, can cause this condition through irritation. Another quite common cause is when a bitch is due, or is in season: this blue eye can suddenly manifest itself and is generally referred to as 'a condition eye'. The occasional affray can of course lead to ulceration through direct injury to the area of the eye itself. Another cause is the presence of enlarged folds of skin under the eye which can actually rub on the surface of the eyeball, once again leading to ulceration. It is not unknown for another set of short eyelashes to grow on the inside rim of the eyelid which can cause irritation, resulting in blueness of the eye.

You will learn from long experience of breeding to recognise these conditions and the most likely causes. With your daily routine of grooming your dog, you will immediately notice any blue haziness on the edge of the eyeball, or a small pin-prick on the eye itself. Your veterinary surgeon will issue you with the necessary ointment which should be administered quickly, repeating as often as possible throughout the day. With immediate and constant care and attention, the eyes should clear and quickly return to normal.

**Ingrowing Lashes** Veterinary assistance is essential for the removal of ingrowing lashes. We did have one dog who had this condition as a youngster and, with the aid of a pair of blunted tweezers, we removed the lashes as they grew again. Eventually they ceased to reappear and he lived to a good age with no further sign of the problem. However, we do not recommend that you rush to get your tweezers and practise on your dog. Leave this to your vet. We were very fortunate in the fact that this particular dog was one that did not mind what you did to him; he had the greatest faith and would sit quite quietly and patiently, never flinching. There are others that we may have had a little more trouble with had they been unlucky enough to suffer from this complaint.

## *Heatstroke*

Owing to its heavy coat and flat face, a Pekingese is liable to feel the heat and so is particularly susceptible to heatstroke. We have described the measures which can be taken to prevent the body temperature rising to a dangerous level in Chapter 9 (*see* page 143). However, should this occur, you will need to take immediate steps to bring the body temperature quickly back down to normal.

A dog suffering from heatstroke shows obvious signs of distress, the panting becomes exaggerated and he has great difficulty in breathing. The expression becomes wild, the dog is on the verge of collapse if he has not collapsed already and, at the same time, the bowel may lose control.

If you are at home immediately put your dog in a freezer chest, or large freezer compartment if you own one, using a towel to protect the dog's feet from the frost. Hold the dog there for long enough for him to become relaxed. Do not shut the freezer door or leave the dog alone. If this method is not possible, immerse the dog up to its neck in a bath of cold water. Hold his head and body so that he does not panic and slip under the water. If someone can get ice-packs or ice-cubes to throw in the bath, then all the better.

Be vigilant in both cases and do not leave the poor animal in case he panics. These are extreme but necessary measures and could possibly cause the dog to go into shock, but at this stage you have no other options open to you. We would advise that once the dog has become a little calmer, and his breathing is less strained and frightening, you ring the vet and ask him to call. Do not take the dog to the surgery as it will do him no good at all to take a ride in a hot car. Even if outwardly your dog seems to have completely recovered, you should still consult your vet and ask for an examination to be carried out. In severe cases of heatstroke the strain on the heart can be immeasurable, so always have the dog checked over for your own peace of mind.

## *Bad Backs*

Whether it is due to the shape of the Pekingese, maybe because of the slightly longer back of some of them, it seems that bad backs are not an uncommon ailment.

The classic symptom of this is the dog emitting a scream if you try to pick him up, tensing himself at the same time. The area around the abdomen appears rigid and taut to the touch. The dog will seem quiet and will possibly try to lie stretched out, usually on a cold floor in some part of the house or kennel. Of course, these symptoms relate to other conditions and if, like the rest of us, you are not a fully qualified vet, then expert help is needed right away, plus the necessary medication to ease any pain or discomfort.

This agony for your dog can be caused by several things, the most common of which is a disc that has slipped out of place, trapping a nerve in the process. A strain on the back can also cause the dog to show great signs of discomfort. Both can cause him to lose his mobility and, in severe cases, collapse completely.

Depending on the severity of the condition, your vet will prescribe certain drugs and in most cases will order the patient to be kept rested in total confinement. The dog is only to be let out to answer the call of nature, and then must be returned to his pen. The area of confinement should be of a size that allows him to turn around and to lie stretched out comfortably. It should not be too large an area, for that will defeat the object of the exercise. Most probably, as the dog begins to show signs of recovery, your veterinary surgeon may allow him to move to larger quarters while still being restrained. With care and attention, and resisting the urge to let the dog rejoin his friends too soon, very often a quite healthy recovery is made. It should be stressed, though, that you must bear in mind that a weakness is still present there. The dog should not be allowed to run about with any dogs that are too boisterous, or be allowed to run up and down stairs for this will only cause the problem to recur at some later date.

## *Stings*

A dog seen snapping at flies is a fairly harmless and amusing sight but, unfortunately, your little dog cannot tell the difference between a fly and a wasp. Bees, of course, are also potentially dangerous, but it seems to be the wasp that causes the most problems.

If a dog is stung externally by a bee you may be able to see the sting left in the skin, usually around the area of the muzzle. With your fingernails, or tweezers, this can be plucked out. If this is done early enough it can help to reduce the swelling slightly. A little bicarbonate of soda dabbed on the wound will help give relief also. Vinegar or lemon juice should be applied to a wasp sting.

The danger becomes more apparent if the dog is stung in the mouth or at the back of the throat when swelling can block the airway. Urgent help is needed if the dog is to be saved. Administer orally half a 4mg Piriton tablet, and immediately rush the dog to the vet where you will need to inform them of the urgency, and emergency measures will be taken. It is always a good idea to stock in your medicine cabinet some anti-histamine tablets, such as Piriton, which can be obtained as a non-prescription drug.

## *Constipation*

This is a condition causing symptoms opposite to those of gastro-enteritis, but equally upsetting and painful for the dog. If you notice that your dog has not passed a motion during the day, keep him under observation to see if this rights itself the following day. If he still does not show any signs of 'performing' and is in discomfort, a little liquid paraffin that can be obtained from your local chemist may be given, administered orally. Alternatively, if this does not work, give the dog a small saucer of cooked liver. If there is no obvious improvement and he is becoming increasingly unhappy then it is best to take him along to the surgery for diagnosis.

## *Cysts*

Two common types of cyst are the *sebaceous* and the *inter-digital*.

**Sebaceous Cysts** These appear on the skin and are often quite deep-rooted. It is possible for them to be cleared by gently squeezing them after bathing with warm water. Some of these cysts appear as small boils initially, eventually bursting. Once the pus has been removed, bathe them with warm water and apply a little medication (obtained from your vet) into the crevice. Sometimes these cysts appear as enlarged pores containing pus. These need to be cleansed of any poison to aid their healing process and treated in the same way.

**Inter-Digital Cysts** These appear between the pads or toes of the feet causing soreness which makes walking very difficult. Poultices applied to the area affected help to draw the poison out and bring some relief but, if the condition does not seem to improve after applying these and a good antibiotic cream, consult your vet as soon as possible.

## *Anal Glands*

An impacted anal gland can cause immense discomfort to the dog and, if left untreated, may result in an abscess which will eventually erupt, exuding a large amount of pus. Signs that the glands are impacted are when the dog drags his bottom along the ground or when he keeps swinging round to bite the area around his tail. Your vet can empty the glands quickly and painlessly and, by having this done regularly, you can prevent abscesses forming.

In the event that an abscess does develop, the area around the anus becomes red and swollen. Bathe regularly with warm water (not so hot to the touch that it burns but warm enough to help draw the abscess) using either cotton wool or a poultice. Eventually the abscess will burst, the area will need to be thoroughly cleaned and a veterinary antibiotic cream applied. Consult your vet who can prescribe the correct medication. There will be a distinct hole where the abscess was before it burst; check this daily for the formation of any poison and draw this off. Bathe the area once again, placing more cream over the spot. Do not allow it to heal over without always checking the abscess daily, for otherwise traces of poison left behind will cause a further condition to develop at a later date.

## Nursing Your Dog

In some cases of severe illness, constant care and attention is needed for your sick dog. You may have to administer the various drugs prescribed by your vet. Generally these will come in liquid or tablet form.

If the symptom of an illness is loss of appetite, there is no point in offering the dog a tablet in a tit-bit; you will need to administer the tablet manually. Open the dog's mouth, taking care to hold his head at a comfortable angle, and place the tablet at the back of the tongue. Close the mouth and, holding the head steady, stroke the throat gently to make the dog swallow. Always double-check that the tablet has been taken for Pekingese are masters of the art of concealing tablets in the side of their mouths.

The simplest way to give a dog any liquid medication is with the aid of a needleless syringe. Placing the syringe towards the back of the mouth, nearer the side, squeeze in a little at a time until the dog has taken the entire dosage. Be prepared for some to be lost during this process; if you give small amounts at a time, though, the loss should be minimal.

When nursing a dog, try to allow yourself an isolation area, space permitting. If this is not practical, try to ensure that the patient is kept in a part of the house where he is unlikely to come into contact with others, especially in the case of a contagious disease.

When the condition is highly infectious always make sure that the dog's bedding is either thoroughly disinfected or disposed of safely, preferably burnt. When he is strong enough to want to go outside to relieve himself, allow him to exercise in an area where no other dog is likely to go.

Incontinence can occur when a dog is ill or aged. Whether the condition is temporary or permanent depends on the cause; some cases respond very well to treatment. But for a dog who is normally clean this can be a very distressing time for him. To help the dog retain a sense of pride and to make it easier for yourself always ensure that there is paper down at easily accessible points.

## Old Age

Old age comes to us all and, unfortunately, in the canine world it seems to come so quickly. Pekingese on the whole enjoy a reasonably good life span and one always hopes that when the time comes for one's little friend to pass on, he will go quietly in his sleep.

Sometimes it is left to you to make the final decision. It is very easy to want to hold onto that little dog for as long as possible: it is only natural to feel this way. However, one has to remember that your friend may not be enjoying life anymore, but is unable to tell you so. Perhaps the back legs are not as strong now as they used to be, and the dog cannot stand properly. Perhaps, too, the will to eat is disappearing very quickly and the dog is losing condition. As with old age in humans, things start to wind down and various organs gradually cease to function properly. Perhaps the little dog's digestion is not working as well as it used to, and he is having great difficulty in keeping any food down.

When that dreaded day comes and, in your heart of hearts, you will realise this, do not let your lifelong companion suffer any more; help this devoted friend by letting your vet perform the kindest act of all.

# 14

# Kennels and Dogs of Today and Yesterday

Over the years since this breed was first introduced into the United Kingdom, several books have been written, especially in the first half of this century, outlining the various great dogs of these years. Many of you, being avid breed fanciers, will have copies of these in your collections, as do we. In this chapter we aim to wander through these annals of history, emerging at the other end with some contemporary dogs and owners. In other words, those in whose hands lies the future of our breed.

There have been so many great dogs and kennels during the twentieth century that it is almost impossible to list them all. Therefore, we pray forgiveness of those who may go unmentioned due to lack of space.

Over the years many dogs have emerged to stamp their mark, be it in the way of success in the ring, or by passing their attributes on to their progeny who have continued to carry the banner for their sire or dam.

Champion Goodwood Lo has to have been one of the most famous dogs in the breed for the pure and simple reason that he was the first in the United Kingdom. We also made mention in Chapter 1 of many of his fellow pioneers who established our breed on these shores all those years ago.

When the breed Pekingese is mentioned, one name that is known as being synonymous with it was of course the Alderbourne kennel, that literally spanned the century. This kennel was started by the late Mrs Ashton Cross and was carried on with the aid of her daughters, principally Marjorie and Cynthia. Cynthia Ashton Cross was the last of this bastion of Pekingese heritage to die, and, although she lived enjoying the breed up to the end, the Alderbournes were no longer active in the show ring. As we have said, she always retained her interest in the breed and judged her last

Championship Show, which she had announced would be her swan-song, in 1977. This was the Invicta Pekingese Club's Championship Show; and her final two CC's were awarded to Cynthia Sterling's Sweet William of Devana, with May Robertshaw's Lotusgrange Shorona winning the bitch ticket.

There were many top-quality dogs bred at the Alderbourne kennel, at their home of Little Shardeloes at Amersham (a house once belonging to Sir Francis Drake) and then later at The Wilderness, Ascot.

Champion Chu-Erh of Alderbourne, of course, needs no introduction, himself a sire of many Champions within the breed. Chu-Erh's brother was Sutherland Ouen Teu T'ang, and we mentioned this famous combination in Chapter 1 as being one of the foundations of the breed in general as well as of this famous kennel.

Another well-known dog from here was Champion Yu Tong of Alderbourne. Those of you who are pedigree buffs will see his name appear behind many generations of today's winning dogs. Many of the Caversham stars were related to this mainstay.

Champion Caversham Ku Ku of Yam (*see* Fig 91) is the breed record holder. A recent survey was held involving Championship Show Judges, and this dog was regarded as the greatest dog of all

*Fig 91 Champion Caversham Ku Ku of Yam, 1955.*

time in the breed. Apart from holding the record of forty Challenge Certificates in the breed, he was also a very dominant sire. His Champion children in the United Kingdom alone came to nine. One of these famous children was in turn another prolific sire, Champion Ku Jin of Caversham.

The Caversham kennel of Pekingese was originally started with great success by Miss Mary De Pledge in 1921. Miss De Pledge eventually went into partnership with Mrs Herminie Lunham who was showing Pekingese in her own right under the prefix of Caleva. This lady became better known in later years as Mrs Herminie Warner Hill. The success and history that these two ladies created is legendary. After Miss De Pledge's death, the kennel name was carried on until Mrs Warner Hill's sudden death a few years ago.

Another of Champion Caversham Ku Ku's children was the Cruft's triple crown winner, Champion Ku Chik-Ku of Loofoo. Coincidentally, this record stands at this time, as does his father's. Ku Chik-Ku was one of several lovely Champions bred at the home of Mrs Richard Jones (known throughout the Pekingese world at home and abroad as Mrs 'Loofoo' Jones). Champions continued to be made up until the 1970s; type and quality still came through, and continued to do so right up until her death.

The Pekingese from Sammy North's Calartha kennel were renowned for their beautiful coats and especially their ear fringes. Many a breeder tried to discover the 'secret' but none ever did. Sammy North lived right down on the peninsula of Cornwall near the coast and bred such lovely dogs that, as with many of those named here, could be so useful to the breed had we them in our midst today. Champion Rikki of Calartha went over to the other side of the Atlantic to live, as did Champion Calartha Wee Bo Bo of Ecila (*see* Fig 92). These two Champions epitomised the dogs that this gentleman bred and nurtured.

Many of the breed's older and more established kennels will remember Roberta Ogle as a very colourful lady and breeder extraordinaire. One name out of just a few lovely dogs produced from this kennel was Champion Goofus Le Grisbie. Once again, this dog was a son of Champion Ku Ku of Yam out of an Alderbourne-bred bitch; this combination proved to be very successful for many of the kennels of yester-year. Another well-known dog that was campaigned successfully in this country, including winning Best of Breed at Cruft's in 1964, was English, American and Canadian Champion Goofus Bugatti, who, as his title suggests, went on to

*Fig 92 Champion Calartha Wee Bo Bo of Ecila. Bred by Mrs E.A. Williams. Owned by Mr S. North.*

further conquests overseas. After coming, seeing and conquering, he returned to his native land shortly afterwards.

William Hindley Taylor's Kyratown Pekingese need no introduction. His association with the breed started while he was still a schoolboy, and was regularly seen at the ringside avidly taking in everything he saw with his satchel slung over his back. He obviously learnt a lot, for his first (of many) Champions was bred while he was still a teenager; she was Champion San San of Kyratown. Another well-known bitch from this kennel was Champion Kyratown Lu Tong of Redstock who for many years held the breed record of being the top winning bitch, with thirty-three CC's.

A contemporary of the aforementioned breeder was Ethel Partridge who resided with her lovely Pekehuis Pekingese, amid the lovely garden setting of her home in Sir Harry's Road, Edgbaston. One of her home-bred daughters now holds the record of being the top winning bitch, which still stands at time of publication. She was Champion St Aubrey Pekehuis Petula (*see* Fig 93) who won in total thirty-seven CC's. The Pekehuis name still flies high although Mrs Partridge is no longer with us. She arranged that her kennel name be transferred to Winifred Mee after her death. Winifred had worked for her almost since leaving school, and was more a companion and

*Fig 93 Champion St Aubrey Pekehuis Petula. Top winning bitch, with 37 CC's. Owned and bred by the late Mrs E. Partridge.*

friend than employee. It was Winifred who piloted Petula to her record, and is also enjoying enormous success in her own right, too. Champion Pekehuis Sir Guy was the last dog to be bred by Ethel Partridge and is chasing the record for being the top living male Champion, which at present stands at twenty-six CC's. Sir Guy at the present time has gained twenty-five. In partnership with Winifred now is the husband and wife combination of Anne and Colin Tennant, although Winifred in the interim period had had considerable success in partnership with Joan Cross. These dogs were shown under the name of Pemyn. The sire of Ch. Sir Guy is a result of this partnership, Champion Pemyn Some Guy.

The original Toydom kennel was started in the early 1920s by Vandella Williams' mother, the late Alex Williams. Many of the people who knew her and remembered her, always remarked on her lovely dogs and her big hats! These hats really were her trademark. The kennel was originally founded in the far north where many of today's successful breeders reside. On moving down from Yorkshire to the South, the success of this kennel continued although, of course, with the outbreak of war showing was suspended. It was Champion Toydom Chien Mein who had the

*Fig 94 Champion Toydom Ts'Zee. Owned by the late Mrs A.C. Williams.*

accolade of being the youngest Champion at the outbreak of war. Other names synonymous with this earlier kennel were the two 'Manzees', Champion Toydom Manzee and his son Champion Toydom Manzee Tu. In fact, a plaster-cast head study was made of the former and it seems they have become quite a collector's item in this modern day.

In the 1950s another star emerged from this line, this time a grey and white parti-colour, who won in all eighteen CC's during his show career, including Best of Breed at Cruft's in 1956. This was a win repeated in 1982 by the new generation. The former was of course Champion Toydom Ts'Zee (*see* Fig 94), followed later by Champion Toydom A Touch of Class.

The St Aubrey kennel of Nigel Aubrey Jones and R. William Taylor have produced and campaigned, over their extensive career, some beautiful top winning dogs and continue to do so. One of these has had a great impact on the breed in the USA: American and Canadian Champion St Aubrey Laparata Dragon (*see* Fig 95) who resided with Ed Jenner of the Knolland Pekingese in the USA. Dragon was bred by Lilian Snooks of the Laparata kennel, who has enjoyed many years of successful breeding and showing in this

*Fig 95 American and Canadian Champion St Aubrey Laparata Dragon. Bred by Mrs L. Snook, owned by Mr E. Jenner.*

country. Champion Laparata Celestial Star, Champion Laparata Precious Madam and, the most recent, Champion Laparata Regal Star are just a few of the winning dogs produced by this clever breeder.

Dragon became a legend in his own time in America. Apart from being hard to beat in the show ring, he sired over one hundred Champions. Shortly after he died, the tributes and obituaries dedicated to him in an American breed magazine, The Orient Express, showed the depth of affection this dog had inspired in his adopted country.

Champion Mr Redcoat of Kanghe and the Honourable Mr Twee of Kanghe are two of the most famous names associated with the dogs bred and owned by the late Miss Queenie Mould. Both these dogs appear behind many of today's successful Pekingese, one of these being Champion Singlewell Wee Sedso (*see* Fig 96), the 'anchor man' of Pam Edmonds' world famous Singlewells. He, of course, is one of many top winning dogs of this famous kennel, and a photograph of another of these, the bitch Champion Singlewell T'Sai Magic can be found on page 88 (*see* Fig 35).

The great Champion Yu Yang of Jamestown has marked his place

*Fig 96 Champion Singlewell Wee Sedso. Owned and bred by Mrs P. Edmond.*

forever in the breed also. Owned by the late Jean Eisenman he encompassed what has since become known as the 'Jamestown' look – great substance and quality, masculine head and large, dark lustrous eyes. All these qualities have since been passed down through generations and still manifest themselves in some highly successful exhibits in the ring today. One of his equally famous progeny was Champion Chyanchy Ah Yang of Jamestown who was owned by the late partnership of Fred and Lily Sawyer. He in turn sired six Champions, while being the winner of a creditable number of CC's himself.

When you mention Jamestown and the two prolific sires Yu Yang and Ah Yang, one has to think of another sadly lamented brilliant Pekingese breeder, Beryl Prior, of the Sungarth kennel. Her lines, which proved highly successful for both herself and others, were founded on these two sires. Champion Sungarth Hi Jinks of Sunsalve was the first Champion for an up and coming young man in the breed in the early 1970s, Terry Nethercott. Sungarth Echo of Jamestown was bred at Sungarth when she resided at the Golden Lion, Winchester. He was, of course, the sire of Champion Shiarita Lingsam and in turn the grandsire of another legend, Champion

*Fig 97 Sungarth Kanga of Toydom. Bred by the late Mrs B. Prior, owned by Miss A. Summers and Miss V. Williams.*

*Fig 98 Champion Belknap El Dorado. Owned and bred by Mrs A. Horn.*

Shiarita Cassidy. Beryl's first Champion in the breed, although she was also a well-known breeder of Bulldogs and Bassets, was Champion Sungarth Camelia, a daughter of Ah Yang. Camelia's dam was Sungarth Anchusa who in turn was the mother of a dog we personally owe so much to – combined with another dominant line from Champion Singlewell Wee Sedso – Sungarth Kanga of Toydom (*see* Fig 97).

Champion Belknap el Dorado (*see* Fig 98) is probably one of the most famous Champions to have emerged from Donhead Hall. Once again, another breeder has found the right combination and continued after many years, consistently producing top winning stock. Two black and tan Champions were campaigned by the Belknaps, a male, Champion Belknap Nero, and a bitch, Champion Scarteena by Belknap. The latter had a very consistent winning puppyhood, gaining two tickets during this time. One day after her first birthday she won her third and qualifying CC which gave her her crown. Champion Suzie Wong of Jamestown was the early foundation in this now world famous kennel. Since those early days they have gone from strength to strength. Our own Champion Toydom Modesty Forbids (*see* Fig 13, page 40) was sired by 'El Dorado' out of Toydom No Secrets (*see* Fig 83, page 172). 'Forbids' in his turn sired the brother and sister combination for the Belknaps, Champion Belknap Bravo and Champion Belknap Blush.

Pauline Bull registered her Changte prefix in 1930 and she must now be one of the very few showing kennels left from that time. The name Changte needs no introduction, for anyone involved in breeding and showing these delightful dogs will have heard this lady's name and will hark back to all the success she has enjoyed over the years. All her knowledge, combined with her breeding programme, came to fruition most spectacularly in the 1970s, although of course she was no stranger to high awards before this.

Champion Tudor Treasure of Changte (*see* Fig 99) is the grandam of one of the Changte's greatest-known sons, Champion Chuffys Charm of Changte (*see* Fig 100), who won seventeen CC's all told. Apart from accruing awards such as these in the ring, he was also an outstanding sire in the breed, being declared the top sire for 1973, 1974 and 1975. At this time, another Changte son was reaching for the stars, Champion Tsungli San Fou of Changte, who coincidentally was also the winner of 17 CC's.

Situated in Wakefield, the Changtes have some equally successful neighbours along the Pennines at Keighley; they are the Micklees.

*Fig 99 Champion Tudor Treasure at Changte. Owned and bred by Mrs P. Bull.*

The Micklee kennel of Joyce Mitchell was registered originally in 1946 and since that time has been campaigned over the years with great merit by Joyce and her husband Jack. Numerous Champions have been made up by this knowledgeable couple: Champion Tameko of Micklee, Champion Micklee Twee Jin, Champion Micklee Tarjeo, Champion Micklee Rocfard and Champion Micklee Rocs Ru-Ago are the latest in a long line of royal breeding.

Nowadays the dogs are registered purely in Joyce's name, for the reason that Jack is now regarded as one of the UK's top toy all-rounders which means that he is constantly sought for appointments in the UK. Because of this, and a Kennel Club rule that states you are unable to exhibit if one of a partnership is judging any other breed at that show, the only alternative was the transfer of these dogs into a single name. Over the years, the Micklees have won to date 152 Challenge Certificates and have bred a total of seventeen English Champions. Amid all this success, at Cruft's Dog Show in

*Fig 100 Champion Chuffys Charm of Changte. Owned and bred by Mrs P. Bull.*

1985, Champion Micklee Rocs Ru-Ago made these devotees of the breed very happy when he was awarded Reserve Best in Show.

Going further westwards along the M62 towards Macclesfield another top British kennel is situated. This is the kennel of Liz and Paul Stannard's Shiaritas. Of course, 'Cassidy' is the star, although these top breeders have produced a galaxy of Champions. To name but a few: Champion Shiarita Peter Pan, Champion Shiarita Hello Dolly and Champion Shiarita Diamond Lil. These three alone have won nearly fifty CC's, while Hello Dolly is, of course, the dam of their great stud dog.

Dorothy Dearn, with her now married daughter Heather Beard, have achieved fame with their Dorodea Kennel. Once again, top winning and producing stock and Champions have been born and campaigned from here. Two of the most famous ones immediately associated with these ladies are the lovely Champion Dorodea Petite Beurre and Champion Dorodea Yu Song.

Two kennels that are situated in the same vicinity are the Beaupres and Lotusgrange Pekingese. The former are now owned solely by Fiona Mirylees after many years success with her late mother

Elizabeth, or Betty, as she was affectionately known throughout the breed. Once again this kennel has reproduced their quality through their stud dogs and acquitted themselves highly in the show ring as well.

Champion Samotha Gay Lad of Beaupres (*see* Fig 101) we suppose has to be the dog one associates most of all with this strain. He sired several winning children including Champion Lady Gay of Beaupres, Champion Beaupres Likely Lad of Patrona, Champion Teijon Ching Ching and Champion Lotusgrange Maybelle. Another name associated with the kennel is Champion Beaupres Belle who was ultimately made BIS All Breeds at Darlington Championship Show in 1975. The amazing fact of this grand bitch was that the vast majority of her wins came when she was over seven years old.

Champion Some Man of Lotusgrange is fast proving to be one of today's major sires. May Robertshaw first registered the prefix Lotusgrange in 1954 and has, since that time, bred six English Champions and won thirty-three CC's. Overall, her stud dogs have proved a force to be reckoned with, their progeny having been credited with forty-eight CC's.

*Fig 101 Champion Samotha Gay Lad of Beaupres. Bred by Mrs Coupland, owned by the late Mrs E. Mirylees and Miss F. Mirylees.*

The Mathena Pekingese enjoyed much success for many many years. The dogs were registered in the name of Yvonne Hoynck Van Papendrecht, but in the last few years of their show career they were primarily shown by her late husband John. Champion Mingulay Seumas of Mathena was the last Champion to be shown by them, but their kennel name lives on, down through two litter sisters, Misha of Mathena at Toydom and Mathena Nanette of Toydom. The former is the dam of three English Champions: Champion Toydom Modesty Permits (*see* Fig 32, page 82), Champion Toydom's Quite Outrageous and Champion Toydom The Drama Queen. Nanette is the dam of Pam Hunter's Champion Tirakau Dream Design, and of her latest glamour girl, Champion Tirakau Royal Replica.

Ella Pilgrim is one of the breed's most respected figures having founded her kennel in 1936. The name Chintoi was taken from the two words 'Chinese Toydog' taking the first four and three letters from each respectively. She does confess that she changed the 'Toy' to 'Toi' to give a more authentic and oriental flavour. Twee Jin of Chintoi encompasses five generations of Chintoi breeding on his maternal side through Che Wei of Chintoi (*see* Fig 102) who was born in 1938. In turn, he has passed his qualities to seven Champion children. Also bred here was the lovely Champion bitch, Champion Cheryl of Chintoi, herself the dam of four Champions.

*Fig 102 Che Wei of Chintoi. Owned and bred by Mrs E. Pilgrim.*

Although the Chintois are nowadays rarely seen in the ring, it was only a few years ago that the last Champion was made up: Champion Chintoi Chelsfield Golden Guinea. He is a son of Champion Belknap El Dorado, bred by Nina Brown and piloted by his owner Ella to his title.

The Copplestone Pekingese were owned by the late Yvonne Bentinck who was a stalwart of the breed. Not only was she involved in showing pedigree Pekingese – one of her most famous being International Champion Copplestone Pu Zin, a glamorous, silver fawn – but she was also a well-known and respected figure in the world of cats.

Two white Champions made their mark in the breed, the first being Champion Silverdjinn Splash, owned and bred by Norah MacFarlane who with her late husband Jimmy were two popular figures in the breed. Their logo of Silverdjinn on their car was always very distinctive. The Hydlewood kennel of Hilda Garwood is also widely remembered for several top-flight dogs and bitches. One of these was the white Champion Pleiku Snowshan of Hydlewood, with two more popular ones being Champion Wingwood Jamie of Hydlewood and the miniature Champion Hydlewood Shantung.

The Kettlemere Pekingese were renowned for their lovely bitch Champions Matilda and Margo of Kettlemere. The kennel was started originally by Lilian Shipley but, since her death, daughter Joyce has continued to keep the name alive by showing and winning, most notably with Champion Lien Prunella of Kettlemere.

The Cheranganis were also of an easily recognisable type; such dogs as Champion Cherangani Chips, Cherangani Dart, Champion Cherangani Chips Chime all had that distinct feature that aligns certain dogs to their distinctive kennel type.

Champion Linsown Ku-Che-Pet and Champion Linsown Ku-Che-Tu (the former being a son of Champion Ku-Jin of Caversham) were owned and bred by Yvonne Pownall. These were both very distinctive dogs, and the latter in particular was a very popular and dominant stud dog in the late 1970s.

The list is endless: Mrs Mabel Fyer's Chungkings, Sammy Lowe's Dell Pekingese, Mrs Lilian Drake and her Drakehurst kennel, and the Greymount kennel of Miss Furneaux-Dawson (again one of our older established kennels but very much in evidence in the show ring today; many will remember Champion Greymount Wee Bambee in the 1970s). Betty Simper has enjoyed much success over the years and is still active today with her Wellbarn kennel name. Also getting a lot of pleasure in going to many shows today is 'Mickey' Brabant-Holbrook whose Brabantas need no introduction. There were the Sunshens of Eleanor Colomb, the Ifields of Ray Chandler, Lady Isabelle Throckmorton's Coughton Pekingese, the delightful Alison Wilson's Wanstrows which included the lovely Champion Salote of Wanstrow. In the 1930s and 1940s the Manstone Pekingese were one of the major kennels, belonging to Mrs Stains. Also notable were Mrs Alison Rae's Perryacres dogs – we could go on and on.

Each and every one of the aforementioned people have played their part, with others we have not even managed to mention. But all of these, whether they are listed here or not, will go down in Pekingese archives as having played their own special part.

Let us return to the present day where the breed is in the hands of some already mentioned and well-known names and some new breeders who have begun to make their way.

Sadie Stagg's Chophoi kennel has been around for as long as most people can remember. Her current star, the male Chophoi Silver Dollar, has to date one Challenge Certificate and several Reserves.

Alan and Ruby Charlton have had many years of experience in the breeding and showing of Pekingese. They had been absent from the United Kingdom for several years, going to, among other places, Australia. Their present star is Brentoy Country Satin, while another Brentoy was awarded her title of Champion, campaigned by their married daughter Brenda Oades, Champion Brentoy Cherry Blossom. This bitch, in fact, returned with the family from overseas where she had also been shown. Their other claim to fame is that they were the breeders of Champion Beaupres Belle.

Another family affair are the combined kennels of Wanscara and Annesuz although they show under their separate prefixes. Jack and June Whitehead have done well with their Wanscaras including winning a CC with Wanscara Buddleia who is also included in many of their pedigrees. Sue Whitehead has also bred a couple of very nice dogs who are well on their way to their titles abroad.

The Wanscaras owe much of their interest originally to the Highfoo kennel of Peggy Winston. Highfoo Precious Shadow won a CC and Highfoo March Morning was another consistent winner for this kennel. The most recent Champion sired by Champion Jay Trump of Sunsalve is Maurice and Sheila Smith's Champion Shobris Toy Boy, who has also several RCC's accredited to him, including Cruft's.

Toyboy lives in the north-east of the country, while two other well known breeders live close by, Judith Risbey's Pascans and Pat Drew with her Mahjon Pekingese.

In the early 1980s a young puppy went to America to live with Bob and Mary Anne Jackson at Fourwinds Farm, near Chicago. This young man did very well for himself both in the ring and by siring some lovely puppies. He became known as American Champion Cassidy T'sun (needless to say who his sire is!).

Pat Drew recently made up her black and tan bitch, Champion Mahjon Oriana, while Judith Risbey also has a bitch who made it all the way to her title, Champion Pascan Perfect Lady.

The Penang Pekingese are not often exhibited these days; their owners Jimmy and Dorothy Simpson have business commitments and are also actively involved in Papillons. Champion Penang Kung Fu emerges from the history books as a name to remember, while there is a more recent star, Champion St Sanja Trumps Upp of Penang. Trumps Upp was bred by Ann and Barry Offilier, who have in the last two years made up two Champions of their own, Champion St Sanja Prim 'n' Proper, Trumps Upp's full sister, and Champion St Sanja The Thought Of You.

The Thought of You is sired by Eileen Newman's prepotent dog Champion Rosayleen Casino Royale. Another daughter of his is the newest star on the horizon for Pam Hunter, Champion Tirakau Royal Replica. Pam returned from New Zealand in the 1970s with her husband Dave, two children and a couple of their favourite Pekingese. One of these was eventually mated to Toydom Trump Card and the result was Tirakau The Seductress who won a RCC. Since then she has campaigned Champion Hidden Talent at Toydom (who is featured in Fig 78, page 163) to his Championship. She has had other successes with Champion Tirakau Dream Design, also winning a CC with a daughter of Hidden Talent, Tirakau Hidden Havoc.

Champion Ebernoe Afterthought won a multitude of CC's for the partnership of Malcolm Watson and Steve Parkinson, being the Top Winning Pekingese, 1986. Malcolm originally handled for Olive Mellor of the Clareview Pekingese when they both lived in Ireland. Champion Clareview Eileen was made an English Champion with Malcolm handling her to her title. Since the partnership that owned 'Afterthought' broke up, she has retired and lives with Olive Mellor. Malcolm still takes an interest in the show scene, although due to other commitments has to restrict his involvement to the occasional judging appointment.

Another breeder who maintains an interest in the breed among other activities is the owner of the Fonalds Pekingese, Erica Crouse, whose Fonalds Perchance To Dream, after having won one CC and two RCC's, had to retire due to a spinal injury.

May Young (who is a highly successful exhibitor of Rough Collies as well, going under the kennel name of Ugony) made up a litter brother and sister into Champions, Champion Adlungs Rah Rah and Champion Adlungs Sweet Charity, both sired by Champion Belknap Bravo. She has also made up another Champion in this breed, Champion Singlewell Little Else, a daughter of Champion Singlewell Wee Sedso. Apparently Pam Edmond christened her this for at that particular time she felt that she had 'little else' to show.

When you say that the strength of a kennel is in its bitches, then Tilly Brickwood's Teijon kennel is proof of that. She very rarely keeps a dog and the success she has achieved over the years comes from her very dominant bitch line, mated to well-bred dogs. Champion Teijon Ching Ching and Champion Teijon Shy Won both won exceptionally well, as did her Champion Teijon Linetta.

Champion Fearnvale Potters Viola, won her title for her owners Gordon and Marian Fearn. Apparently the first parti-colour Champion to be bred and shown by the owners, this beautiful bitch won many hearts and quickly gained her crown. They are now enjoying success with another home-bred daughter, Fearnvale Angel Star, a daughter of Champion Laparata Regal Star. Their Teijon Pansi Potter at Fearnvale who was bred by Tilly Brickwood is the mother of four CC-winning children, Fearnvale Ebony Baroness, Fearnvale My Lady Potter, Fearnvale Bravado and their Champion bitch also.

Lyn Taylor (Rarta) is another up and coming kennel and has founded her breeding lines on Champion Jay Trump of Sunsalve and Toydom lines. The Silverwillow kennel of John and Barbara McNulty have one Champion to date, Champion Silverwillow Gretel a daughter of Champion Shiarita Cassidy, while their male by him, Silverwillow Ku-Jin, has at present one CC also.

The Algol kennel of Anne Tompkins is now situated in the Midlands, after having resided for most of her life in the south of the country. She has mainly based her breeding programme on the lines of the Singlewell strain. Her long-time travelling companion and once near neighbour is Eileen Maycock. Eileen originally started out with a strong black line of good brood bitches. Quite a strong Belknap influence is predominant in these bitches. From these beginnings have come some consistently winning dogs, including

Dratsum Midshipman Hendrix 1CC, while her Dratsum Captain Courageous also notched up some very worthy wins.

As mentioned in Chapter 9, distance is no object. People literally travel miles and miles. From Northern Ireland and Eire, breeders make the journey to the shows on the mainland of Britain. Mrs Watter's Yankuis hold their own well in all competition, while a not so frequent visitor nowadays but consistently so up to a few years ago was Winifred Crowe of the Colindene Pekingese.

Several regular exhibitors come over from the Channel Isles, including Pat Dale (Ksarina), Christine Mace (Kalastina) and Eileen McFadden (Mearnskirk). All year round, these intrepid travellers pack their dogs and show gear and head for the airport. Sometimes the plane only holds a few people and they may have a long journey to the show from wherever they land, but they are never daunted.

Talking of island folk, we also have breeders on the Isle of Wight who come over on the early morning ferry, and then set off to drive to the show site wherever that may be. Carol Greenaway and Mrs Marlow-Matthews are regular travelling companions. Another islander, Betty Kettell, is a regular visitor to shows on the mainlaind too.

Champion Ikoura Benjamin was campaigned to his title by George Baxter who has a long haul down the motorways from Scotland to various parts of England or Wales or, alternatively, across the sea to take in the Irish shows also.

Oakmere is a prefix widely known and belongs to that dedicated and popular duo Arnold and Olive Clay. Not only have they bred some top winning dogs in their time, but they are dedicated to the extent that they are involved in many aspects of the administration side of the dog world, turning their hands to most things. Committee work, stewarding and printing, nothing daunts them. One of the breed's great favourites was owned by them – Oakmere Dolly Daydream of Upcot – an enchanting little parti-colour bitch that did extremely well in the show ring here.

Some of us like to be at the shows and in the ring, while there are others that, although they enjoy this as well, are behind-the-scenes people. Clare Scott is one such person; we are sure that she would not mind us referring to her as so. When she shows her Tonbuk Pekingese, she achieves good results, although we suspect she prefers the rearing of her puppies and everything that pertains to this.

Bill and Maureen Grant have become more involved in the show world since Bill retired from the RAF. He is now engrossed in running his own business but, as this is to do with printing and a large section of his work is devoted to pedigrees and all stationery related to dog people and shows, this helps them combine work with pleasure. They won a Challenge Certificate with Sushima Jetsetter under breed specialist Lilian Snook and are also doing quite well with their young male Sushima True Blue.

Phil and Jackie Jones made up their first Champion in the breed in 1988, Champion Bramblefields Berangaria, although they have been involved in the breed for many years now. They have recently started another young lady on the ladder towards stardom; this is another home-bred bitch, Bramblefields Organza.

Another successful breeder is Joan Stokoe of the Josto Pekingese who has had years of experience in this breed and in the process bred some magnificent stock. Champion Josto Airs 'n' Graces, Champion Josto Royal Flush and Champion Josto Madam Gaye at Sunsalve – these names speak for themselves. Nowadays this lady finds the travelling to shows a little beyond her, and now has a partner in Audrey Dungey who shows the dogs for her all over the country.

Anne Whitehead of the Weesann Pekingese has really been hitting the high spots in the last twelve months or so, after several years in the breed. Her Etive Sonnet of Weesann, who was bred by Di Holman of Etive fame, has a clutch of RCC's to her credit. Anne is known for her fascinating advertisements, with all her dogs sounding like characters from Wind in the Willows. They are very entertaining and light-hearted which can't be bad!

Champion Wei Sing Prai Pollyanna was owned and bred by Nancy Kerkin, winning a total of twelve CC's. Another top-flight bitch from this kennel was Champion Pixie of Wei Sing Prai who is herself the grandam of another Champion, Leonie Rolfe Hazell's Champion Sunsalve Queen Bee of Lejervis, bred by Terry Nethercott.

The husband and wife partnership of Don and Daphne Lee started in the breed with a Champion Pocket Peke son, Josto Red Toff. To say he was his own worst enemy in the ring, we feel, would be an accurate description. He was a quality little dog who more than often threw a very good chance away. Being thoroughly captivated by him and the breed, they persevered and through him have come to learn the meaning of success. Jennifer Sim's first English Champion, Charlot the Harlot, was sired by him.

Two of the breed's present-day success stories belong to the Jonsville Pekingese and the Yakee Pekingese, the former with their second Champion in the breed, Champion Jonsville Daytime Lover, owned and bred by John, Doreen and Gary Thomas, who was

*Fig 103 The end of a good day. International and Nordic Champion Royceland Lapaloma for Toydom. Second top dog, all breeds, Norway, 1987 and 1988; Nordic Winner 1987. Top dog, all breeds, 1989.*

named as Top Toy Dog 1988. Bert Easdon and Philip Martin continue to produce and show top winning Pekingese, the most notable being Champion Yakee For Your Eyes Only. Let us not forget, though, Champion Yakee Patent Pending, Champion Yakee Gentlemen Prefer and Champion Yakee The Hoi Polloi.

Geoffrey Davis of the Genderlee Pekingese has been showing and has been associated with this breed for as long as many can remember. Apart from enjoying success with his own kennel, he was seen showing up to a few years ago, and with great results, some of the Cheranganis for Eileen Stewart, who was unable to get to many shows at the time.

Two more devoted and dedicated breeders who travel the length and breadth of the country from their home in South Wales are Mr and Mrs Symmonds who, with home-bred son Eirlyn Fly Cracker, a Champion Jay Trump grandson, have amassed several RCC's.

To present a Pekingese is a task that needs a lot of care and attention; to present a white Pekingese needs even more dedication. Masters of this are the husband and wife team Ron and Tina Bacon who show their Bahho Petite Ajax to absolute perfection.

Another lady who showed her dogs to the peak of perfection and was so elegant herself was the late Lyd Kinnersley who died quite recently. She was a breeder who never lost interest in the breed, and even up until recent times would attend a local Club Show with the help of a relative. Her parti-colour dog Champion Tushos Pao Pei Boy of Pendarvis was the most recent success of her involvement in this breed when he won Best of Breed at Cruft's for two consecutive years, and in one of these years was also declared Best In Show at the great northern show, the Manchester Championship Show.

We cannot forget to mention one of our oldest breeders, Iris Driscoll of the Ladycross Pekingese. This amazing lady shared her love and successes in the breed with her late husband, and even now well into her nineties she still manages to go to some of the Club Shows near her home, looking quite sprightly. She is the patron of the parent club of the breed, the Pekingese Club, and still attends some of the meetings. They say that breeding and showing keeps you young, and Iris really is proof of that.

As we near the end of our journey through this delightful and entrancing breed, we hope we have managed to introduce you to its history along with the various aspects of breeding and showing. Also, we hope that we have been able to introduce you, in some small way, to the Pekingese fraternity of breeders and exhibitors alike.

We all have our ups and downs along the way but that is all part and parcel of avid competition. Let us leave you with the thought that you can make some very good friends in the dog world and in the process also have a hobby that completely absorbs you.

And when the day is over, the most wonderful aspect is that you have the undivided loyalty and complete devotion of a truly magnificent animal, the Pekingese, one-time companion of Emperors.

# Appendix 1

## Clubs and Associations within the United Kingdom

**Birmingham Pekingese Association**
Secretary: Mrs O.M. Clay, 5 Lammascote Road, Stafford ST1 63TA
Tel. 0785 42940

**Bristol, Bath and West of England Pekingese Association**
Secretary: Mrs. B. Keen, 33 Lower Down Road, Portishead, Avon.
Tel. 0272 848231

**British Pekingese Club**
Secretary: Mrs D. Dearn, Ramore, 192 Queen Victoria Road, Tupton, nr. Chesterfield S42 6DW.
Tel. 0246 864261

**Forth and Tay Pekingese Club**
Secretary: Mr J.S. Matthews, 5 Sharp Terrace, Grangemouth, Lothian Region KF3 8PN.

**Invicta Pekingese Club**
Secretary: Mr D. Chance, 36 High Street, Caythorpe, Grantham, Lincs NG32 3DS.
Tel. 0400 72622

**London and Provincial Pekingese Club**
Secretary: Mrs S. Stagg, Springfield House, Pavilion Road, Aldershot, Hants.
Tel. 0252 28143

**North of Ireland Pekingese Club**
Secretary: Mrs W. Crowe, Colindene, 674 Crumlin Road, Belfast 14.
Tel. 0232 744347

**North of Scotland Pekingese Club**
Secretary: Mr and Mrs Gunn, Kirkden House, Letham, Angus DD8 2QF.
Tel. 030 781 296

**North of England Pekingese Club**
Secretary: Mr M. Smith, F. Boll P.B. Phil, 84 Woodlands Road, Shotley Bridge, Co. Durham.
Tel. 0207 504269

**The Pekingese Club**
Secretary: Mrs J. Mitchell, Brow Cottage, Whalley Lane, Denholme, nr. Bradford, Yorks 8DB 4LJ.
Tel. 0274 834968

**Pekin Palace Dog Association**
Secretary: Mrs L. Snook, 13 Briarscroft Road, Brighton, E. Sussex BN2 6LL.
Tel. 0273 32096

**Pekingese Reform Association**
Secretary: Miss V. Williams, Berrylands Farm, Stanford, Pirbright, Surrey GU24 ODG.
Tel. 0483 233377

**Pekingese Sleeve Dog Club**
Secretary: Mrs O. Clay, 5 Lammascote Road, Stafford ST1 63TA.
Tel. 0785 42940

**Red Rose Pekingese Club**
Secretary: Mrs B. McNulty, 16 Fairhurst Drive, Little Hulton, Walkden, Manchester.
Tel. 061 702 8295

**Scottish Pekingese Association**
Secretary: Mr G. Baxter, 154 Halbeath Road, Dunfermline, Fife KY11 4LB.
Tel. 0383 724368

**South Wales Pekingese Association**
Secretary: Mrs J.S. Jones, Ynshir Farm, Quakers Yard, Treharris, Mid Glam.
Tel. 0443 410563

**Ventura Pekingese Club**
Secretary: Mrs M. Lyster, 62 Fleetwood Avenue, Holland on Sea, Essex.
Tel. 0255 812403

**Yorkshire and Eastern Counties Pekingese Club**
Secretary: Mr B. Offiler, Ivy House, 35 Leeds Road, Methley, nr Leeds LS26 9EH.
Tel. 0977 515377

# Appendix 2

## Clubs in the United States of America and Canada

**Allegheny Pekingese Club**
Corresponding Secretary: Robert Schuerch, RD1, Box 567, Ruffsdale, PA 15679.

**Arizona Pekingese Club**
Secretary: Pat Monahan, 6210 W. Earll Drive, Phoenix, AZ 85033.

**Canton Ohio Pekingese Club**
Secretary: Joyce Lietzke, 607 E. Lincoln Way, Lisbon, OH 44432.

**Citrus Capital Pekingese Club**
Secretary: Lois K. Lane, 1068 Venetian Parkway, Venice, FL 34292.

**Colony Pekingese Club of the Southern Tier**
Leo O'Leary, 803 Morlando Drive, Endicott, NY 13760.

**Delta Pekingese Club**
Secretary: Kathy Masilla, 2 Cleveland Court, Meitairie, LA 70003.

**Derbytown Pekingese Club**
Secretary: Betsy Jones, 2140 Bonnycastle Avenue, Louisville, KY 40205.

**Evergreen State Pekingese Club**
Secretary: Anne L. Samek, 3025 NE 137th, #211, Seattle, WA 98125.

**Greater Pittsburgh Pekingese Club**
President: Ruthe Painter, 270 Arona Road, RD3, Irwin, PA 15642.

**Houston Area Pekingese Club**
Secretary: Becky Carney, 3210 Forest Glen, Spring, TX 77380.

**Imperial Pekingese Club of Greater Flint**
Corresponding Secretary: Harrison D. Viele, 12016 Davison Road, Box 153, Davison, MI 48423.

**North Central Illinois Pekingese Club**
Secretary: Patricia Mullendore, 53 Royce Drive, Oswego, IL 60543.

**Pacific Coast Pekingese Club**
Secretary: June E. Strange, 16031 Archwood Street, Van Nuys, CA 91406.

**Pekin Palace Dog Association**
Secretary: Alice Scott, 220, Toynbee Tr., Scarborough, Ontario, Canada, M1E 1G9.

**Pekingese Club of Alabama**
Secretary: Marsha G. Allison, 205 Hazel Green Drive, Wetumpka, AL 36092.

**Pekingese Club of America**
Secretary: Hetty Oringer, 3 Carolyn Terrace, Southboro, MA 01772.

**Pekingese Club of Central California**
Secretary: Neal McCauley, 4767 Midway Road, Vacaville, CA 95688.

**Pekingese Club of Georgia**
Secretary: Leslie M. Dees, 2103 Springlake Drive NW, Atlanta, GA 30305.

**Pekingese Club of Southern New Jersey**
Secretary: Gloria Henes, 17 Hope Road, Tabor, NJ 07878.

**Pekingese Club of Texas**
Secretary: Don Sutton, 507 S. Manus Drive, Dallas, TX 75224.

**Pilgrim Pekingese Fanciers**
Secretary: Carolann Cinelli, PO Box 170, East Boston, MA 02128.

**Potomac Valley Pekingese Club**
Secretary: Dan Fischer, 4212 Anthony Street, Kensington, MD 20895.

**Rose City Pekingese Club**
Secretary: Mary L. Burke, 2414 E. 20th Street, Vancouver, WA 98661.

**Western Canada Pekingese Club**
Secretary: Louise Pearce, 27760 Quinton Avenue, Adergrove, BC, Canada, XOV 1AO.

# Appendix 3

## UK Pekingese Rescue List

**Mrs Jackson and Mrs Ware**
25 Crofton Avenue, Orpington, Kent, BR6 8DU.
Tel. 0689 51666

**Mrs M. J. Fieldhouse**
154 Lichfield Road, Brownhills, Walsall, West Midlands.
Tel. 0543 377147

**Mrs M. Walford**
116 Military Road, Colchester, Essex.
Tel. 0206 45533

**Mrs V. M. Williamson**
87 Winchester Street, Botley, Southampton, SO3 2EB.
Tel. 0489 22902

**Mrs I. Marshall**
21 Primrose Street, Carnoustie, Scotland.
Tel. 0241 52703

**Mrs W. Middleton**
18 Cairnfield Place, Aberdeen.
Tel. 0224 632465

**Mr G. MacLennan**
41 Firthview Road, Inverness.
Tel. 0463 226260

**Mrs D. Gunn**
Kirkden House, Letham, Angus, DD8 2QF.

# Index